JOHN WESLEY
Friend of the People

Other Books by Oscar Sherwin

PROPHET OF LIBERTY, The Life and Times of Wendell Phillips

UNCORKING OLD SHERRY, The Life and Times of Richard Brinsley Sheridan

GOLDY, The Life and Times of Oliver Goldsmith

JOHN WESLEY
Friend of the People

OSCAR SHERWIN

Twayne Publishers, Inc.
New York

Library of Congress, Catalogue Card Number: 61-15094

Manufactured in the United States of America.
Type set by Elroy Typesetters, New York.

To
Francis Neilson
and
The Coterie

TABLE OF CONTENTS

JOHN WESLEY
Friend of the People

CHAPTER ONE

BLIND GUIDES

"Nine tenths of the men in England," said John Wesley, "have no more religion than horses, and perish through total contempt of it."[1] Earlier in 1736 Bishop Berkeley of tar-water fame remarked: "The age of monsters is not far off." Morality and religion had collapsed "to a degree that was never known in any Christian country."[2] The torrent of evil Berkeley attributed to irreligion of the better sort. "Our prospect is very terrible."[3]

To sap a creed with solemn sneer was considered not only clever but praiseworthy.[4] Addison in No. 37 of the *Freeholder* declared that there was "less appearance of religion in England than any other neighboring state or kingdom."[5]

Religion was considered a backwater having no vital connection with the main stream of the river. At the beginning of the century men worshipped the idol of Good Taste; at its end they fell down before the Baal of Commerce and Industry.[6] Of the higher classes of society Montesquieu wrote, "Everyone laughs if one talks of religion."[7] Crowds flocked to see that great curiosity, a religious bishop.[8]

But if gold rust, what shall iron do? For at least five or six decades poltroons and pedants, timeservers and sycophants, pluralists and place-hunters reveled almost unrestrainedly in the heyday of their theological and ecclesiastical opportunism.[9] "I read," says Thackeray in "George the Second," "that Lady Yarmouth (my most religious and gracious King's favorite) sold a bishopric to a clergyman for £5,000. She betted him £5,000 that he would not be made a bishop and he lost and paid her."[10]

"Archbishops of the eighteenth century," says Rowden, "were great potentates, if not princes. A coach and six horses, a private state barge on the Thames with its liveried crew properly belonged to such a dignitary."[11] Only two eighteenth century primates were even half worthy of their sacred office.[12] Bishop Hurd (nicknamed the Beauty of Holiness) traveled from his palace to his cathedral, a bare quarter of a mile, in his episcopal coach with his servants in full-dress liveries. When he went to Bristol Hot Wells, he never moved without a train of twelve servants.[13] John Potter, stilted and starchy, primate at the time of Wesley's conversion, loathed the manifestation of new "enthusiasm." But true to the current fashion of the ruling class into which he (a draper's son) had been lifted, he left behind him £90,000 which he had saved out of the church.[14] Archbishop Moore secured well-feathered nests for his five sons. One of these for more than fifty years was recipient of an annual income from the church of not less than £12,000. Moore's own revenue averaged £11,000 a year, almost a thousand times the customary stipend of a self-sacrificing missionary teacher who went as a servant of Christ to the Indians in the wilds of North America.[15]

Frederick Cornwallis married a great lady and Lambeth Palace was full of such notorious routs and feastings that the celebrated Selina, Countess of Huntingdon, lodged a protest with the King and Queen which resulted in a forcible letter to the primate. The king spoke of the "grief and concern with which my breast was affected" at receiving the news, held "these levities and vain dissipations as utterly inexpedient, if not unlawful, to pass in a residence for many years devoted to divine studies, religious retirement, and the extensive exercise of charity and benevolence," and ordered that they be suppressed immediately. Cornwallis published little or nothing and died rich.[16] Lord Campbell informs us that in spite of Lord Thurlow's living openly with a mistress, his house was not only frequented by his brother the bishop, but by ecclesiastics of all degrees.[17] Jonathan Trelawney, Bishop of Winchester, who died in 1721, used to excuse himself for his excessive swearing by saying he swore as a baronet and not as a bishop.[18]

Preferment and absenteeism were the bane of the clergy. Preferment was bestowed chiefly for political or family influence. The pastoral care of parishioners was confided to a curate whose services were enlisted at a stipend oftentimes far lower than that of a groom or coachman. Only three questions were asked by worldly clerics: Where would they be most comfortable? What were the chances of further preferment? How could they best please the court and ministers in office?

Richard Watson, Bishop of Llandaff, made no secret of the fact that he was in receipt of £2,000 a year which he derived in part from the titles of two churches in Shropshire, two in Leicestershire, two in his diocese, three in Huntingdonshire. He was appointed only because the Earl of Shelburne hugged himself with the hope that Watson become a useful partisan. Though appointed to the see at Llandaff in 1782, from that time on till 1816 he resided on the margin of lakes in Westmoreland, spending his life principally in building farmhouses, blasting rocks, enclosing wastes, in making bad land good, in planting larches, and in planting in the hearts of his children principles of piety, of benevolence, and of self government—quite laudable if extended to all not just a few.[19]

Dr. Thomas Newton, who occupied the see of Bristol from 1761 to 1782, records in his *Autobiography*: "But, alas! never was the church more shamefully neglected." The bishop several times had been there for months together without seeing the face of a dean or prebendary or anything better than a minor canon.[20] The curate dining with Bishop Pearce was asked when he usually went into residence at the Cathedral of Rochester. "Oh, my lord," said he, "I reside there the better part of the year." "I am very glad to hear it," replied the good bishop in blissful ignorance of the fact that the respondent resided in Rochester only during the week of the audit.[21]

Nichol's *Literary Anecdotes* records the following epitaph:

Here rests all that was mortal of
Mrs. Elizabeth Bate,
Relic of the Reverend Richard Bate,
A woman of unaffected piety
And exemplary virtue . . .
She was honorably descended
And by means of her alliance to
The illustrious family of Stanhope
She had the merit to obtain
For her husband and children
Twelve several employments
In Church and State.
She died June 7, 1751
In the 75th year of her age.[22]

"No man can now be a bishop for his learning and piety," said Dr. Johnson. "His only chance of promotion is his being connected with some one who has parliamentary interest."[23] Yet perversely Johnson justified this condition. The government having too little power must make all appointments in its own support and it could not reward merit. The church became a department of state. And prelates wrote pamphlets instructing the poor that it was their high privilege "cheerfully to perform their various duties" in "those stations of life in which it had pleased God to place them."[24] As for the Industrial Revolution these "blind guides" were as insensitive to its challenge as if it were taking place on the moon.

D'Alembert, the famous mathematician and one of Diderot's foremost editors of the *Encyclopédie,* depicting the pre-Revolution France of his day, with withering sarcasm wrote: "The highest offices in the Church and State resemble a pyramid whose top is accessible to only two sorts of animals, eagles and reptiles." [25] The aphorism was equally applicable to Protestant England. Certainly it contained enough truth to bite.

Swift portrays one prelate mounting fast towards the top of the ecclesiastical ladder without the merit of a single virtue: "He treated all his inferiors of the clergy with a most sanctified pride," and had neither eyes nor ears for the faults of the rich. Power in whatever hands or whatever party was always sure of his most charitable opinion. This good cleric could be "soberly drunk, at the expense of others, with college ale, and at such times he was always most devout." He was in the habit of dropping in his own half crown among the collection and taking it out when he disposed of the money. "He paid his curates punctually at the lowest salary and partly out of the communion money, but gave them good advice in abundance."[26]

Meanwhile the hungry sheep looked up and were not fed. The main body of the clergy was dead and lifeless. Instead of animating one another they rather seemed to lay one another asleep.[27] Wesley flamed: "A worldly clergyman is a fool above all fools, a madman above all madmen. Such vile, infamous wretches as these are the real ground of the contempt of the clergy. Indolent clergymen, pleasure taking clergymen, money loving clergymen, praise loving clergymen, preferment seeking clergymen—these are the wretches that cause the order in general to be contemned. These are the pests of the Christian world, the grand nuisance of mankind, a stink in the nostrils of God."[28]

Oxford and Cambridge were at the lowest ebb of scholarship. As Southey expressed it, "The waters of Helicon were too much polluted by the wine of Bacchus."[29] There was a head of Oriel who was continually obliged to be assisted to bed by his butler.[30] Dr. Taylor in 1730 spoke of Cambridge as pervaded by solemn slumbers interrupted mainly by whist and politics.[31] Lloyd, the Poetry Professor, about 1760, mentioned

> "Fellows who've soaked away their knowledge
> By sleepy residence at college,"

men whose attachment to the grave pursuits of eating and drinking left little time "for the impertinence of thinking."[32] Southey who went to Oxford "with a view to orders" learned there two things: "to row and to swim."[33] Gibbon referred to his Oxford days as "fourteen idle and unprofitable months" and said his tutor "remembered he had a salary to receive, but forgot he had a duty to perform."[34] The historian records a passing regret that he had not embraced the lucrative pursuits of the law or of trade, the chances of civil office or India [sic] adventure, or even the fat slumbers of the church."[35]

True, theological pamphlets and books in the Deist controversy had a staggering sale, and a constant demand for purely devotional literature existed in quiet country parsonages.[36] But apathy and torpor were the prevailing tone.

Whereas parliamentary corruption could at least be debated in the House of Commons and exposed by the opposition, ecclesiastical corruption battened under cover. While many a hard-drinking, fox-hunting parson with family and political influence "swallowed more livings than he could chew," the vast majority of the humbler clergy were half starving on from £20 to £60 a year.[37] Goldsmith's father was "passing rich on £40 a year," and Samuel Wesley, the father of John and Charles, a capable, thrifty, hard-working priest, for months was in a debtor's jail.[38] The rural clergy became prototypes of Parson Trulliber, or Adams, or even of Mr. Gilfil, an excellent old gentleman who smoked very long pipes and preached very short sermons. Parson Adams, a pious, capable clergyman, at the age of fifty with a wife and six children was "provided with a handsome income of £23 a year." [39] In the reign of Queen Anne, out of 10,000 livings, 5597 livings were worth less than £50 a year; in the reign of George III, Massey estimates the number of livings under £80 per annum at over 5,000.[40]

Any common footman with £7 yearly and 7s a week board-wages and vails was better off than the curate. There were many clergymen, says one writer, who just sustained themselves "by God's mercy and man's charity," and sometimes by menial duties or coarse manual labor. Parson Trulliber in a laborer's smock feeding his pigs may be matched by Churchill in his Welsh cure eking out his scanty maintenance by the management of a little cider shop. When Mackay about 1722 made a tour through Britain, he found that in Wales the alehouse was kept by the parson "for their livings are very small."[41] The poor brethren, grown old in the service, objects of extreme wretchedness, lived in garrets and appeared in the streets with tattered cassocks. They were hired to read prayers for two pence and a dish of coffee, to preach a sermon for 12d and a Sunday dinner, and to do other occasional offices at a proportional rate.[42] Contrast Parson Woodforde's stocked granary: "1776. Sept. 14. Very busy all day with my barley, did not dine till 5 in the afternoon, my harvest men dined here today, gave them some beef, and some plumb pudding, and as much liquor as they could drink. This evening finished my harvest and all carried into the barn—8 acres. Dec. 3. My frolic for my people to pay tithe to me this day. I gave them a good dinner, sirloin of beef roasted, a leg of mutton boiled and plumb puddings in plenty."[43]

The social gulf between the rich and poor clergy was almost as wide as in medieval times. The domestic clergy had sunk to the plebeian class. The chaplain was thought a fit mate for a lady's maid, ate only at the second table, and was expected to lend a hand to carry his patron to bed at night after the wine bottles had been emptied, while turning a conveniently deaf ear to the blasphemy and oaths which flowed as freely as the wine.[44] On working days he went about in a grazier's coat and assisted at harvest time. Macaulay's picture of the clergy from the Restoration to the accession of James II applied with equal force word for word to one half the rural clergy of England in the eighteenth century. It was a white day on which he was admitted to the kitchen of the great house and regaled by the servants with cold meat and ale. His children were brought up like the children of peasants. His boys followed the plough and his girls went out to service. Study he found impossible and he might be considered lucky if he had ten or twelve dog-eared volumes among the pots and pans on his shelves.[45]

In the French Revolution the common clergy were on the side of the peasants. That was inconceivable in England. As the curé's windows looked to the village, the parson's windows looked to the hall. Even when resident and conscientious, as he often was, and always ill-paid, he moved like a pluralist rector in the orbit of the rich. He was in that world, though not of it. All his hope hung on the squire. To have taken the side of the poor against him would have meant ruin, and the English church was not a nursery for that kind of heroism.[46]

Here and there anchored in lonely parishes were found men who as the poet Thomson said of his father were "with no titles blest, but that best title, a good parish priest."[47] But while such men—the salt of their order—lived, they were necessarily exceptional. "Our ember weeks," wrote Bishop Burnet in 1713, "are the burden and grief of my life. The much greater part of those who come to be ordained are ignorant to a degree not to be apprehended by those who are not obliged to know it."[48] Arthur Young in his *Inquiry into the State of the Public Mind among the Lower Classes* remarked caustically: "A man must have traveled very little in this kingdom who does not know that country towns abound with curates who never see the parishes they serve but when they are absolutely forced to it by duty."[49] "If the whole body of the clergy were like ourselves," said an old Surrey fox-hunting parson, "the world would see that we were of no use and take away our tithes, but a few of these pious ones redeem our credit and save for us our livings." [50]

Unfortunately it cannot be said of the average country parson of the eighteenth century as Chaucer was able to say of the parish priest of his day—

> Cristes lore and his apostles twelve,
> He taughte, but first he folwed it hymselve,

but rather that he entered the temple and drove out the worshippers. "There never was such license among the shepherds of the flock or such toleration in the flock for such shepherds."[51] There were parsons like the Rev. Horne Tooke who flaunted abroad in gold lace and sky blue and scarlet and who apologized to Wilkes for having suffered "the infectious hand of a bishop to be waved over him." There were Duelling Parsons like the Rev. Mr. Bate, chaplain to a cavalry regiment, who went out and was killed in a fair duel, "a most promising young man," said the papers with commiseration. There were the clergymen known pleasantly as "The Three Fighting Parsons"—Henley, Bate, and Churchill, and Bruising Clergymen like the one mentioned in Grose's *Olio*.[52] The Rev. Mr. Patten, curate of Whitstable by the sea, had originally been a sea chaplain and contracted much of tar-like roughness. He openly kept a mistress and on any one going into church in sermon time and showing him a lemon, he would instantly conclude his discourse and adjourn to the alehouse.[53] The story of the unfortunate Macaroni parson, Dr.

Dodd, was in everyone's mouth as well as that of the infatuated Hackman. The profane joke was uttery untrue, but significant of the tone of the day: Lord Sandwich's bet about twelve clergymen who were dining with him, all of whom he coarsely insisted had corkscrews in their pockets but not one a prayerbook.[54]

Portraits of clerics in novels and essays were hardly exaggerated. It was not astounding that Roderick Random found a cheat in canonicals in a village inn, was scandalised at the oaths he swore and the songs he sang. The divine was Mr. Shuffle, the curate of a neighboring parish who could shift a card with such dexterity it was impossible to discover him.[55] In *Tom Jones,* Mr. Supple the curate and Squire Western make a libation of four bottles of wine to the good of the country.[56] The Chinese Essay, No. 58, describes a visitation dinner that was composed of three courses and lasted as many hours, till the whole company from the lord bishop to the Rev. Dr. Marrowfat was "unable to swallow or utter anything more."[57] Colman and Thornton have limned a typical country parson of this period in their sketch of Rev. Jack Quickset, a divine who saw "his dearest action on the field" and who boasted that he had in his stable a brace of hunters as good as ever leg was laid over, whose life was mostly spent in hunting and shooting, who found the Sunday dull and tedious, and who made up for loss of it by "going out a-cock-shooting very early the next morning." His thoughts were taken up more with the stable or dog kennel than the church.[58]

The country parson regarded his office as little better than a sinecure. One found among them poachers and fox hunters who having spent the morning scampering after the hounds, dedicated the evening to the bottle, and "reeled from inebriety to the pulpit." "Such advertisements," said Arthur Young, "were never seen in France as I have heard of in England: 'Wanted a curacy in a good sporting country where the duty is light and the neighborhood convivial.' "[59] Then that cassock wearing scapegrace, the

Rev. Dr. Warner, bosom friend of George Selwyn, was quite an ornament to the Establishment. He was always in high spirits whether quizzing "canting pot-bellied justices," contemplating with equanimity "a fine corpse at Surgeon's Hall," or looking with hopeful vivacity to the time when he would be a "fine grey-headed old jollocks of sixty-five."[60] Careless and witty the Doctor took religion easily, retailed scandal, and played the jester. At christenings he got fuddled with claret, and when in the country on Saturday evenings joined the neighboring parsons in a convocation, and then he says in a letter to his patron, "for whist, backgammon, and tobacco till we can't see."[61]

Dr. Alexander Carlyle, minister of Inveresk, when he visited Harrogate in the summer of 1763, was astonished that the spa abounded with more clergymen than he had ever seen before, and that in general they were divided into two classes—bucks and prigs, the first, though ignorant, unassuming, the other not to be endured, half-learned, narrow-minded, pedantic, and overbearing.[62] Dr. Knox, headmaster of Tunbridge School, himself a divine of the English Church wrote that the public of his day had "long remarked with indignation that some of the most distinguished coxcombs, drunkards, debauchees, and gamesters, who figure at the watering places and all public places of resort, were young men of the sacerdotal order."[63]

Cowper had nothing better to say of the parish priest than that he was

> Loose in morals, and in manners vain,
> In conversation frivolous, in dress
> Extreme; at once rapacious and profuse,
> Frequent in park with lady at his side,
> Ambling and prattling scandal as he goes,
> But rare at home and never at his books.

While in another place he speaks of

The things that mount the rostrum with a skip,
And then skip down again, pronounce a text,
Cry—hem! and reading what they never wrote,
Just fifteen minutes, huddle up their work,
And with a well-bred whisper close the scene.[64]

Crabbe says of the parson of his *Village*—it was his custom to give "to fields the morning and to feasts the night."[65] That the Bishop of Winchester upon one occasion examined candidates for ordination in a field during the progress of a cricket match was not altogether destitute of foundation.[66]

When Dr. Johnson met an old college friend Edwards in 1778, the following conversation took place: Edwards. "I wish I had continued at college." Johnson. "Why do you wish that, sir?" Edwards. "Because I think I should have had a much easier life than mine has been. I should have been a parson and had a good living, like Bloxham and several others, and lived comfortably."[67] A saintly man was looked on as a fanatic.

If the force of religion was practically dead under the early Georges, the royal example was not calculated to revive it. The custom certainly was to have prayers said daily in the palace, but they were performed by parsons in a room next to the Queen's dressing room while she was at her toilet, the door being open only "enough for those parsons to think we may hear and shut enough that we may not hear quite so much—these creatures pray so loud we cannot hear oneself speak."[68] "No wonder," says Thackeray, "Whitefield cried out in the wilderness, that Wesley quitted the insulted temple to pray on the hill-side. . . . Which is the sublimer spectacle—the good John Wesley surrounded by his congregation of miners at the pit's mouth, or the Queen's chaplains, mumbling through their morning office in their ante-room under the picture of the great Venus with the door opened into the adjoining chamber where the Queen is dressing, talking scandal to Lord Hervey, or uttering sneers at Lady Suffolk who is kneeling with the basin at her mistress's side?"[69]

As for Kings George I and II alike, their profligacy was so notorious that they did not care to conceal it. The first had shut up his wife in the lonely castle of Ahlden on the Lüneburger Haide, thirty miles from Hanover, and lived among his mistresses in uninterrupted pleasures. The second was on good terms with his Queen, but she cared so little for him herself that even her daughter could remark openly upon the retirement of Lady Suffolk, one of the numerous royal flames, "I wish with all my heart that he [the king] woud take somebody else, that mamma might be a little relieved from the ennui of seeing him always in her room." [70] The King himself was sulking like an ill-bred bear because he had to leave his favorite mistress Madame von Walmoden (afterwards Countess of Yarmouth) in Hanover while he returned for the winter to England. The Queen was calmly advised by Walpole to supply her royal husband with a fresh mistress, Lady Tankerville, to balance the attractions of his German concubine.[71]

"Now what can an impartial person think concerning the present state of religion in England?" asked John Wesley. "Is there a nation under the sun which is so deeply fallen from the very first principles of all religion? Where is the country in which is found so utter a disregard to even Heathen morality, such a thorough contempt of justice and truth and all that should be dear and honorable to rational creatures?"[72]

People behaved in church with an irreverence that shocked the least religious. They lolled and talked in the pews, sat on the communion table, stood on chairs to bow and smile to their acquaintances. Very few attended church at any time. Nothing was more dreaded than the reproach of being mystical or zealous. *The Spectator* constantly refers to irreverence in church. The Starter posted himself upon a hassock and from this point of eminence impertinently scrutinized the congregation and put ladies to the blush.[73] The Gigglers burst into laughter behind their fans.[74] Will Honeycomb seldom came in till the prayers were about half over, and when he entered his seat, instead of joining with the congregation he devoutly held his hat before his face for three or four moments, then bowed to all his acquaintances, sat down, took a pinch of snuff, and spent the remaining time in surveying the congregation.[75] Then there were the Rattlers who, if a sermon was not suited to their taste, signaled to one another, or, if in the same pew, conferred in such loud and clamorous tones as not to be silenced but by the bells.[76]

High, square, curtained pews to which churchgoers in the Georgian era were devotedly attached, constituted excellent sleeping compartments and convenient places where flirtations could be carried on.[77] Lady Booby in *Joseph Andrews* occupied a pew which the congregation could not see into.[78] During a church service Bishop Sumner once sent for a blacksmith to take off the locks from certain pews. He asked the congregation to "sing a hymn while the blacksmith performed his task."[79]

But they all preached. What was the character of their sermons? Martyrdom and Restoration sermons preached annually both before the House of Lords and the House of Commons and also in parish churches throughout the country, spoke of Cromwell and his colleagues as "that hypocritical brood of infernal vipers," denounced the "hypocrisy and fanaticism" of the Puritans, and dubbed Charles I, "the worthiest gentleman, the best master, the best friend, the best husband, the best father, and the best Christian that the age in which he lived produced."[80] Their emphasis on submission to God-appointed inferiors gained the support of those who looked upon the clergy as faithful watchdogs and dependable police corps for vested interests, but alienated from the church the allegiance and respect of the working multitude.[81] "The King's sacred life" became the monotonous chant in Commemoration sermons. The popular poem ran—

> Kings are Gods but once removed. . . .
> So that for Charles the Good to have been tryed
> And cast by mortal votes was Deicide.[82]

Even Bishop Warburton who, whatever his sins, and he was far from a saint, was no puppet of party or class—"the soulless plutocrat he could not abide"—even Warburton joined the general chorus. In his Martyrdom Sermon before the Lords, 1760, he dismissed the Commonwealth period as "that disgraceful epoch in our story" when the subjects "renounced the protection of their Common Sovereign and invaded and insulted his imperial crown." [83] Swift rehashes the same perennial mumbo-jumbo. In a typical sermon he does obeisance before "that excellent King and blessed martyr Charles I who rather chose to die on a scaffold than betray the liberties of his people wherewith God and the laws had entrusted him."[84]

Dr. George Stinson, preaching to the Commons, called the Commonwealth era "a fit of frenzy" and urged "dutiful submission to authority." The chords are familiar. In one breath the highest ecclesiastics appealed for suppression of all opposition to oligarchic government in church and state as "licentiousness and outrage" while in the next they besought people to fall down in obeisance before "our excellent constitution, both civil and religious.[85]

Bishop Newton, preaching the Martyrdom Sermon before the House of Lords, took as a text the importance of moderation. Of this same genial bishop Leslie Stephen says that his intimacies with great men enabled him "to worm himself into the high places of the church."[86] In the sphere of self-seeking preferment Newton conveniently forgot all about moderation. Enthusiasm was the unpardonable sin to him. Methodism, which dared approach the denizens of the unwashed underworld and teach them they had souls, he lampooned as "a bastard kind of popery." He prided himself that he lived above the loathesome "immoderations" of the vulgar menial herd.[87]

After 1688 the refusal of Jacobites to recognize William as King—they regarded him only as Regent—led to a deification of the constitution. One Dr. Binckes, preaching before the Lower House of Convocation, went so far as to argue that the execution of Charles I "transcended in enormity the murder of Christ."[88] Yet the grand trouble with the first Charles Stuart was that he "would not keep faith with any man or institution on earth."[89] Concerning the "tinkers, cobblers, and draymen" of Commonwealth days, the aforesaid brood of infernal vipers, those "dreadful dissemblers with God and Heaven," John Richard Green has this to say: "The whole history of English progress since the Restoration on its moral and spiritual sides has been the history of Puritanism."[90] The Martyrdom and Restoration sermons, folly allied to idolatry, represent the most foolish and servile church preaching in the eighteenth century.

The Whole Duty of Man, a manual which for nearly a century held undisputed sway alongside the Prayer Book reverted constantly to its underlying theme that rigid class distinctions were divinely ordained. Men were exhorted "to order themselves lowly and reverently to all their betters." [91] Wesley before his spiritual emancipation held *The Whole Duty of Man* in the highest esteem. But after his "new birth" he cast aside the religious manual as a pedantic, hypocritical heap of rubbish which nullified the Brotherhood of Man.[92]

Little wonder that the industrial population came to regard the parish clergy among the most merciless of all forces of reaction and subjugation. If the workingman attended the Established Church his recognized place was the rough, rude bench in the gloomiest corners of the edifice and his spiritual diet instruction on how to reverence his "betters" worshipping amidst sumptuous cushions and carpets in locked pews.

Sir William Blackstone, the eminent jurist, had the curiosity to go from church to church and hear every clergyman of note in London. What was the result? His reaction to all these sermons was that he failed to hear a single discourse which had more Christianity in it than the writings of Cicero, and that "it would have been impossible for him to discover from what he heard whether its preacher were a follower of Confucius, of Mohammed, or of Christ."[93]

Church sermons were in an unknown tongue to the common man, and most preachers seemed to care very little what effect their preaching had on their audiences. In fear of being overzealous the average sermon became overtame and colorless, "too stiff and formal, too cold and artificial." Two texts were worn threadbare by the preachers of the day: "Let your moderation be known to all men," and "Be not righteous overmuch."[94] Numbers of clergymen did not preach sermons at all, while many who did fell back on manufactured sermons modeled on those of Dr. Tillotson and Dr. Hugh Blair. As early as 1709 Bishop Horsley in his *Charge to the Diocese of St. David's* complained: "We make no other use of the high commission we bear than to come abroad one day in seven dressed in solemn looks and the external garbs of holiness to be the apes of Epictetus."[95] God was an idol compounded of fragments of tradition and frozen metaphysics.

"A sermon in France," Voltaire wrote home from England, "is a long declamation scrupulously divided into three parts and delivered with enthusiasm. In England a sermon is a solid but sometimes dry dissertation which a man reads to the people without gesture and without any particular exaltation of voice."[96] "We have no sermons," said Dr. Johnson, "addressed to the passions that are good for anything."[97] Memorable is Wesley's caustic gibe: "So we are forbidden to go to Newgate for fear of making them (the inmates) wicked and to Bedlam for fear of driving them mad."[98]

The sermons, artful to a degree, smooth and polished as marble, at heart were as cold and dead as marble. They offered no redemption from inward sin, no deliverance from outward wretchedness, no dynamic for social reform. They fell back on theories, dogmas, formalities, rules, and precepts. And the result? They were little more than washed out retailers of platitudes. Of what inspiration then was this religious pedantry "to the miner in the bowels of the earth, to the mechanic amidst the grime and sweat of the workshop, or the foundryman daily facing an inferno of flame?" Absolutely nothing.

CHAPTER TWO

THE FALL OF MAN

It was an age of beastliness and debauchery, savagery and violence. The moral fibre of the nation was vitally decayed. "These unhappy creatures," said a writer in the *Gentleman's Magazine* of 1791 of the brutish Bristol colliers, "married and buried amongst themselves and often committed murders with impunity." [1] In 1735 a sailor was convicted of having killed his wife in Bristol. He poisoned himself in jail and was buried at the crossroads outside the city. Bristol men, deprived of their prey, went to the crossroads, dug up his body, "dragged his guts about the highways, poked his eyes out," broke his bones, and then put what was left in a very deep grave near the gallows.[2] Shepherd was hanged at Tyburn in the presence of two hundred thousand spectators.

Government insulted humanity by the brutal ferocity of its criminal code. There were more than two hundred crimes punishable by death. Prisons were indescribably filthy. Those who escaped the gallows came out emaciated and diseased.[3]

Gin was the curse of the poor and the grand destroyer of life. In 1684 only 500,000 gallons of gin were distilled. Thirty years later the annual amount increased to two million. Twenty years more and it rose to five million gallons. In 1749 it was calculated there were 17,000 private gin shops in London alone. Lecky called the practice of gin drinking the most memorable event in the eighteenth century. Certainly it was more deadly than Frenchman or

Jacobite. Every sixth house in London was a public house. Signs invited the poor to get drunk for a penny, dead drunk for two pence, and have straw on which to lie and recover free. Drunkenness was a national vice. Dr. Johnson speaks of the time when all the decent people of Lichfield got drunk every night and were not the worse thought of.[4]

Purity and fidelity were sneered out of fashion. George II "united the morals of a rake with the tastes of a boor." Walpole as prime minister set an example of shameless profligacy.[5] The mania for gambling ran unabated. Stakes were played high at the King's palace. Lord Ilchester lost £13,000 at one sitting. Statesman Fox was reduced to poverty. The brutal pastimes of bull-baiting, bear-baiting, and cock-fighting constituted the delight of all classes. It was unsafe to travel or walk in London streets. Roads were vile. In 1769 Arthur Young asserted that in the whole of England there were but four good roads; as for the rest it was "a Prostitution of Language to call them turnpikes." [6] Citizens drew up their wills before they left London.

This was the plain, naked fact as Wesley saw it: a flood of general wickedness and universal misery—fraud and wrong, deceit and violence, the dire thirst of gold, lust to possess, rapine—threatened to engulf mankind. "It strikes the eye of the most careless inaccurate observer. . . . Now it is certain the generality of men do not wear their worst side outward. Rather they study to appear better than they are and to conceal what they can of their faults. What a figure then would they make were we able to touch them with Ithuriel's spear!" [7]

"But," added Wesley, "that the former days were better than these, that his contemporaries now lived in the dregs of time when the world was, as it were, grown old, that everything in it was in a declining state—a common cry from generation to generation—that concept was absolutely false. The generality of men were not one jot wiser in ancient times than they were in his day; the Egyptians had no deeper meaning in worshipping cats than our schoolboys have in baiting them." [8]

Yet in the "Doctrine of Original Sin," 1756, Wesley bitingly surveys the past and present of mankind, with special reference to the Irish and English. Of the first: "Now what knowledge have these rational animals? They know to plant and boil their potatoes, to milk their cow, and to put their clothes on and off, if they have any besides a blanket, but other knowledge they have none, unless in religion. And how much do they know of this? A little more than the Hottentots and not much."

As for the English: "The generality of English peasants are not only grossly but stupidly, I had almost said, brutishly ignorant as to all the arts of this life. Neither in their tempers or conversation, do they rise one jot above the pitch of a Turk or a Heathen. Perhaps, it will be said, 'Whatever the clowns in the midland counties are, the people near the sea coasts are more civilized.' Yes, great numbers of them are, in and near all our ports, many thousands there are civilized by smuggling. These are, therefore, general robbers. They rob you and me and everyone of their countrymen, seeing had the king his due customs, a great part of our taxes might be spared. A smuggler then . . . is a thief of the first order, a highwayman or pickpocket of the worst sort.

"Can we say of the soldiery in general that they are men of reason and religion? I fear not. Are not the bulk of them void of almost all knowledge divine and human, . . . Is there any more knowledge or virtue in that vast body of men, the English sailors? Surely no. It is not without cause that a ship has been called 'a floating hell.' . . . I doubt whether any heathen sailors, in any country or age, Greek, Roman, or Barbarian, ever came up to ours for profound ignorance and barefaced, shameless, shocking impiety. . . .

"But all men are not like these. No, it is pity they

should. And yet how little better are the retailers of brandy or gin, the inhabitants of blind alehouses, the oyster women, fish wives, and other good creatures about Billingsgate, and the various clans of peddlers and hawkers that patrol through the streets or ply in Rag-fair and other places of public resort? These, likewise, amount to several thousands, even within the Bills of Mortality. And what knowledge have they? What religion are they of? What morality do they practice? . . .

" 'But these have had no advantage of education, many of them scarce being able to write or read.' Proceed we, then, to those who have had these advantages, the officers of the excise and customs. Are these, in general, men of reason who think with clearness and connection, and speak pertinently on a given subject? Are they men of religion, sober and temperate, fearing God and working righteousness? . . . How many do you find of this kind among them?—men that fear an oath, that fear perjury more than death, that would die rather than neglect any part of that duty which they have sworn to perform. . . . These only are wise and honest men. Set down all the rest as having neither religion nor sound reason.

"But surely tradesmen have! Some of them have both and in an eminent degree. Some of our traders are an honor to the nation. But are the bulk of them so? Are a vast majority of our tradesmen whether in town or country, I will not say religious, but honest men? Perhaps you think St. Paul is too strict. Let us appeal then to Cicero, an honest heathen. Now, when he is laying down rules of honesty between man and man, he proposes two cases—

"1. Antisthenes brings a shipload of corn to Rhodes at a time of great scarcity. The Rhodians flock about him to buy. He knows that five other ships laden with corn will be there tomorrow. Ought he to tell the Rhodians this before he sells his own corn? 'Undoubtedly he ought,' says the Heathen, 'otherwise he makes a gain of their ignorance, and so is no better than a thief or a robber.' . . .

"Now how many of our tradesmen come up to the Heathen standard of honesty? Which of our countrymen would not have sold his corn or other wares at the highest price he could? Who would have sunk his own market by telling his customers there would be plenty the next day? Perhaps scarce one in twenty. That one the Heathen would have allowed to be an honest man, and everyone of the rest, according to his sentence, is no better than a thief or a robber. . . .

"That there is honor, nay, and honesty, to be found in another body of men, among the gentlemen of the law, I firmly believe, whether attorneys, solicitors, or counsellors. But are they not thinly spread? Do the generality of attorneys and solicitors in chancery love their neighbor as themselves and do to others what (if the circumstances were changed) they would have others do to them? . . . A lawyer who does not finish his client's suit as soon as it can be done, I cannot allow to have more honesty (though he has more prudence) than if he robbed him on the highway.

"But whether lawyers are or no, sure the nobility and gentry are all men of reason and religion. If you think they are all men of religion, you think very differently from your Master. . . . Much money does not imply much sense, neither does a good estate infer a good understanding. As a gay coat may cover a bad heart, so a fair peruke may adorn a weak head."

Of the thousands of ministers in the Established Church, the Dissenters, the Roman Catholics: "Of these I would only ask: Is their heart right with God? Is their eye single? Is it their sole intention to glorify God and to save souls? . . .

"The very foundations of all things civil and religious are utterly out of course in the Christian as well as the Heathen world. There is a still more horrid reproach to the Christian name, yea to the name of man, to all reason and humanity. There is war in the world! war between men. Men in general can never be allowed to be reasonable creatures till they know not war any more. So long as this monster stalks uncontrolled, where is reason, virtue, humanity? They are utterly excluded; they have no place; they are a name and nothing more. . . ." [9]

This was the plain, glaring, apparent condition of human kind. Men are unhappy because they are unholy. To believe is to walk in the light of eternity.[10]

CHAPTER THREE

THE MESSAGE OF EQUALITY

John Wesley taught liberty, equality, fraternity long before the French Revolution.

Methodism was a religion of the common people, a movement of and by the poor—"not many mighty, not many noble."[1] Methodism was republican in government. Opportunities for laymen to exercise their gifts, to assume responsibilities and to occupy official positions attracted the working classes. The fellowship was voluntary. It attracted men because it gave them something to do, made them feel they had a share in the success of the movement. Working men and women were made into class leaders, local preachers, exhorters, prayer leaders, trustees, and stewards. They could exercise their votes in the Leaders' Meeting, the Society Meeting, perhaps in the Trustees' Meeting, the Preachers' Meeting, and the Quarterly Meeting. All this opportunity and trust were offered to the poorest of the poor who were made most welcome. Hence it happened that years before the people were offered the political vote they were offered the religious franchise.[2]

The leaders were not imposed from above. Methodism made its leaders. Many had but the slightest education. Class leaders rose from the rank and file and represented every conceivable occupation. There was no financial qualification. The chief qualifications were common sense, a flair for initiative, and a positive religious experience. By the end of the century there were at least eight thousand of these leaders of small groups. Founders might include at random a carpenter, a schoolmaster, a shepherd, a retired soldier, an upholsterer, a tailor, a taverner, a piece maker, a handloom weaver, a cordwainer, a cooper, a grocer, a breadbaker, and a brazier.[3] Even women could and did attain to positions of leadership. All over the country societies were formed on the initiative of women who needed no other authority than their own impulse and determination. A servant girl, an itinerant carder and spinner, or a housewife was no less acceptable than a woman of social position and influence. This was a bold innovation and an example of leveling sentiment even in an age of bluestockings. In these and other ways the gifts and enthusiasm of a large number of earnest people were enlisted in Wesley's cause.[4]

The system of class meetings was the very life of Methodism. These consisted of small groups of Christians who met regularly together for mutual help and fellowship. Their meeting place was sometimes a private house or room in the local chapel. Membership of the class always carried with it membership of the Methodist Society. The weekly meeting was not only a religious meeting but also a social or family gathering. There was usually a free and easy atmosphere about the place. All who attended were encouraged to assist one another. Those who could not subscribe a penny a week were helped by those who could.

> Help us to help each other, Lord
> Each other's cross to bear,
> Let each his friendly aid afford
> And feel his brother's care.

Each person who attended was expected to take some part in the devotions. All members were expected to use, not hide their talents, their faith to be expressed in works.[5]

Far from being an anodyne the urgent and compelling message of Wesley was a summons to put sloth aside and accept duties and responsibilities and play a full part in the arena. To carry out Wesley's injunction meant that every Methodist became in some degree a teacher, a judge, and a preacher, something new to the illiterate masses of the eighteenth century. Whatever they were in the mine or mill, here in the chapel they were men—with worth and dignity in the eyes of God and their brethren—free and equal. This confirmation of human values, the recognition of the common man, was one of the most far reaching and potently significant elements in Wesley's work. Gray's short and simple annals of the poor were told in reverse; hidden resources were tapped and utilized. In a sense the century of the forgotten man had begun;[6] in a sense, too, Wesley's was the first neurological clinic.[7]

Wesley taught the laboring poor that they too were precious in the sight of God and that they had a soul to save and maintain equally with the richest in the land. For the crushed and despised to be told over and over again that God loved them, that they could be saved, sounded strange in their ears and filled them with astonishment. The effect on mind and heart, the revolution in outlook on life and society was phenomenal. Many changed themselves and tried to change and improve their environment.[8]

In Methodist societies members learned "earnestness, sobriety, industry, and regularity of conduct," ready to take their places in the industrial world. These were serviceable social fruits indeed. In the chapel life, too, working men first learned to speak and organize, to persuade and trust their fellows. "It was in the Little Bethel that many of the working class leaders were trained." From the very beginning of the Trade Union Movement, among all sections of the wage earners, says Sidney Webb, "it is men who are Methodists whom we find taking the lead and filling the posts of influence. From their ranks have come an astonishingly large proportion of the Trade Union leaders."[9]

2.

Methodism was a child of the Industrial Revolution. Its growth was slow when industrial endeavor was sleepy and sluggish. Its expansion increased as the use of machinery was extended. It had a key to the heart of new England growing up in towns and industrialized villages. Workers who migrated to centers where economic opportunity offered a livelihood constituted the "very social material Methodism was wont to lay hold upon." They were a virgin field for the new teaching. Large sections of the manufacturing population heartily embraced Wesley's doctrines.[10]

To a certain extent Wesley neglected the country districts. It was the policy of Methodist preachers to go to places where there was no spiritual shepherd and that meant to towns where the population was thickest. Villages were left to the care of the Anglican clergy. Agricultural areas were correctly described as the Methodist wilderness. Wesley disliked farmers as a class and refused to idealize the farmer's life. Besides the sparse peasant population bound to their field work failed to provide large audiences.[11]

The center of population had shifted from the south to the north. The discovery that iron might be smelted with coal led to an extraordinary growth of population in Lancashire and Yorkshire. The growth of towns may be seen by comparing various estimates of the population of six provincial towns in the years 1685 and 1760: Liverpool grew from 4,000 to 40,000, Manchester from 6,000 to 40,000, Birmingham from 4,000 to 30,000, Sheffield from 4,000 to 30,000, Leeds from 7,000 to 150,000 (in 1841), and Bristol from 29,000 to 100,000.[12]

The Established Church was parochial and conservative —loath to leave old pathways, slow to seize new opportunities. Among the vast population of the mining areas and in rapidly growing textile towns, it scarcely existed for the poor. Not a new parish had been created; no additional churches had been built. Methodism, on the other hand, with no tradition and no prejudices had not become stabilized and rigid and so was better able to adapt itself to new conditions.[13]

The provision of the Established Church was ridiculously inadequate. Manchester reported in 1817 a population of 109,457 and church accommodations of only 14,850. In Oldham the figures were 18,000 against 1,700, in Stockport 33,973 compared with 2,000. Sheffield in 1819 had fifteen times as many people as churches could hold, Leeds six times.[14] The inability of the state church to meet the hunger and urge of new populations was a factor in the growth of Methodism.

"We went forth to seek that which was lost, more eminently lost," says John Wesley, "to call the most flagrant, hardened, desperate sinners to repentance. To this end we preached in the Horsefair at Bristol, in Kingswood, in Newcastle, among the colliers in Staffordshire and the tinners in Cornwall, in Southwark, Wapping, Moorfields, Drury Lane, at London. Did any man ever pick out such places as these in order to find serious, regular, well-disposed people? How many such might there be in any of them I know not. But this I know, that four in five of those who are now with us were not of that number but were wallowing in their blood, till God by us said unto them 'Live.' "[15]

Established religion was a soporific of the poor. Again a modified mercantilism argued that supine obedience of the masses to the few was alone consistent with the national welfare. On this ground they should be accorded a subsistence level of life. Class lines were rigidly drawn—it was not an integrated but a segmented society—and the lower classes were economically helpless, demoralized, and irresponsible. They were not only a continuous burden on the poor rates but also a permanent threat to the social order. Religion urged the poor to look to the distant future for redress, emphasized the virtues of poverty as compensatory gains. But as Burke said: "The deserts of the poor would be adjusted in the final proportions of eternal justice."

Gin to Burke was a great medicine for the poor — of their cares and sorrows. If there was no food gin greatly alleviated the want of it. He was against the idea that it is within the competence of the government taken as a government or even of the rich as rich to supply to the poor those necessaries (food, clothing, and shelter) which it has pleased the Divine Providence for a while to withhold from them. "All crimes are safe," said Dr. Johnson, "but hated poverty." [16]

In gist the typical attitude was rooted in the helplessness of the unpropertied, the irresponsible character of the poor, the physical structure of society, the dominance of the Calvinistic tradition, the national system of economics built upon the exploitation of labor.[17] No wonder that Thorold Rogers scathingly remarked: "I contend that from 1563 to 1824 a conspiracy concocted by the law and carried out by parties interested in its success was entered into to cheat the English workman of his wages, to tie him to the soil, to deprive him of hope, and to degrade him into irremediable poverty." [18]

What then were the zeal, the folly, the extravagance of Wesley and his disciples? The real offence lay in the missionary aspect of Methodism. Methodism was one of the great people's movements. The *Gentleman's Magazine* described it as a "system which tended to overthrow Church and State." The Bishop of Rochester suspected that sedition and atheism were the real objects of its institution.[19] "I thank your ladyship for the information concerning the Methodist preachers," writes the Duchess of Buckingham to Lady Huntingdon. "Their doctrines are most repulsive, and strongly tinctured with impertinence and disrespect towards their superiors, in perpetually endeavoring to level all ranks, and do away with all distinctions. It is monstrous to be told that you have a heart as sinful as the common wretches that crawl on the earth. This is highly offensive and insulting, and I cannot but wonder that your ladyship should relish any sentiment so much at variance with high rank and good breeding." [20]

While the gospel was being preached to the poor and vulgar, the churches were half empty. The church believed not only in the unquestioning servitude of the poor and vulgar, but in the simple policy of leaving them alone. The contrast is striking: The church offered a religion of learning and elegance to the rich and genteel; Wesley offered a simple soul to the poor, democratic opportunities, worth, and dignity. To whom would they naturally turn?

Between the Trent and Tweed, Wesleyanism and Industrialism were soon to forge a new world.[21] "They were the first preachers since the days of the Franciscan friars in the Middle Ages," says Hugh Price Hughes of Wesley and his helpers, "who ever reached the working classes. In England as in France, Germany, and everywhere else the Reformation was essentially a middle class movement. It never captured either the upper classes or the working classes. That explains its limitations." Wesley brought the Reformation to its logical fulfillment in England—he recovered the reform tradition of Wyclif.[22]

3.

The land of England bloomed waving with yellow harvests, but in the miner's black pit, the workers toiled in anguish and desperation. The hours of labor were never less than eleven and often fourteen and upwards. A large proportion employed in the coal mines were under thirteen years of age. Children began to work at four. Ventilation and drainage systems were lamentably defective. Some of the work meant solitary confinement. Accidents were numerous and of a fearful nature. Conditions were dreadful. Girls were often employed at pulling or "hurrying," that is, pulling the baskets or wagons of coal along the ground by means of a chain. Like four-legged animals, half-naked girls creeping on their hands and feet with a chain between their legs were compelled to work for many hours on their burdensome track. When the road was wet, they often had to pass through dirty water and filthy clay.[23]

Amongst these people of the pit Wesley and his followers came to exercise their most beneficent influence. The religion they preached came to the miners not only as a form of religious dissent but also as welcome in a dark and dismal environment. In the gospel of spiritual opportunity, the fellowship of all men, they tasted the sweetness of democracy.[24]

Wesley rode to Blanchland about twenty miles from Newcastle. The rough mountains round about were still white with snow. In the midst was the small winding valley through which the Derwent runs. On the edge of this little town stood little more than a heap of ruins. Wesley stood in the churchyard and prayed, and all the congregation knelt down on the grass. "A row of chilldren (they were gathered out of the lead mines from all parts) sat under the opposite wall all quiet and still. The whole congregation drank in every word with such earnestness in their looks that I could not but hope that God will make this wilderness sing for joy. . . ." [25]

Among the tin miners of Gwennap twenty to thirty thousand people gathered in the open air to hear him. . . .[26]

Amazing the personal influence of this restrained, immaculate, erudite Oxford don whose speech was classical English, whose bearing was always that of a Christian gentleman, upon soldiers, sailors, publicans, miners, fishermen, smugglers, and the roughest industrial workers. He was the Friend of the People. By the mouth of the pit, before the door of worship, vast throngs of horny-handed and face-begrimed toilers removed their hats and stood in rapt and reverent attention.[27]

"The fields in every part of England are indeed white for the harvest. There is everywhere an amazing willingness in the people to receive either instruction or exhortation." [28]

CHAPTER FOUR

THE ALPHABET OF THE GOOD LIFE

"They are poor only because they are idle," said Wesley, is "wickedly, devilishly false."[1] He summed it up on one occasion when distress was acute in the community: "Let everyone avoid luxuries; let everyone work; provide employment for all."[2]

The most persistent charge leveled against the laboring poor was their improvidence and untrustworthiness, their carelessness of their own welfare, their mean, sordid, indecent spirit. Wesley addressed himself more effectively to the problem than any other force in the eighteenth century.[3] "To set the state of perfection too high," said Wesley, "is the surest way to drive it out of the world."[4] He therefore introduced to the poor the alphabet of the good life, the bare introductory phrases—industry, cleanliness, diligence, frugality, self-reliance, honesty—the tangible ideals which the masses could understand and lay hold of. Often Methodist preachers were welcomed for the effect they had upon the laborers.[5]

"My part," Wesley remarked, "is to improve the present moment."[6] To the miners he came as a civilizing influence. The Methodist chapel gave the collier a homely and joyous religion. It also provided a happy fellowship and means of education. "The typical miner," says Webb, "was drunken, dissolute, and brutalized, tyrannized over by his employers and their underlings."[7] The majority had never received any education whatever. To these people Wesley and his preachers brought the Bible and

Methodist Hymn Book. There came to them a desire for learning and improvement which had to be gratified. They sent their children to Sunday School, and not content with that, often accompanied them. Wesley drove into the minds of a naturally improvident race that extravagance was in itself a sin. No longer were wages squandered in alehouses and cockpits, or sums wasted in pawning and borrowing. Drunkenness disappeared. No small part of the riotous opposition to Wesley and his societies was instigated by alehouse keepers who complained of loss of their customers. Their antagonism was justified.[8]

"What have been the consequences of the doctrines I have preached for nine years last past?" demanded Wesley. "By the fruits shall ye know those of whom I speak. . . . The habitual drunkard that was is now temperate in all things; the whoremonger now flees fornication; he that stole, steals no more, but works with his hands; he that cursed or swore perhaps at every sentence has now learned to serve the Lord with fear and rejoice unto Him with reverence. . . ."[9]

Industriousness was not merely a duty; it was woven into the doctrine of moral transformation. The Methodist brought to his work an habitual seriousness of purpose. He worked and lived austerely and found satisfaction in it. He worked in a mood of devotion. The sheer association of religious zeal and daily work made it natural that the economic ideal should acquire meaning and power. Methodist workmen felt no self-consciousness in undertaking to persuade even their masters to become Methodists just as Methodist masters often led their employees to enter the societies not by compulsion of prestige but by sincere personal zeal. This union of religious enthusiasm, Puritan austerity, and sanctification of work sank deeply into the character of the faithful member. He had a more hopeful and more purposeful hold upon life. The converts of Wesley could look forward to a new heaven and new earth.[10]

"Sir, I willingly put the whole cause on this issue," said Wesley. "What are the general consequences of this preaching? Are there more tares or wheat? more good men destroyed (that is the proper question) or wicked men saved? . . . Now let any man inquire at Rhode, Bradford, Wrexall, or among the colliers at Coleford, 1) What kind of people were those before they followed these men? 2) What are the main doctrines they have been teaching for this twelvemonth? 3) What effect have these doctrines upon their followers? What manner of lives do they lead now? And if you do not find 1) that three in four of these were, two years ago, notoriously wicked men, 2) that the main doctrines they have heard since were, 'Love God and your neighbor, and carefully keep his commandments, and 3) that they have since exercised themselves herein, and continue so to do, I say, if you or any reasonable man, who will be at the pains to inquire, does not find this to be an unquestionable fact, I will openly acknowledge myself an enthusiast, or whatsoever else you shall please to style me." [11]

"No Indians," added Wesley, "are more savage than were the colliers of Kingswood, many of whom are now an humane, hospitable people full of love to God and man, quiet, diligent in business, in every state content." [12]

The eighteenth century was not slow to observe the effects of Wesley on the laboring section of the community. Methodists and non-Methodists, friendly observers and unfriendly critics, bore witness to the making of self-respecting, trustworthy, disciplined, and orderly working men in all the industrial centers. "To you," declared Priestley in *An Address to the Methodists*, "is the civilization, the industry, the sobriety of great numbers of the laboring part of the community owing." [13] "The Methodists," another remarked of the Cornish miners, "have perseveringly taught, gradually reclaimed, and at length, I almost venture to say, completely reformed a large body of men" otherwise immersed in "the grossest moral turpitude." [14] The moment they became religious their brutality subsided. Even children employed in factories, the most profligate in the town, were transformed by contact with Methodism.

In a different industrial section a different set of factors held true—new opportunity for initiative, economic improvement, and social mobility. "Yet if any doubt it," declared an official apologist of the movement in 1785, "let them go to Kingswood and Cornwall; let them go to Newcastle, Coleford, Wednesbury, and Whitehaven; let them go to Leeds, Sheffield, Manchester, and Liverpool; let them go to Birmingham, Wolverhampton, and Chester; let them go to Norwich, Bath, and Bristol—and they will soon be satisfied that multitudes," once dissolute and undependable, "are now sober holy Christian men." [15]

Even in the army and navy Methodist soldiers and sailors were commended for their steadiness and reliability. Officers often welcomed Methodist preachers to their camps and barracks. Methodist sailors on Nelson's ship, *Victory,* owned the distinction of being "the best sailors on the ship." [16]

"I like him for a workman," it was said of a pious society member, "but I hate his religion." Yet there was a direct relation between Methodist discipline of character and material success. Methodists were given posts of responsibility, an intermediate stage to positions of economic independence and power. "Actuated by interest, proprietors of factories chose sober and pious men for their foremen and overlookers." [17] Sir Robert Peel the Elder was reported to have testified in 1787: "I have left most of my works in Lancashire under the management of Methodists and they serve me excellently well." [18] In one case Methodists were imported into a district to found an ironworks.[19] Afterwards the leading ironmasters throughout the country were prominent Wesleyans.

Personal austerity and a rigid moral code by which the Methodist ordered his conduct in his business activities acquired the force of a settled reputation. Strict integrity resulted from adherence to the cause. In an industrial community the term Methodist came to be altered from one of opprobrium to one of respect. "How few of them ever failed in business!" it was said, and therein was revealed how much pride the societies took in maintaining their reputation in the world of industry and trade.[20]

Wesley pressed the point of business integrity even more closely home. Did the Methodists, he asked, profit from the ignorance or need of others? "Do you walk by this rule? Do you never do unto any what you would not they should do unto you? . . . Suppose you were engaged in trade: do you demand, do you receive no more than the real value of what you sell? Do you demand, do you receive no more of the ignorant than of the knowing, of a little child than of an experienced trader? If you do, why does not your heart condemn you? You are a barefaced extortioner! Do you demand no more than the usual price of goods, of any who is in pressing want—who must have, and that without delay, the things which you only can furnish him with? If you do, this is also flat extortion. Indeed you do not come up to the righteousness of a Pharisee." [21]

The disposition of money was undertaken in exactly the same spirit of responsibility with which gain was attempted. Methodists came to be distinguished and known by their attention to the poor and their generosity in case of need. Sometimes they gave a large proportion of their earnings on principle.[22]

Woodrow Wilson has well said: "The Church was dead and Wesley awakened it; the poor were neglected and Wesley sought them out; the gospel was shrunken into formulas and Wesley flung it fresh upon the air once more in the speech of common men." [23]

2.

Wesley was not the man to be elated by being noticed

by the rich, the noble, and the great. He was thankful for their help, but far from being proud of their approbation. "To speak a rough truth, I do not desire any intercourse with any persons of quality in England, I mean for my own sake. They do me no good, and I fear I can do none to them. If it be desired, I will readily leave all those to the care of my fellow laborers." [24] Not seldom when he was invited to dine with them he politely declined and went on his way. "O how hard it is to be shallow enough for a polite audience!" [25] "I was a little out of my element among lords and ladies. I love plain music and plain company best." [26] He repeatedly speaks of the "ignorance," even "gross ignorance" he had observed in rich and genteel people throughout the nation.[27] In June, 1739, when he came to Bath, the general excitement drew many of the rich and great to his preaching. After his sermon several fine ladies followed him to his lodging desiring a conversation with him. "I do not expect," he told them tersely, "that the rich and great should want either to speak with me or to hear me, for I speak the plain truth—a thing you hear little of, and do not desire to hear." [28]

Surprisingly it was the man who came from a humble home, Whitefield, who could or sought to attract the high born whom the aristocratic Wesleys failed or did not care for the most part to touch.[29]

The illustrious vulgar were too proud to be saved and too foolish to understand. Said Charles Wesley of the man about town—

> "What is a modern Man of Fashion?
> A man of taste and dissipation. . . .
> In sleep and dress and sport and play
> He throws his worthless life away;
> Has no opinions of his own,
> But takes from leading *Beaux* the *ton*; . . .
> With a disdainful smile or frown
> He on the riff-raff crowd looks down:

The world polite—his friends and he,—
And the rest are—Nobody!
Custom pursues his only rule,
And lives an APE and dies a FOOL."[30]

"I love the poor," added John Wesley. "In many of them I find pure genuine grace, unmixed with paint, folly, and affectation. . . . The poor are the Christians." [31]

The charge and cure were reiterated: "none but a Christian is happy; none but a real inward Christian. A glutton, a drunkard, a gamester may be merry, but he cannot be happy. The beau, the belle may eat and drink, and rise up to play, but still they feel they are not happy. Men or women may adorn their own dear persons with all the colors of the rainbow. They may dance and sing and hurry to and fro and flutter hither and thither. They may roll up and down in their splendid carriages and talk insipidly to each other. They may hasten from one diversion to another, but happiness is not there—

'Tis a dull farce, an empty show,
Powder, and pocket glass, and beau.[32]

"But a dissipated life was not merely that of a powdered beau, a petit-maître, a gamester, a woman hunter, a playhouse hunter, a fox hunter, or a scatter brain of any kind." It was the life too of an honorable statesman, a gentleman, or a merchant "that is without God in the world. A *dissipated* age is an age wherein God is generally forgotten. And a *dissipated* nation (such as England is at present in a superlative degree) is a nation, a vast majority of which have not God in all their thoughts." [33]

In a softer moment Wesley admitted, however: "The chief disadvantages of an elevated situation is this: it removes us from the scenes of misery and indigence. We are apt to charge the great with want of feeling, but it is rather want of consideration. The wretched are taught to avoid and the poor fear to accost them, and in the circles of perpetual gaiety they forget that these exist." [34]

"Riches," Wesley concluded, "are equally a hindrance to the loving our neighbor as ourselves, that is, the loving all mankind." [35]

CHAPTER FIVE

THE GREAT ADVENTURE

"Two young men without a name, without friends, without either power of fortune, set out from college with principles totally different from those of the common people to oppose all the world, learned and unlearned, to combat popular prejudices of every kind. Our first principle directly attacked all the wickedness, our second all the bigotry in the world. Thus they attempted a reformation not of opinions (feathers, trifles not worth the naming), but of men's tempers and lives, of vice in every kind, of everything contrary to justice, mercy, or truth. And for this it was that they carried their lives in their hands, that both the great vulgar and the small looked upon them as mad dogs and treated them as such, sometimes saying in terms, 'Will nobody knock that mad dog on the head?' "[1]

Between 1732 and the end of the century 606 anti-Methodist publications were printed. "Malicious invective," "a profane and filthy production," "a violent tirade" runs the comment of Richard Green who compiled a bibliography of anti-Methodist literature in the eighteenth century. Other productions were extremely dull and theological. The *Scots Magazine* for 1739 called the Wesley brothers "movers of sedition and ringleaders of the rabble."[2] Malicious squibs in newspapers and pamphlets of all kinds painted them as unheard of monsters—"sanctified devils, scoundrels, quacks, canting, hypocritical villains."[3] The printer of the *Dublin Chronicle* called John

Wesley "a double-tongued knave, an old crafty hypocrite who used religion merely for a cloak, saying one thing and meaning another." [4] Abused in the press, assaulted and stoned in the streets, Wesley still went on testifying salvation by faith. As his opponents grew more violent and abusive, he grew calmer and more reasonable. He never lost his temper or good manners in a controversy. And it was nearly always the eighteenth century apostles of good taste rather than the Methodists that seemed to be the foaming enthusiasts.

The ever memorable Toplady who his admirers said "stands paramount in the plentitude of dignity above most of his contemporaries," was scurrilous and intemperate. Wesley, said Toplady, was guilty of "Satanic shamelessness," of "acting the ignoble part of a lurking, sly assassin," of "uniting the sophistry of a Jesuit with the authority of a Pope," and of sinking the discussion "to the level of an oyster woman." [5] It seemed, said Southey of Toplady, as if he had imbibed the spirit of sectarian scurrility from the truculent libelers of the puritanical age.[6] Wesley treated Toplady's attack with contemptuous silence. Yet elsewhere he retorted to his critics: "Suppose we really were enthusiasts, suppose our doctrines were false and unsupported either by reason, Scripture, or authority, then why hath not someone who is a wise man and endued with knowledge among you attempted at least to show us our guilt in love and meekness of wisdom. . . . The wisdom that is from above is pure, peaceable, gentle. . . . Does this spirit appear in one single tract of all those which have been published against us? Is there one writer that has reproved us in love?" [7] But Wesley might have added: "To those who know the world, hardly anything that is wrong or foolish in it appears strange." [8]

"Pray tell Mr. Wesley that I shall not give him the Sacrament, for he is not fit," were the words of the Epworth rector in the very parish where, says Wesley, "I had so long lived a Pharisee." [9] "Heark ye, Clinker," counsels Squire Bramble, "you are a most notorious offender. You stand convicted of sickness, hunger, wretchedness, and want." When Clinker is put into prison on the charge of highway robbery, he preaches to the felons, much to the annoyance of the turnkey who says, "I don't care if the devil had him." [10]

Smollett's portrait is tinged with admiration, an apologia for Methodism as well as a criticism. But Horace Walpole's is dipped in acid: "Methodism is more fashionable than anything but Brag; the women play devilish deep at both." [11] Methodism to Walpole was "a revival of all the folly and cant of the last age." [12] His first remark is a witty counterpart to Dr. Samuel Bowden's satirical poem entitled, "The Mechanic Inspired," which bespatters the Wilshire Methodists—

Ye vagabond Levites who ramble about,
To gull with your priestcraft an ignorant rout,
Awhile your nonsensical canting suspend,
And now to my honester ballad attend.
The dupes of sly Romish, itinerant liars,
The spawn of French Prophets and mendicant friars,
Ye pious enthusiasts! who riot and rob,
With holy grimace and sanctified sob. . . .[13]

Reading that, we are less apt to cavil at Wesley's remark: "Let every one, then, speak as he finds. As for me, I cannot admire either the wisdom or virtue or happiness of mankind. Wherever I have been, I have found the bulk of mankind, Christian as well as heathen, deplorably ignorant, vicious, and miserable." [14]

2.

No one set out on a great adventure with more determined foes to overcome than John Wesley. Against him were the Mob, the Clergy, the Aristocracy, and the Press. But Wesley's will was heroically adamant. Through bleak

Yorkshire moors, over the somber Cornish wastes, through the mountain solitudes of Wales—in stables and inns and barns, in churchyards and under market crosses, in streets and lanes of cities he preached the doctrine of repentance and personal faith.[15]

We get a picture of Wesley's style of operation on his first visit to Newcastle. After finding an inn and putting up his horses, he refreshed himself with a cup of tea and went out to look at the town. Newcastle was not the immense place it is today. Wesley had never seen such a rabble of squalid, noisy, drunken, blaspheming wretches. Even the grubby children cursed and swore and fought and tumbled in the gutters.

On Sunday morning at seven, walking down to the poorest and most contemptible part of the town with one companion, he took his stand at the end of a street and began singing the 100th Psalm. Three or four persons came to see what was the matter. Soon four or five hundred joined them. Before he was through, there were twelve to fifteen hundred. They stood gaping and staring at him in astonishment. When he had finished preaching, he told them, "If you desire to know who I am, my name is John Wesley. At five in the evening, with God's help, I design to preach here again." At five the hill on which he was to preach was covered from top to bottom. When he was through speaking, his listeners were ready to tread him under foot "out of pure love and kindness." [16]

In June, 1742, he arrived at Epworth and the curate to whom Samuel Wesley had shown the greatest kindness refused to allow the son of his old benefactor "to assist him by preaching or reading prayers." That same evening John Wesley, not being permitted to preach in the church, preached in the churchyard, standing on his father's tombstone. "Accordingly at six I came and found such a congregation as I believe Epworth never saw before. I stood near the east end of the church upon my father's tombstone, and cried, 'The kingdom of heaven is not meat and drink, but righteousness, and peace, and joy in the Holy Ghost.' "[17]

But the reception accorded Wesley by the people was often not "loving and kind."

During the first three decades ugly and riotous interference of mobs was more or less continuous. Meetings were attacked by drunken, brawling rabbles armed with clubs, whips, clods, bricks, staves, stones, stink bombs, wildfire, and rotten eggs. Southey refers to egg shells filled with blood and stopped with pitch.[18] Drums were beaten, horns blown, churchbells jangled, guns let off, fiddlers and ballad singers hired, mill dams let out, and blacksmiths hired to ply their noisy trade in order to drown the voice of the preacher. One man was sent to cry fresh salmon at a little distance from the multitude of "unawakened" hearers at Leicester, but no one regarded him.[19] Wesley tells us that a woman went about with a sponge effacing obscene words on houses, doors, walls, etc.[20]

At Charles' Square the mob drove an ox into the midst of a congregation, starting a scene of wild disorder. The poor animal was wiser than his tormentors, for "he ran round and round one way and the other, and at length broke through the midst of them clear away, leaving us calmly rejoicing and praising God." [21] At Pensford the rabble, which had been baiting a bull, concluded their sport by driving the torn and tired animal full against the table on which Wesley was preaching. "They strove several times to throw it down by thrusting the helpless beast against it, who of himself stirred no more than a log of wood. I once or twice put aside his head with my hand that the blood might not drop upon my clothes." [22] On Feb. 22, 1746, he says: "I preached at five. As we went home, a great mob followed and threw whatsoever came to hand. I was struck several times, once or twice in the face—but not hurt at all." [23] Visiting Leominster several months later he preached on a tombstone close to the south side of the church. "The multitude roared on every side, but my voice soon prevailed, till they began ringing the bells." [24] In Rochdale he found the streets lined on both sides "with multitudes of people shouting, cursing, blaspheming, and gnashing with their teeth." [25] On Sunday evening, May 5, 1745, he preached at Goston's Green, Birmingham, when "it was dangerous for any who stood to hear, for the stones and dirt were flying from every side, almost without intermission for near an hour." [26] At Natwich he was "saluted with curses and hard names," and soon afterwards the mob pulled down the chapel.[27] At Hull the mob stoned him in a crowded coach, "but a large gentlewoman, who sat in my lap, screened me so that nothing came near me." [28]

Bristol and Kingswood at the time contained a population the most primitive, brutal, and ignorant in all England. At Chowden, as he entered the village for the first time he says, "Twenty or thirty wild children ran round us as soon as we came, staring as in amaze. They could not properly be said to be either clothed or naked. One of the largest (a girl about fifteen) had a piece of a ragged, dirty blanket some way hung about her, and a kind of cap on her head, of the same cloth and color. My heart was exceedingly enlarged towards them, and they looked as if they would have swallowed me up." [29] At Plymouth and Bolton "howling fanatics dancing with rage such as had never been seen before in creatures called men hunted the preacher like a pack of wolves." At the Cross in Bolton they pushed Wesley from the steps several times. Repeatedly he returned and finally finished his discourse. Here he tells an instance of "how God overrules even the minutest circumstances," that when preaching at the Cross "one man was bawling just at my ear when a stone struck him on the cheek, and he was still. A second was forcing his way down to me till another stone hit him in the forehead; it bounded back, the blood ran down, and he came no farther. The third, being got close to me, stretched out his hand, and in the instant a sharp stone came upon the joints of his fingers. He shook his hand and was very quiet till I had concluded my discourse and went away." [30]

The savage mob of the day found as much pleasure in persecuting Wesley and his preachers as baiting a bear or watching a cock fight.

The clergy and squires aroused the mob. The *Journal* of April 17, 1743, runs thus: "While I was speaking, a gentleman rode up very drunk, and after many unseemly and bitter words labored much to ride over some of the people. I was surprised to hear he was a neighboring clergyman." [31]

Rev. George White, curate of Colne, Lancashire, who subsequently drank himself to death, invited, to ensure a roisterous anti-Methodist mob, all interested to repair to a specified pub where "each man shall receive a pint of ale in advance, and other proper encouragements." A terrible reception awaited Wesley on this occasion at Roughlee. When he began to preach, "a drunken rabble came with clubs and staves in a tumultuous and riotous manner." The deputy constable requested him to go to the house of Rev. Mr. White. "I had scarcely gone ten yards," says Wesley, "when a man . . . struck me with his fist in the face with all his might. Quickly after, another threw his stick at my head. Another man, cursing and swearing in the most shocking manner, cried out, 'Bring him away.'" After leaving the house, the mob followed him with oaths, curses, and stones. One of them beat him to the ground. When he rose again, the whole body came about him like lions and forced him back into the house.[32]

But the clergy were puppets of parish squires who in most cases controlled their livings. Wesley traced the majority of mob riots to the doors of magistrates, squires, and gentlemen. A *Journal* entry (May 7, 1743) says: "The sons of Belial gathered themselves together, headed by one or two wretches called gentlemen, and continued shouting, cursing, blaspheming, and throwing showers of stones almost without intermission." [33] At North Taunton a clergyman and two or three gentlemen brought a huntsman with his hounds, "but the dogs were wiser than the men, for they could not bring them to make any noise at all." [34] The entry of September 19, 1769, is amusing: "The beasts of the people were tolerably quiet till I had nearly finished my sermon. They then lifted up their voice, especially one called a gentleman, who had filled his pockets with rotten eggs, but a young man coming unawares, clapped his hands on each side and mashed them all at once. In an instant he was perfume all over, though it was not so sweet as balsam." [35] On another occasion a gentleman hired a company of boys to shout and "made a poor man exceeding drunk, who bawled out much ribaldry and nonsense while he himself played the French horn." [36] Some gentlemen magistrates advised mobs to "do what you will" with the Methodists, "so you break no bones." [37] Others issued general warrants for the arrest of itinerant preachers.

Wesley never lost his temper. Repeatedly when struck by stone or cudgel, he quietly wiped away the blood and went on preaching without so much as a frown on his face. Not courage alone saved Wesley, but serenity—cool, steady, courteous behavior. If he had to walk through the mob, he would uncover his head so that they might see his face, and then the singing mass would give way before him. His favorite method was to go up to the ring-leader and take him by the hand. Never did he show the least sign of being rattled. On one occasion when he was just about to preach, an excited friend rushed into the room and warned him that the house was surrounded and that the mob proposed to burn it down. "Then our only way is to make use of it while it is still standing," Wesley replied quietly, and he proceeded to expound the tenth chapter of St. Matthew.[38]

He was a master of mob psychology. He knew that the mob must be led and not driven. He knew how to attract its attention and how to coax it into respect. Here is a typical scene: an open street, a curious, hostile crowd watching Wesley who is just about to preach. Suddenly he whips off his hat and in clear, easy accents addresses them. "Friends, let every man do as he pleases, but it is my manner when I speak of the things of God, or when another does, to uncover my head." [39]

In his *Journal* he says he made it a rule confirmed by long experience "always to look a mob in the face." He saved his life more than once by acting on this rule. Never was he in greater danger than in Falmouth in the summer of 1745. The Pretender was marching south from Scotland, and a ridiculous rumor that Wesley was an emissary of the Pretender reached Cornwall. Wesley was calling on an invalid and the house which he had entered was beset on all sides by the rabble who "roared with all their throats, 'Bring out the Canorum! Where is the Canorum?'" (meaning Methodist).

They forced the outer door and filled the passage. Only a thin partition separated them from the room in which Wesley awaited their attack. He was urged to hide, but answered, "No, it is best for me to stand where I am." Setting their shoulders to the inner door, the robbers cried out, "Avast, lads, avast!" Away went the hinges, and the door fell back into the room.

Wesley stepped forward at once into the middle of the mob and said, "Here I am. Which of you has anything to say to me? To which of you have I done any wrong? To you? Or you? Or you?"

A mob sings well in chorus, but it is not good at providing solos. "I continued speaking," says Wesley, "till I came, bareheaded as I was (for I purposely left my hat that they might all see my face) into the middle of the street, and then, raising my voice, said, 'Neighbors, countrymen! Do you desire to hear me speak?' 'Yes! yes!' they cried vehemently. 'He shall speak. He shall. Nobody shall hinder him.' . . . I never saw before," adds Wesley, "no, not at Walsall itself, the hand of God so plainly shown as here . . . although the hands of perhaps some hundreds of people were lifted up to strike or throw, yet they were one and all stopped in the mid-way, so that not a man touched me with one of his fingers; neither was anything thrown from first to last, so that I had not even a speck of dirt on my clothes." To the leader of the mob Wesley said, "I wish you a good night," to which the wretch replied, "I wish you were in hell," and then turned away with his companions.[40]

Wesley's caution was no less conspicuous than his courage. It was a fair day when he visited Pocklington in April, 1752. The room provided for preaching was only five yards square, and Wesley was anxious to have a bigger place. Someone suggested the yard. But when he went to see it, he found that "it was plentifully furnished with stones, artillery, ready at hand for the devil's drunken companions." Fortunately a gentleman offered a large barn.[41]

The *Journal* mentions Wesley's expertness in the crushing retort. Told at Bath that Beau Nash meant to interfere, Wesley was entreated not to attempt to preach. Wesley, however, was not the man to yield to a swaggering dandy. He had gone to preach, and preach he would, and did, the threatenings of Nash having made his congregation much larger than was expected. Soon after Wesley began his sermon, the Beau in his immense white hat appeared, and coming close to him, told Wesley he preached contrary to Acts of Parliament. "Besides your preaching frightens people out of their wits." "Sir," said Wesley, "did you ever hear me preach?" "No." "How then can you judge of what you never heard?" "I judge," he answered, "by common report." "Common report," replied Wesley, "is not enough. Give me leave, sir, to ask, is not your name Nash?" "It is," he said. "Sir," retorted Wesley, "I dare not judge of you by common report." The master of ceremonies paused a while, and having recovered his composure, asked what the people wanted. Upon which an old woman begged Wesley to allow her to answer him. Amid her taunts the resplendent king of the pump room sneaked away.[42]

In October, 1743, Wesley was at the scene of disturbances in Wednesbury, Staffordshire. A mob besieged the house in which he was staying, yelling for him to be put out. Wesley requested the leader of the crowd to come into the house. The popular hero rashly accepted the challenge, but quickly succumbed to Wesley's seductive reasoning. The lion had become a lamb. He was asked to bring in one or two of his more angry companions. "He brought in two who were ready to swallow the ground with rage, but in two minutes they were as calm as he." Wesley then went outside to face the crowd. Mounting a chair, he asked, "What do any of you want with me?" They wanted him to go with them to a justice. He agreed to do so, but went on speaking, and in a few seconds had them clamoring to spill their blood in his defense. Some two or three hundred still insisted, however, that he go with them to the justice. He consented and after a two mile tramp in the rain, they arrived at Bentley-Hall, the residence of Mr. Lane, the justice. The excited vanguard announced to the astonished magistrate that they were bringing Mr. Wesley. "What have I to do with Mr. Wesley?" asked his honor. "Go and carry him back again!" and he went to bed. The main body of the mob now came straggling up and began banging on the door. The magistrate's son soon appeared. What was the disturbance about? A spokesman answered, "To be plain, sir, if I must speak the truth, all the fault I find with him is that he preaches better than our parsons." Another said, "Sir, it is a downright shame; he makes people rise at five in the morning to sing psalms. What advice would your worship give us?" "Go home," said Lane the younger, "and be quiet."

The mob now hurried Wesley to Walsal to another justice. It was now seven o'clock and dark. Mr. Persehouse also refused to see them. Its civic conscience appeased, there was nothing for the mob to do but trudge back again. About fifty of the crowd undertook to be Wesley's escort, but before they had gone a hundred yards, a fresh mob from Walsal rushed the converted mob. Some were pelted, others fled, and Wesley was left alone in the hands of the victorious ruffians. Some tried to seize him by the collar and pull him down. One ruffian rushed through the crowd, lifted his arm to strike but on a sudden let it drop and only stroked Wesley's head saying, "What soft hair he has!" As they dragged Wesley from one end of the town of Walsal to the other, he tried to dart into an open door, but was pulled back by the hair. He tried it again, but was stopped by the owner of the house. He managed to make a stand in an open doorway and harangued the crowd until his voice failed him. "Are you willing to hear me speak?" Many cried, "No, no! knock out his brains! Down with him! Kill him at once!" Wesley asked, "What evil have I done? Which of you all have I wronged in word or deed?" Again they cried, "Bring him away, bring him away!" Wesley began to pray aloud, and a man who just before had headed the mob, turned and said, "Sir, I will spend my life for you; follow me and not one soul here shall touch a hair of your head."

The leader of the mob with two or three of his comrades, one of them a noted prizefighter, now closed around Wesley and brought him safely back to Wednesbury, "having lost only one flap from my waistcoat and a little skin from one of my hands," he reports. But one of the mob had struck him on the mouth with such force that the blood gushed out. A big lusty fellow behind him struck him several times with an oaken club, and another hit him on the breast. Yet he felt no more pain "than if they had touched me with a straw. . . . From beginning to the end I found the same presence of mind as if I had been sitting in my study. . . . Only once it came into my mind that if they should throw me into the river, it would spoil the papers that were in my pocket. For myself I did not doubt but I should swim across having but a thin coat and a light pair of boots." [43]

The same coolness impressed the mob that tried to break up his meeting at Whitechapel by throwing stones, one of which struck Wesley between the eyes. But again he felt no pain, and when he wiped away the blood, he went on preaching, "Testifying that God hath given to them that believe not the spirit of fear but of power and love and of a sound mind." His behavior disarmed the hoodlums.[44]

From Manchester on one journey in 1757 he rode over the mountains to Huddersfield. "A wilder people I never saw in England. The men, women, children filled the street as we rode along, and appeared just ready to devour us. They were, however, tolerably quiet while I preached; only a few pieces of dirt were thrown, and the bellman came in the middle of the sermon. I had almost done when they began to ring the bells." [45] At Gawksham there was a lone house on the side of an enormous mountain "where the congregation stood and sat, row above row, in the sylvan theatre. I believe," he adds, "nothing on the post diluvian earth can be more pleasant than the road from hence between huge, steep mountains, clothed with wood to the top, and washed at the bottom by a clear, winding stream." Leaving Gawksham, he went to Radiham and preached to "a large, wild congregation." At Glasgow he preached in the yard of the poorhouse.[46]

At Dunbar he went into the street and began speaking to a congregation of two men and two women which was soon joined by about twenty little children, and not long after by a large number of young and old. On a sudden the sun broke out and shone full on his face. At Kelso he went to the market house, but neither adult nor child came near him. At length he began singing a Scotch psalm. In due time a congregation gathered. Wesley used "keen and cutting expressions." Coming to Placey he writes, "The society of colliers here may be a pattern to all the societies in England. No person ever misses his band or class." [47]

In Cornwall his labors were Herculean. Though now in the sixty-sixth year of his age, for eight days together he preached mostly in the open air three or four times a day and said, "I hardly felt any weariness, first or last." [48] At Polperro his bedroom was filled with pilchards and conger eels, which made him glad to accept the offer of another room. At Plymouth a silly man talked without ceasing during the sermon until Wesley desired the people "to open to the right and left and let him look his garrulous disturber fairly in the face," upon which the noisy prater pulled off his hat and quietly went away. Between Charlton and Lympsham the rivers were so swollen that Wesley's horse had to swim and Wesley himself had to be taken to lodgings on an "honest man's shoulders." [49]

When the *Dublin Chronicle* viciously attacked him years later, Wesley replied in a touching summation of his saintly and heroic labors. "This is my answer to them that trouble me and will not let my grey hairs go down to the grave in peace. I am not a man of duplicity. I am not an old hypocrite, a double-tongued knave. . . . I now tell a plain tale, that the good which is in me may not be evil spoken of. I have no temporal end to serve. I seek not the honor that cometh of men. It is not for pleasure that at this time of life I travel three or four thousand miles a year. It is not for gain.

> No foot of land do I possess,
> No cottage in this wilderness;
> A poor wayfaring man,
> I lodge awhile in tents below,
> Or gladly wander to and fro,
> Till I my Canaan gain." [50]

The scoffers vanished away. Neither house nor yard would contain the congregation and all were serious. Near Todworden the people stood row above row on the side of the mountain. "They were rough in outward appearance, but their hearts were as melting wax." [51] At Stoneseygate a large congregation filled both the yard and the road to a considerable distance. Many were seated on a long wall adjoining, but as it was built of loose stones, in the middle of the sermon all fell down at once. "I never saw, heard, nor read of such a thing before. The whole wall and the persons sitting upon it sunk down together, none of them screaming out and very few altering their posture. . . . Nor was there any interruption either of my speaking or of the attention of the hearers." [52] At Shore, four miles south, halfway down a huge, steep mountain, Wesley preached again to a "loving, singlehearted people." At Congleton Cross it rained most of the time that he was speaking, but that did not hinder an abundance of people from quietly attending.[53] He arrived at St. Ives before morning prayers and walked to the church without so much as one huzza. "How strangely," adds Wesley, "has one year changed the scene in Cornwall. They give us good words almost in every place. What have we done that the world should be so civil to us?" [54]

From the beginning Wesley had loved soldiers, and he found it always a pleasure to preach to them. Soldiers came in troops and at times made up a considerable part of the congregation.[55] While he was preaching in the square at Plymouth a regiment of soldiers with military music marched into it. No sooner, however, did the commanding officer perceive the preacher than he stopped the music and drew up his men to listen. "They were all still as night," says Wesley, "nor did any of them stir, till I had pronounced the blessing." [56]. . .

Wesley had seen dark days, but now the sun was shining.

2.

"I preached," says Wesley, "to a huge multitude in Moorfields on 'Why will ye die, O house of Israel?' It is field preaching which does the execution still; for usefulness there is none comparable to it." [57]

Wesley, a pragmatist, was quick to adopt the good and discard the bad. He disliked field preaching, but was converted by the test of practical results. "What marvel," he writes, "the devil does not like field preaching. Neither do I. I love a commodious room, a soft cushion, a handsome pulpit. But where is my zeal if I do not trample all these under foot in order to save one more soul?" [58] It was cooping themselves up in rooms, he remarked to James Rea, Methodist preacher, that damped "the work of God, which never was and never will be carried on to any purpose without going out into the highways and hedges and compelling poor sinners to come in." [59]

But as he says in *A Further Appeal to Men of Reason and Religion,* forbidden to preach in any church, he had no desire or design to preach in the open air till after the prohibition, that when he did, it was no matter of choice or premeditation, that field preaching was therefore a sudden expedient, a thing submitted to rather than chosen, and submitted to because he thought preaching even thus was better than not preaching at all.

"Things were in this posture when I was told I must preach no more in this, and this, and another church; the reason was usually added without reserve. 'Because you preach such doctrines.' . . . When I was at any of the societies, I spoke more or less though with much inconvenience to as many as the room I was in would contain. But after a time, finding those rooms could not contain a tenth part of the people that were earnest to hear, I determined to do the same thing in England which I had often done in a warmer climate, namely, when the house would not contain the congregation, to preach in the open air. This I accordingly did, first at Bristol where the society rooms were exceeding small, and at Kingswood where we had no room at all, afterward, in or near London.

"And I cannot say I have ever seen a more awful sight than when on Rose Green or the top of Hannam Mount some thousands of people were calmly joined together in solemn waiting upon God while

> They stood and under open air adored
> The God who made both air, earth, heaven, and sky.

And whether they were listening to his word with attention still as night, or were lifting up their voice in praise as the sound of many waters, many a time have I been constrained to say in my heart, 'How dreadful is this place! This also is no other than the house of God! This is the gate of heaven!' "[60]

CHAPTER SIX

REGIMEN

"What is important for us," says Woodrow Wilson, "is the method and cause of John Wesley's success. His method was as simple as the object he had in view. He wanted to get men and he went directly to them, not so much like a priest as like a fellow man standing in a like need with themselves." [1]

If ever spirit refused to be shackled by the flesh, it was that which drove or carried him over hundreds of thousands of miles through storms at sea, through blizzards on land, and torrents in rivers. In 1753 that same spirit caused him to survive unimpaired an attack of consumption so severe that to prevent as he said a "wild panegyric," he composed his own epitaph. From his youth he had inured himself to weather. Besides, what he willed, he willed.[2] He was as indifferent to the doubts expressed by Hume as if the two men lived in different hemispheres or centuries.[3]

His accomplishments were due to methodical habits. He made schedules weeks in advance and nothing could deter him from fulfilling his engagement. The ice cut like a sword,[4] the rain ran in the main street with a stream capable of turning a mill,[5] his clothes were wet through and through most of the day,[6] he had a pain in the left side and in his shoulder, his windpipe seemed nearly closed,[7] he was violently sick or feverish, preaching as if his feet were in cold water,[8] but he never disappointed. "Press on, break through," he urged one of his preachers.

"Let not a little hindrance or inconvenience put you out of your way." [9]

On Februray 23, 1745, the causeways in many places were impassable. The hard frost succeeding the thaw had made the ground like glass. Wesley was often obliged to walk, it being impossible to ride, and several times his horse fell down while he was leading him. It was eight before he got to Gateshead Fell which appeared a great pathless waste of white, the snow filling up and covering all the roads. "Many a rough journey have I had before, but one like this I never had, between wind, and hail, and rain, and ice, and snow, and driving sleet, and piercing cold, but it is passed. Those days will return no more, and are therefore as though they had never been." [10] In this sort of weather he rode 280 miles in six days.

On the way to Newcastle in February, 1747, the hail drove so vehemently in their faces that they could hardly breathe. The northwind blew so hard and keen that when he and his companions got to Hatfield they could scarcely use either hands or feet. Next day the storm of snow and hail changed to a violent storm of rain and hail, driving through their coats and boots and freezing as it fell. Their eyebrows hung with icicles. The wind rose higher and higher until it threatened to overturn both man and beast. When they came to an inn at Stilton, they were exhausted.[11]

At another time, after an illness of fever and convulsion, his hand shook so that he could hardly write his name, "but after I had been well electrified by driving four or five hours over very rugged broken pavement, my complaint was quite removed and my hand was as steady as when I was ten years old." [12] Near the road at Wells, just as he began to preach, a wasp stung him upon the lip. "I was afraid it would swell so as to hinder my speaking, but it did not. I spoke distinctly near two hours in all and was no worse for it." [13] One day on the way to Dullen he was on horseback from 5 a.m. till nearly 11 o'clock at night with but an hour or two intermission. And yet only five hours after this, he again set out and made the longest day's journey he ever rode—about ninety miles. At eighty-three he set out in a snowstorm on a journey that occupied more than the next four months. His first halt was at Newbury, where he had "a large and serious congregation," but where he passed such a night as he had not passed for forty years, his lodging room being as cold as the outward air. "I could not sleep at all till three in the morning. I rose at four and set out at five." The next fortnight he spent at Bristol and vicinity. Then he started off to Scotland, where the roads were blocked with snow and the weather was intensely cold.[14]

His saddlebags were filled with books, which he read as he rode along in good weather. History, poetry, and philosophy he commonly read on horseback, having other employment at other times.[15] (Once riding to Newcastle he finished the tenth book of the *Iliad.*) [16] Only a few times was he thrown head over heels. In riding vast distances he scarcely ever remembered a horse (except two) to fall or stumble while he rode with a slack rein.[17] But if over the roughest paths and fells, he tumbled, treacle and brown paper provided a sovereign cure for bruises.

It must have been a remarkable sight—a small man in scrupulously neat clerical dress, jogging somewhat awkwardly along the road, the reins hanging loosely on his horse's neck, a book in one hand and a busy pencil in the other, marking through a word here, a phrase there, a sentence or paragraph yonder, now and then writing in the margin or changing the punctuation to suit the requirements of the abbreviated sentences. Often on the back of his best ridden horses he prepared other men's work for republication. When he was sixty-three friends gave him a carriage and pair. He nailed up one side of the coach and built in shelves which were filled with books and a board which could be let down to serve as a desk.

His chaise became a study, an office, a book shop, a library, and also a private chapel.[18]

In an era when the chief thoroughfares of England were infested with highwaymen, he never once was robbed on the road. If inhospitably treated at an inn, as he was at first in Cornwall, he could feed on blackberries. If there were no bed to lie on, well, he would lie on boards. Once, after about a fortnight of such sleeping, he turned round in the night to his companion and, clapping him on the side, said, "Brother Nelson, let us be of good cheer, for the skin is off but one side yet." [19]

"In my present journey," he remarks, "I leap as broke from chains. I am content with whatever entertainment I meet with and my companions are always in a good humor because they are with me. This must be the spirit of all who take journeys with me. If a dinner ill dressed, or hard bed, a poor room, a shower of rain, or a dusty road will put them out of humor, it lays a burthen upon me greater than all the rest put together. By the grace of God I never fret. I repine at nothing. I am discontented with nothing. And to hear persons at my ear fretting and murmuring at everything is like tearing the flesh off my bones. I see God sitting upon His throne and ruling all things well." [20]

2.

Wesley's industry was almost without parallel. The mere outlines of his work are sufficient to make one gasp with astonishment. During his itinerant ministry, he traveled (mostly on horseback) over a quarter of a million miles (a distance equal to nine times round the world), preached no less than 52,400 times between 1738, when he returned from Georgia, and 1791, when he preached his last sermon eight days before he died. In addition he organized and superintended hundreds of societies in every part of the kingdom, wrote 233 books and pamphlets and helped in the writing and editing of two hundred more, kept a journal and private shorthand diary, carried on a huge correspondence, organized various forms of relief for the poor and unemployed and had always time to talk or pray with anyone who needed him.[21] "Looking at his traveling the marvel is how he found time to write, and looking at his books, the marvel is how he found time to preach." [22] He was always moving and yet in the midst of ceaseless toils, he betrayed no more bustle than a planet in its course. His mission was too great to allow time for trifles. Rising with the lark, traveling with the sun, he always acted in harmony with his own well-known utterances. "The world is my parish!" [23] He reappears in nearly half a hundred towns for thirty times and more, while he records forty visits each to Canterbury, Bolton, Chester, Salisbury, Sheffield, between fifty and seventy to Leeds, Manchester, Birmingham, Newcastle-on-the-Tyne, over a hundred to Kingswood, one hundred and seventy-five to Bristol, and two hundred recorded visits to London. He sent forth preachers to proclaim the love of religion to every inhabitant throughout the land while he himself regularly ranged the three kingdoms and Wales "stirring the stagnant current of human life." [24]

His labors in Ireland were almost incredible. All over the isle he went preaching every day and often twice or thrice a day, not only in Methodist meeting houses, but in churches, Presbyterian chapels, in factories, in bowling greens, in assembly rooms, in court houses, in barns, in sloping meadows, in shady orchards, in groves and avenues, in linen halls, in churchyards and streets—everywhere he had a chance. We know with certainty that minute as are the details of his journals he by no means mentions every sermon that he delivered and every society that he visited.[25]

The story of a single typical day is the story of the whole fifty years. He rose at four o'clock, read his devotional books until five, preached in the open air to the colliers or other workers who had to go to their tasks at half past six. After breakfast at seven he mounted his horse and drew rein for a few minutes from time to time to read a page in some book he was analyzing. After a twenty or thirty mile ride, he preached in the public square or some churchyard at noon. He dismissed his hearers at one o'clock that they might return to work, then rode rapidly, often twenty miles, to his next appointment where he preached at five. After supper, when evening twilight fell, he preached again or held a service that lasted until nine or ten o'clock.

Always and everywhere he was ready to turn passing incidents to practical account. "Pray, sir, let us go," said one of his friends while two women near Billingsgate market were quarreling most furiously, and using language far more forceful than pious. "Pray, sir, let us go. I cannot stand it." "Stay, Sammy," replied Wesley, as he looked at the viragos who were evidently inspired, though not from heaven. "Stay, Sammy, stay and learn how to preach." [26]

Although it was Wesley's constant rule that no preacher preach more than twice a day unless on Sunday or an extraordinary occasion—to do oftener than this was "a degree of self murder"—he himself frequently delivered three or four sermons in a day. A letter to James Hutton on his activities, June 23, 1739, reads: "At four I preached to about two thousand at the Bowling Green on 'Do all to the glory of God,' at seven in the morning to four or five thousand, and at ten to about three thousand at Hanham." As he was riding to Rose Green, his horse pitched on its head and rolled over and over. Wesley received a little bruise on the side, which made him lame for two or three days.[27]

The practice of preaching at five or earlier was begun in order not to interfere with the working hours of his hearers. The miners of Newcastle came to hear him at night and slept on the benches of the old meeting house so that they might hear him again at five in the morning before going to the pithead.[28] Wesley considered preaching at five the healthiest exercise in the world. These early morning services, he said, were "the glory of the Methodists," a glory that made them "a peculiar people." No other church or community in England had a service like this. If Methodists failed to attend, they would lose their zeal and become a fallen people.[29]

"It is no exaggeration to say," remarked one biographer, "that Wesley preached more sermons, rode more miles, worked more hours, printed more books, and influenced more lives than any Englishman of his age or perhaps of any age. And the performance did not even tire him!" In 1786 he writes, "I have entered upon the eighty-third year of my age. I am a wonder to myself. I am never tired either with preaching, writing, or traveling." [30]

Perhaps the secret of Wesley's intense accomplishment lies in this: "Do all things with a single eye as I have done from the beginning." [31]

3.

On December 6, 1726, Wesley hoisted his flag—"Leisure and I have taken leave of one another. I propose to be busy as long as I live if my health is so long indulged me." The flag never drooped till death overtook him in 1791.[32] Even when he badly sprained his ankle on the ice in the middle of London Bridge he was never idle. He spent the week in prayer, in reading, in conversation, and in writing *Lessons for Children,* and compiling a Hebrew grammar.[33]

Dr. Johnson complained about Wesley's activity. "John Wesley's conversation is good, but he is never at leisure. He is always obliged to go at a certain hour. This is very disagreeable to a man who loves to fold his legs and have out his talk as I do." [34] Wesley explained the manner of his life to Miss March, December 10, 1777: "Though I am always in haste, I am never in a hurry because I never undertake any more work than I can go through with perfect calmness of spirit. It is true I travel four or five thousand miles in a year. But I generally travel alone in my carriage and consequently am as retired ten hours in a day as if I was in a wilderness. On other days I never spend less than three hours (frequently ten or twelve) in the day alone. So there are few persons in the kingdom who spend so many hours secluded from all company." [35]

Inflexible temperance was linked to unexampled economy of time. At seventy-three Wesley wrote this paean of himself: "I am seventy-three years old and far abler to preach than I was at three and twenty. What natural means has God used to produce so wonderful an effect? 1. Continual exercise and change of air by traveling about four thousand miles in a year. 2. Constant rising at four. 3. The ability, if ever I want, to sleep immediately. 4. The never losing a night's sleep in my life. 5. Two violent fevers, and two deep consumptions. These, it is true, were rough medicines, but they were of admirable service, causing my flesh to come again as the flesh of a little child. May I add lastly, evenness of temper? I feel and grieve, but by the grace of God I fret at nothing." [36]

To Sally Wesley, to readers and listeners, he marked the pitfalls of excessive indulgence in sleep. "All are intemperate in sleep who sleep more than nature requires, and how much it does require is easily known. There is, indeed, no universal rule, none that will suit all constitutions. . . .

"Healthy men in general need a little above six hours' sleep, healthy women a little above seven in four and twenty. I myself want six hours and a half, and I cannot well subsist with less.

"If any one desire to know exactly what quantity of sleep his own constitution requires, he may very easily make the experiment which I made about sixty years ago. I then waked every night about twelve or one and lay awake for some time. I readily concluded that this arose from my lying longer in bed than nature required. To be satisfied I procured an alarum, which waked me the next morning at seven (near an hour earlier than I rose the day before), yet I lay awake again at night. The second morning I rose at six, but notwithstanding this I lay awake the second night. The third morning I rose at five, but nevertheless I lay awake the third night. The fourth morning I rose at four (as by the grace of God I have done ever since) and I lay awake no more. And I do not now lie awake (taking the year round) a quarter of an hour together in a month."

But what were the ill consequences of lying longer in bed—suppose nine hours in four and twenty?

"It hurts the body. . . . it as it were soddens and parboils the flesh and sows the seeds of numerous diseases, of all nervous diseases in particular. . . .

"It hurts the mind, it weakens the understanding. It blunts the imagination. . . .

"Take exactly so much sleep as nature requires. If you need between seven and eight hours, then in the name of God, begin! This very night lie down at ten o'clock and rise between five and six whether you sleep or no."

No avenue of escape is provided, no grace to human weakness. "In spite of the most dear and agreeable companions, in spite of their most earnest solicitations, in spite of entreaties, railleries or reproaches, vigorously keep your hour. Rise up precisely at your time, and retire without ceremony. Keep your hour, notwithstanding the most pressing business; lay all things by till the morning. Be it ever so great a cross, ever so great self-denial, keep your hour, or all is over.

"I advise you, Be steady. Keep your hour of rising without intermission. Do not rise two mornings and lie in bed the third, but what you do once, do always. 'But my head aches.' Do not regard that. It will soon be over. 'But I am uncommonly drowsy; my eyes are quite heavy.' Then you must not parley; otherwise it is a lost case, but start up at once. And if your drowsiness does not go off, lie down for a while, an hour or two after. But let nothing make a breach upon this rule, rise and dress yourself at your hour." [37]

Wesley was one of the most abstemious men of the eighteenth century. He says in one place that for four years he lived entirely on potatoes. Horace Walpole half way through the century describes a court beauty as having "two acres of cheek spread with crimson, an ocean of neck that overflowed and was not distinguishable from the lower part of the body." [38] Thackeray observes, "Swift was fat, Addison was fat, Gay and Thomson were preposterously fat; all the fuddling and lunch drinking, that club and coffee house boozing, shortened the lives and enlarged the waistcoats of the man of that age." Fox and Walpole and the Royal Georges were all massively corpulent. Johnson was huge. Garrick declares that most actors ate and drank themselves into unseemly unshapes." [39]

Wesley's *Thoughts on Nervous Disorders* aimed at providing a remedy for lowness of spirit and a sound specific for a vigorous, temperate, and healthy life. "First. Sacredly abstain from all spiritous liquors. To others they may sometimes be of use, but to nervous persons they are deadly poison.

"Secondly. If you drink any, drink but little tea, and none at all without eating, or without sugar and cream. 'But you like it without.' No matter; prefer health before taste.

"Thirdly. Every day of your life take at least an hour's exercise, between breakfast and dinner. If you will, take another hour before supper, or before you sleep. If you can, take it in the open air; otherwise in the house. If you cannot ride or walk abroad, use, within, a dumb-bell or a wooden horse.

"Fourthly. Take no more food than nature requires. . . . It is not generally the quality but the quantity of what we eat which hurts us. Dine upon one thing—except pudding or pie. Eat no flesh at supper, but something light and easy of digestion.

"Fifthly. Sleep early and rise early, unless you are ill, never lie in bed much above seven hours. Then you will never lie awake. Your flesh will be firm and your spirits lively.

"Sixthly. Above all,

> 'Give not your passions way,
> God gave them to thee under lock and key.'

Beware of anger, beware of worldly sorrow, beware of the fear that hath torment, beware of foolish and hurtful desires, beware of inordinate affection." [40]

"Do you know why that cow looks over that wall?" Wesley asked a friend. The man had been speaking about his troubles and saying that he knew not what he should do. "Do you know why that cow looks over that wall?" "No," replied his friend. "I will tell you then," replied Wesley. "She looks over the wall because she cannot look through it. And that is what you must do with your troubles—look over them." [41]

4.

Be earnest! Be earnest! was the main lesson of Wesley's life. Wisely said the ancients, "The soul and body make a man; the spirit and discipline make a Christian." [42] Wesley's indomitable devotion to duty was magnificent. Here was no ordinary man, but a God-like man, never flinching, never disheartened, always buoyed up by faith, always gentle and kind. "Duty is all I consider. *Trouble* and *reproach* I value not," he wrote.[43] "I must follow my own conscience." [44] To Mrs. Barton he sent words of courage: "Continue to be useful in your generation. As you have time to do good unto all men, comfort the afflicted, support the weak, exhort the believers to go on to perfection. Never be weary of well doing."[45] He always found time to visit the sick and the poor, "and I must do it, if I believe the Bible. . . . Where there is time and opportunity for it, who can doubt but this is matter of absolute duty?" [46] He took as his motto Bishop Stratford's prayer, "Lord, let me not live to be useless." [47] His concern for man's welfare was to bring no towering rank, no monetary reward. An instance of Francis Asbury's greatness caused no end of annoyance. "How can you," he wrote to Francis Asbury in America, "how dare you suffer yourself to be called Bishop? I shudder, I start at the very thought! Men may call me a knave or a fool, a rascal, a scoundrel, and I am content, but they shall never by my consent call me Bishop." [48]

But Wesley's devotion to duty neither scarred his nature and countenance nor desiccated his blood. If ever man dwelt in constant sunshine, it was John Wesley. He was always the Christian gentleman — placid, benevolent, and full of anecdote. Though never trifling, he was always cheerful, sometimes saying, "I dare not fret than curse or swear." His sprightliness among his friends never left him. In the midst of gigantic toils, he was blithe and happy.[49] "I am convinced true religion or holiness cannot be without cheerfulness . . . and that true religion has nothing sour, austere, unsociable in it. Are you for having as much cheerfulness as you can? So am I. Do you endeavor to keep alive your taste for all the truly innocent pleasures of life? So do I likewise. Do you refuse no pleasure but what is a hindrance to some greater good or has a tendency to some evil? It is my very rule." [50]

Wesleyans followed that rule. They were a happy people, but their happiness was seasoned with a tight-lipped determination. "I do not remember," Wesley remarked in 1780, "I do not remember to have felt lowness of spirits from one quarter of an hour since I was born." [51] Alexander Knox, who knew Wesley, said, "He was, in truth, the most perfect specimen of moral happiness that I ever saw." [52] And his biographer, the Rev. Luke Tyerman, concludes on the same note, "Happy, happy old man." [53]

That—the cheerfulness of religion—was the substance of his reproof to William Law: "Let me beg you to consider whether your extreme roughness and morose and sour behavior can possibly be the fruit of a living faith in Christ." [54] To his mother he wrote: "I can't think that when God sent us into the world He had irreversibly decreed that we should be perpetually miserable in it. . . . What are become of all the innocent comforts and pleasures of life if it is the intent of our Creator that we should never taste them? If our taking up the cross implies our bidding adieu to all joy and satisfaction, how is it reconcilable with what Solomon so expressly affirms of religion—that her ways are ways of pleasantness and all her paths peace?"[55]

5.

Whenever Whitefield passed, he left memories of overwhelming passion and eloquence. Whenever Wesley passed, he left more enduring memorials in the shape of schools, mission rooms, meeting places, and unions for prayer, for charity, and for self help.[56] "No preacher ought to stay either at Portsmouth or Sarum or any other place a whole week together," said Wesley. "That is not the Methodist plan at all." [57] Channels of endeavor, areas of fervor were marked out at the first visit; at each return these were bolstered until they became bulwarks.

Wesley's passion for order led him to become the great organizer. The societies were almost semi-military; the whole Methodist organization was benevolently autocratic. But no great religious leader was less of a doctrinaire, less of a dictator. No founder of a great religious movement was more open to conviction: "I have no more right to object to a man for holding a different opinion from mine than I have to differ with a man because he wears a wig and I wear my own hair, but if he takes his wig off and shakes the powder in my eyes, I shall consider it my duty to get quit of him as soon as possible." [58] Wesley was a great general who had the interest of his disciples at heart, and they admired and respected him.

He was no milksop. Those who had business dealings with him soon found out what sort of man they had to do with. "Sir," he wrote to a landowner at Newcastle, "I am surprised. You give it under your hand that you will put me in possession of a piece of ground, specified in an article between us, in fifteen days time. Three months are passed, and that article is not fulfilled. And now you say you can't conceive what I mean by troubling you. I mean to have that article fulfilled. I think my meaning is very plain. I am, Sir, your humble servant." He got the piece of ground—for an orphan house.[59]

Wesley strove to visit all his societies at least once a year, and his visits generally involved a review of local affairs. He expelled or accepted members, appointed local preachers, and confirmed or rejected the appointments of those who had begun to preach without his express sanction. Among all who were his fellow workers, he was the head.

He stamped his personality on every part of the machine he made. At the annual conference of itinerant preachers in 1766, when someone complained of his power, he replied: "I did not seek any part of this power; it came upon me unawares. But when it was come, not daring to bury that talent, I used it to the best of my judgment; yet I was never fond of it. I always did and do now bear it as my burden, the burden which God lays upon me and therefore I dare not yet lay it down. But if you can tell me any one or any five men to whom I may transfer this burden, who can and will do just what I do now, I will heartily thank both them and you. . . .

"It is nonsense to call my using this power, 'shackling free-born Englishmen.' None needs to submit to it, unless he will, so there is no shackling in the case. Every preacher and every member may leave me when he pleases. But while he chooses to stay, it is on the same terms that he joined me at first. 'But this is arbitrary power; this is no less than making yourself a Pope.'

"If by arbitrary power you mean a power which I exercise singly, without any colleagues therein, this is certainly true, but I see no hurt in it. Arbitrary in this sense is a very harmless word. If you mean unjust, unreasonable, or tyrannical, then it is not true."

Wesley believed himself called by God to the work of spreading and organizing Methodism and his grasp of authority was never a selfish grasp. The mass of Methodists knew that John Wesley was not mistaken in his estimate of his own abilities.

Yet Charles was restive under the supervision of his brother whom in letters he called King or Pope. John felt he could not count upon the loyal cooperation of his fellow worker. "O brother," wrote John, "pretend no longer the thing that is not. You do not, will not, act in concert with me. . . . for ten years last past and upwards, you have no more acted in connection with me than Mr. Whitefield has done." Charles indorsed the letter, "Trying to bring me under his yoke." Yet while John was writing his own epitaph to protect his memory against "vile panegyric," Charles made it clear to people that he "neither could nor would stand in his brother's place, if God took him to Himself, for he had neither a body, nor a mind, nor talents, nor grace for it."

The lack of cooperation between the two brothers was due to three causes: Charles's highhanded actions in wrecking John's proposed marriage with Grace Murray, the growing influence of Charles's wife Sally (now at forty, he took no step without consulting his "dearest partner"—this despite twenty years' difference in age. Every decision was in her hands), and, lastly by the brothers' divergent attitude towards the Church of England.[60]

John thought separation from the Established Church

inexpedient; Charles thought it heinous. John was inclined to treat the disaffected with gentleness and persuasiveness; Charles was for the adoption of strong and compulsory measures.

To one intinerant preacher who favored joining the ranks of dissent, Charles intemperately wrote, "I love thee from my heart; yet rather than see thee a dissenting Minister, I wish to see thee smiling in thy coffin." Elsewhere he said, "My brother's first object was the Methodists and then the Church. Mine was first the Church, and then the Methodists." [61]

But John had the mortification of seeing his work thwarted by that church which he loved so dearly. One of his last letters was a manly appeal to the Bishop of Lincoln. "My Lord, I am a dying man, having already one foot in the grave. Humanly speaking I cannot creep long on earth, being now nearer ninety than eighty years of age. But I cannot die in peace before I have discharged this office of Christian love to your lordship. I write without ceremony, as neither hoping nor fearing anything from your lordship or from any man living. And I ask, in the name and presence of Him to whom both you and I are shortly to give an account, why do you trouble those that are quiet in the land, they that fear God and work righteousness?

"Does your lordship know what the Methodists are? that many thousands of them are zealous members of the Church of England and strongly attached not only to his Majesty but to the present ministry? Why should your lordship, setting religion out of the question, throw away such a body of respectable friends? Is it for their religious sentiments? Alas! my lord, is this a time to persecute any man for conscience's sake? I beseech you, my lord, do as you would be done to. You are a man of sense; you are a man of learning; nay, I verily believe (what is of infinitely more value) you are a man of piety. Then think and let think. I pray God to bless you with the choicest of His blessings." [62]

Four years after Wesley's death the Methodist organization separated from the Established Church.

6.

Wesley was wrong at times, but he was always generous and never bitter. Not power alone made him dominant. It was something else—the devotion he inspired in his followers. They adored him, called him Rabbi, because the quality in him they would all have shared, if they could, was his infinite charity. He never spared himself. All the time he gave, gave everywhere, of the spirit that was in him, and it was abundant. Because of this he came to be the best loved man in all England and Ireland.

Wesley was neat and tidy, his linen spotless and his shoes regularly shined, however wet the weather or muddy the road. In an age of powdered and monstrous wigs he was content to wear his natural hair.[63] Immaculateness and simple comeliness were the outstanding marks of his person. Although small in stature (5 ft. 4 in.) he was finely proportioned, muscular and strong. He wore a narrow plaited stock, a coat with small upright collar, no buckles at the knee, no silk or velvet in any part of his apparel and the ordinary shovel hat of a clergyman. In youth his hair was black; in old age it was as white as snow.

The face of Wesley mellowed with the years, shining with the beauty of holiness—serene, resolute, gracious, beatific—white, silken, wavy locks; aquiline nose; clear, ruddy complexion; penetrating, kindly eyes; and radiant cheerfulness. But Cromwellian firmness was mingled with sweetness.[64]

Towards the close of his career Wesley began every New Year by distributing coal and bread and clothing among the poor of the society. For five days in January, 1785, when he was eighty-two years old, he walked the streets of London begging £200 while his "feet were steeped in snow nearly from morning till evening." He got the money and a few days' illness.[65]

Persecution had ceased. His popularity was greater than ever. Everywhere he was greeted with welcoming crowds. On Sunday, August 23, 1789, this "decayed" old man of eighty-six preached in the amphitheatre at Redruth, Cornwall, to an audience estimated at 25,000, but he doubted whether all could hear. At Falmouth the streets were lined by a crowd from one end of the town to the other, "out of stark love and kindness, gaping and staring as if the king were going by." [66]

In the last year of his life what he had said in 1785 was still more clearly demonstrated: "I am become, I know not how, an honorable man." [67]

CHAPTER SEVEN

STYLE AND ORATORY

Wesley could not hold a candle to Whitefield as an orator, but his sentences seemed to clutch at men's hearts. When a man heard Whitefield, he said, "What an actor! What an actor! I think he is sincere," but when he heard John Wesley he felt that he was alone with him, and Wesley's grave, penetrating words were addressed to him personally. Whitefield had the air of a man that could play well upon an instrument, but Wesley stroked back his hair and looked into your eyes. John Nelson felt his heart beat like the pendulum of a clock when he heard Wesley at Moorfields and thought that the whole discourse was aimed at him. His words were often "as a hammer and a flame."[1]

Wesley preached *ex tempore* from an outline and he preached the same sermon over and over. Irrelevance and trivialities dropped out until finally every word sped like a bullet to its mark. The sermons were admirable, clear, plain, practical, and earnest, expressed in pure forcible language, full of good common sense without any tawdry ornament. They lacked the splendors of Jeremy Taylor or Barrow, but the last thing Wesley desired was to pose as a perfervid orator. St. John's First Epistle, where he found "the strongest sense and the plainest language, simplicity and sublimity together," was his model. He began with an elaborate style, but as his intelligent servant Betty could not understand him he changed it.[2] His aim was to address the bulk of mankind, those who cared nothing for the art of speaking, but who were nevertheless shrewd judges of what was necessary for their happiness. He wished to utter plain truth for plain people. Therefore he abstained from all refined philosophical speculations, from all intricate reasonings, and as far as possible, from even the show of learning. He labored to avoid all words which were not easily understood or not used in common conversation.[3]

"Is there need to apologize to sensible persons for the plainness of my style? . . . I dare no more write in a fine style than wear a fine coat. But were it otherwise, had I time to spare, I should write just as I do. I should purposely decline what many admire, a highly ornamental style. I cannot admire French oratory; I despise it from my heart. Let those that please be in raptures at the pretty elegant sentences of Massillon or Bourdalouc, but give me the plain, nervous style of Dr. South, Dr. Bates, or Mr. John Howe. . . . Let who will admire the French frippery; I am still for plain sound English.

"I think a preacher or a writer of sermons has lost his way when he imitates any of the French orators, even the most famous of them. . . . Only let his language be plain, proper, and clear, and it is enough. And let him aim at no more ornament than he finds in that sentence which is the sum of the whole gospel, 'We love him because he first loved us.' "[4]

Abstinence from ornate and turgid language, he said, might check that kind of devotion which found expression in "loud shouting, horrid, unnatural screaming, repeating the same words twenty or thirty times, jumping two or three feet high, and throwing about the arms or legs both of men and women in a manner shocking not only to religion, but to common decency."[5]

Wesley's manner was calm, but it was the calm of restrained emotion. His power lay in the reasonableness and clarity, the quiet sincerity of all he said. There was no escape from relentless logic as he drove home each point, using the simplest and most homely metaphors and similes to illustrate his statements. He grew calmer and more reasonable as he came to his main arguments. Probably it was this spiritual diagnosis couched in colloquial language that could not be misunderstood that affected his hearers so strongly in the eighteenth century.[6]

He generally preached on very practical matters and frequently on simple morality and ethics—thirteen sermons on Application of the Sermon on the Mount, many on such subjects as self denial, the use of money, evil speaking, a caution against bigotry, on dress, on the danger of riches, on the education of children, on obedience to parents, on worldly folly, on the reformation of manners.[7]

People hung upon his words, for he was speaking of things intensely real to him as to them—the tone of absolute conviction held them. He hit upon the secret that "a controlled and reasoning fanaticism is one of the most powerful means of stirring the feelings of man." [8] In preaching he reasoned: "I believe and reason too, for I find no inconsistency between them." He prized his dialectical ability highly. "I would as soon gut out my eyes to secure my faith as lay aside my reason." [9]

He used his voice with skill. "Speak with all your heart," he warned his preachers, "but with a moderate voice. Be a follower of me. I often speak loud, often vehemently, but I never scream. I never strain myself." [10]

He called his preachings love feasts.[11] But he was never content merely to preach. Preaching was a preliminary to societies and classes. He would not speak anywhere that he could not strike the second blow. He was not creating a new religious sect, he insisted, but an order, a fellowship.[12]

Dr. Johnson said of Methodist preaching in reply to Boswell: "Sir, it is owing to their expressing themselves in a plain and familiar manner which is the only way to do good to the common people, and which clergymen of genius and learning ought to do from a principle of duty, when it is suited to their congregations, a practice for which they will be praised by men of sense."[13]

Dinah Morris in *Adam Bede* describes an open air meeting she witnessed. "It was on just a sort of evening as this, when I was a little girl, and my aunt took me to hear a good man preach out of doors, just as we are here. I remember his face well; he was a very old man, and had very long white hair; his voice was very soft and beautiful, not like any voice I had ever heard before. I was a little girl and scarcely knew anything, and this old man seemed to me such a different sort of man from anybody I had ever seen before that I thought that he had perhaps come down from the sky to preach to us, and I said, 'Aunt, will he go back into the sky tonight like the picture in the Bible?' " [14]

Lecky said of Wesley's preaching that it was of greater historic importance than all the splendid victories by land and sea won under Pitt.[15]

2.

Whitefield was all thunder, emotion, and tears; Wesley was logical and analytical. Yet the effect produced by Wesley was more violent and lasting—effects that to him were highly gratifying, but extremely repugnant to many of his friends. The manifestations were all of an hysterical nature—shrieks, groans, trances, and convulsions. The most general sound was a loud breathing like that of people half strangled and gasping for life. Great numbers wept without any voice, others fell down as dead; some sank in silence, some with extreme noise and violent agitation. Prayer and song usually restored them to a happier frame of mind.[16]

The first instance of this manifestation in Wesley's preaching occurred on April 17, 1739, in Bristol. Wesley was expounding the fourth chapter of Acts concerning the healing of a lame man by John and Peter. At the conclusion of the sermon he called upon God "to confirm his word." That was the cue to a woman standing close to him, who raised an outcry as if in the agonies of death. The congregation continued to pray until she recovered and sang a Methodist hymn. Two others followed in the same manner; they too ended with praise to God their Saviour.[17] At Bristol, on May 1, Wesley's voice could hardly be heard above the groans and cries of sinners calling for salvation.[18]

Some said the bad air of crowded rooms helped to bring on fits, but it was noted that the converts began screaming and dropping in the open air. One named Thomas Maxfield roared and beat himself against the ground so that six men could hardly hold him. On this day there were seven cases in the morning out of doors and twenty-nine in the evening in a room.[19] At Bezore a young man "cut to the heart" cried aloud, then another and another, "till my voice was quite lost." [20] Again at Everton there were only silent tears at first on every side, but it was not long before several were unable to refrain from weeping aloud; then a stout young man dropped down and roared.[21] At Stroud, a young gentleman interrupted Wesley's preaching by crying out, "I am damned," and falling to the ground. A second repeated this action quickly after. "We joined in prayer but had not time (it growing late) to wrestle with God for their full deliverance."[22]

At Newgate he was led to pray that God would bear witness to His word. "Immediately one and another and another sunk to the earth; they dropped on every side as thunderstruck. One of them cried aloud." [23] While he was preaching at Newgate a woman broke out into strong cries and tears. Great drops of sweat ran down her face, and all her bones shook, "but both her body and soul were healed in a moment." [24] At Baldwin Street his voice could scarcely be heard amidst the groanings of some and the cries of others. "A Quaker who stood by was very angry, and was biting his lips, and knitting his brows, when he dropped down as thunderstruck. The agony he was in was even terrible to behold. We besought God not to lay folly to his charge, and he soon lifted up his heart and cried aloud, 'Now I know thou art a prophet of the Lord.' "[25]

Wesley encouraged these hysterical outbursts. The aim of a revivalist is to create an atmosphere of contagious emotion in which worldly reason, the counsels of selfish prudence and material welfare are inhibited. The mental condition desired is akin to that induced by Coleridge—"that willing suspension of disbelief for the moment which constitutes poetic faith." Make the individual want to believe with all his heart; "make him feel that he ought to believe, and also that others round him are believing, and he will believe."[26]

But as the Methodist cause progressed, hysterical manifestations became less and less frequent.

3.

Wesley's intimate knowledge of his preachers enabled him to use their various gifts to the utmost advantage. He moved amongst them like a father. He stimulated their studies, guided their reading, took an interest in their families, and did everything in his power to appoint them to places where they could do their best services.[27]

His letters to them show how far he was typical of gentlemen of his time, how insistent he was on order, restraint, and decorum. How pointed and personal his remarks could be is shown in a letter to an Irish preacher, giving a list of "little things to remember."

"1. Be active, be diligent; avoid all laziness, sloth, indolence. Fly from every degree, every appearance of it; else you will never be more than half a Christian.

"2. Be cleanly. In this let the Methodists take pattern by the Quakers. Avoid all nastiness, dirt, slovenliness, both in your person, clothes, house, and all about you. Do not stink above ground. This is a bad fruit of laziness; use all diligence to be clean, as one says,

Let thy mind's sweetness have its operation
Upon thy person, clothes, and habitation.[28]

"3. Whatever clothes you have, let them be whole; no rents, no tatters, no rags. These are a scandal to either man or woman, being another fruit of vile laziness. Mend your clothes, or I shall never expect you to mend your lives. Let none ever see a ragged Methodist.

"4. Clean yourselves of lice. These are a proof both of uncleanness and laziness; take pains in this. Do not cut off your hair, but clean it, and keep it clean.

"5. Cure yourself and your family of the itch; a spoonful of brimstone will cure you. To let this run from year to year proves both sloth and uncleanness. Away with it at once. . . .

"6. Use no tobacco unless prescribed by a physician. It is an uncleanly and unwholesome self indulgence. . . .

"7. Use no snuff unless prescribed by a physician. I suppose no other nation in Europe is in such vile bondage to this silly, nasty, dirty custom as the Irish are. But let Christians be in this bondage no longer. Assert your liberty and that all at once. . . .

"8. Touch no dram. It is liquid fire. It is a sure though slow poison. It saps the very springs of life." [29]

In *Minutes of Several Conversations* further advice is given to Wesley's followers in the form of question and answer. In answer to question 26: What are the rules of a helper? he replies: "Do not affect the gentleman. You have no more to do with this character than with that of a dancing master. A preacher of the gospel is the servant of all. Be ashamed of nothing but sin: not of fetching wood (if time permit) or drawing water, not of cleaning your own shoes or your neighbor's." [30]

"Be mild! Be serious!" Wesley urged elsewhere. "Remember soft and fair goes far." [31]

Wesley's "small advices" on preaching include:

"1. Be sure never to disappoint a congregation unless in case of life or death.

"2. Begin and end precisely at the time appointed. . . .

"4. Always suit your subject to your audience.

"5. Choose the plainest texts you can.

"6. Take care not to ramble, but keep to your text, and make out what you take in hand.

"7. Be sparing in allegorizing or spiritualizing. Do not suffer the people to sing too low.

"8. Take care of anything awkward or affected either in your gesture, phrase, or pronunciation.

"9. Sing no hymns of your own composing. . . .

"13. Exhort everyone in the congregation to sing, not one in ten only. . . .

"20. Beware of clownishness either in speech or dress. Wear no slouched hat.

"21. Be merciful to your beast. Not only ride moderately but see with your own eyes that your horse be rubbed, fed, and bedded.

"After preaching take a little lemonade, mild ale, or candied orange peel." [32]

Insistent was Wesley's demand, "Be temperate! be temperate!" in speaking "else Satan will befool you, and on pretense of being more useful, quite disable you from being useful at all. . . . If you would not murder yourself, take particular care never to preach too loud or too long. Always conclude the service within the hour. Then preaching will not hurt you." [33]

Again he warned: They must speak as earnestly as they could, but they must not scream. It was disgusting to the hearers; it gave them pain not pleasure. "Scream no more at the peril of your soul. . . . It was said of our Lord, 'He shall not *cry*'; the word properly means, 'He shall not *scream*.'" [34]

The chief faults of speaking, after speaking too loud, was speaking in a thick, cluttering manner, speaking too fast, too slow, or speaking with an irregular, uneven voice.

"But the greatest and most common fault of all is the speaking with a tone. Some have a womanish, squeaking tone, some a singing or canting one; some a high, swelling theatrical tone, laying too much emphasis on every sentence; some have an awful solemn tone, others an odd, whimsical, whining one, not to be expressed in words.

"To avoid all kinds of unnatural tones, the only rule is this—Endeavor to speak in public just as you do in common conversation. Attend to your subject, and deliver it in the same manner as if you were talking of it to a friend. . . .

"If you would be heard with pleasure, first study to render your voice as soft and sweet as possible and the more if it be naturally harsh, hoarse, or obstreperous, which may be cured by constant exercise.

"Secondly, labor to avoid the odious custom of coughing and spitting while you are speaking.

"Above all, take care, thirdly, to vary your voice according to the matter on which you speak. Nothing more grates the ear than a voice still in the same key.

"The best way to learn how to vary the voice is to observe common discourse. Take notice how you speak yourself in ordinary conversation and how others speak on various occasions.

"Never clap your hands nor thump the pulpit. . . . Your hands are not to be in perpetual motion; this the ancients called the babbling of hands." [35]

Ease was the first, second, and third points in preaching. It was also the first, second, and third points in style. Stiffness, apparent exactness, artificiality of style were the main defects to be avoided next to solecism and impropriety. "Dr. Middleton is no standard for a preacher. His diction is stiff, formal, affected, unnatural. The art glares and therefore shocks a man of true taste. Always to talk or write like him would be as absurd as always to walk in minuet step. O tread natural, tread easy, only not careless. Do not blunder or shamble into impropriety. If you will imitate, Mr. Addison or Dr. Swift."[36] ("True simplicity," Fenelon says, "is that grace whereby the soul is delivered from all unprofitable recollections upon itself.")[37]

But speaking and writing were to proceed from a bursting granary of knowledge. Wesley enjoined his preachers the necessity of spending at least five hours in twenty-four in reading the most useful books.[38] He warned them too that one could no more be a deep preacher than a thorough Christian without extensive reading. Fifty volumes of his famous Christian Library were edited specifically for the general education of his preachers, helpers, and followers. The Minutes of the Conference for 1774 give the list of books that his preachers were expected to study as the following: Sallust, Caesar, Tully, Erasmus, Castellio, Terence, Virgil, Horace, Vida, Buchanan, the Greek Testament, Epictetus, Plato, Ignatius, Ephraem, Syrus, Homer, the Greek Epigrams, Dupont, Bishop Ussher's Sermons, Arndt, Boehm, Nelson, Pascal, Franckl, R. Gell, the Methodist tracts.[39]

Every preacher was made a distributor and seller of books. "You should take particular care that your circuit be never without an assortment of all the valuable books, especially the *Appeals*, the *Sermons*, Kempis, and the *Primitive Physic* which no family should be without."[40] It was true that most of the Methodists were poor, but what then? "Nine in ten of them would be no poorer if they were to lay out an whole penny in buying a book every other week in the year. By this means the work of God is both widened and deepened in every place." "O why is not this regarded?" Wesley asks elsewhere.[41]

The preachers must diligently ride their circuits. "It is a shame," he writes, "for any Methodist preacher to confine himself to one place. We are debtors to all the world. We are called to warn everyone, to exhort everyone, if by any means we may save some."[42] Again: to preach once in a place and no more seldom did any good. "It only alarms the devil and his children and makes them more upon their guard against a first assault."[43] The indolence of one preacher who lingered elicited this curt response: To Francis Wolfe: "Frankly, are you out of your wits? Why are you not at Bristol?"[44] "Ours are *traveling* preachers," he remarked.[45]

Rules on what to eat and drink, how to dress and act, how to write and speak were gingered with quaint advice on specific ills, health remedies which Wesley was fond of sprinkling in his pointed, practical notes.

"I suppose" [this to John Valton] "nettle tea is the best bracer in the world, and next that, elixir of vitriol (ten drops in a glass of water at ten or eleven in the morning)."[46] Or to Ellen Gretton: "I never knew any disorder in the bowels which might not be speedily cured by drinking plentifully of lemonade unless in a few peculiar constitutions which could not bear lemons. And the drinking nettle-tea (instead of common tea) will commonly perfect the cure."[47] As for gravel and nervous disorders: "The gravel may be easily prevented by eating a small crust of bread the size of a walnut every morning, fasting. But your nervous disorders will not be removed without constant exercise. If you can have no other, you should daily ride a wooden horse, which is only a double plank nine or ten feet long, properly placed upon two tressels. This has removed many distempers and saved abundance of lives."[48]

This fantastic cure: "Mr. Whitefield had for a considerable time thrown up all the food he took. I advised him to slit a large onion across the grain and bind it warm on the pit of his stomach. He vomited no more. Pray apply this to my brother's stomach the next time he eats."[49] Followed by this sensible counsel: "I do not advise you to drink any sea water. I am persuaded it was never designed to enter any human body for any purpose but to drown it."[50]

4.

No leader of a great religious movement was ever more

happy in his helpers that Wesley.[51] He was in command of an army of nearly seven hundred local preachers. He was not one to beat down his subordinates while preserving a broad respectful back to his superiors. He was as open and outspoken to cabinet ministers as to his lay preachers.[52]

Practically all his regular teachers sprang from the single social stratum between unskilled labor and the middle class. But the middle class, smaller then, was much better educated in the eighteenth than in the nineteenth century outside London, though not so in London. All teachers had the basis of an elementary education and a few of them the bare rudiments of a classical one. Yet their education was a continuous growth. Their early years, however, gave a bias to their outlook which their leadership affirmed in the movement. They belonged to a class just below the middle class—skilled artisans, small farmers, and tradesmen in business for themselves in a modest way. Their parents were preponderantly Anglican and only sparsely Dissent. All preachers showed religious hunger in youth. But almost without exception they were men (and women) who were accorded a natural leadership by their fellow members in the small groups. They were an instance of complete equality of opportunity and democratic mobility.[53]

They all lived vigorously, and many of them continued laborious pursuits until advanced old age. They were not fretting under disappointments or depressed with the ennui of prematurely worn-out emotions, or burdened and bowed down by the sorrows of youth. There was one dynamic need: to advance the cause, and one requisite: "No person must be allowed to preach or exhort among our people whose life is not holy and unblamable." [54]

The regular clergy looked down on Wesley's lay preachers. One clergyman told a lay preacher in the north country that he was not qualified to preach. The lay preacher retorted: "Qualified! You say that? Why, without your gown you dare na, and without your book you could na, and without your pay you would na, and I do without all three!" [55] The pay of laymen who were local preachers at first was nothing. They were lodged and fed by members, but they went in rags. Later the preachers received £3 per quarter for clothing and books. It is not surprising then to find that many of the early preachers died young and more than half of them soon ceased to itinerate. They pursued their calling in utter disregard of their lives or safety. Every helper sought to be as far as possible another John Wesley.

Yet the majority who filled the pulpits had abandoned their trade to follow what they believed to be their vocation. This threw a heavy burden upon the infant society, compelled to support not only them, but also their families. Charles's solution was a drastic one. He would have every preacher work at his own trade or business during the week preparing his sermons in his spare time and delivering them on Sundays in neighboring chapels without fee or award. This program was faithfully followed by the great army of Methodist preachers. Perhaps another and less noble motive on Charles's part was to break John's power; their not depending on him for bread might reduce his authority within due bounds as well as guard against that "rashness and credulity" of his. John knew nothing of Charles's hidden motives and begged his brothers, "not to check the young ones without strong necessity." [56]

Addressing himself to his brother clergy John Wesley asked: "For what price will you preach (and that with all your might, not in an easy, indolent, fashionable way) eighteen or nineteen times every week and this throughout the year? What shall I give you to travel seven or eight hundred miles, in all weathers, every two or three months? For what salary will you abstain from all other diversions than doing good and the praising of God? I am mistaken if you would not prefer strangling to such a life, even with thousands of gold and silver." [57]

In answering the objections to lay preachers Wesley compared the physician who though university bred and licensed to practise has failed to cure many of his patients, many dying under his hands, and the man who having some little skill in physic and a tender compassion for those who are sick all around him, cures many of those the doctor could or did not cure. "Will you object that he is no physician nor has any authority to practise? . . . I think he is a physician who heals." [58]

But Wesley's helpful, sympathetic, vigorous, dynamic letters constantly urged work to be done, workers to go on. "No, Aleck, no!" he writes to one preacher. "The danger of ruin to Methodism does not lie there. It springs from quite a different quarter. Our preachers, many of them, are fallen. They are not spiritual. They are not alive to God. They are soft, enervated, fearful of shame, toil, hardship. . . . Give me one hundred preachers who fear nothing but sin, and desire nothing but God, and I care not a straw whether they be clergymen or laymen; such alone will shake the gates of hell and set up the kingdom of heaven upon earth." [59]

CHAPTER EIGHT

THE CORE OF RELIGION

"I shall endeavor to show," declared John Wesley in the delivery of his fourth discourse on the Sermon on the Mount, "that Christianity is essentially a social religion, and that to turn it into a solitary one is to destroy it."[1] The core of religious ethic was a socialization of will. "The Gospel of Christ knows of no religion but social, no holiness but social holiness."[2]

No mouthing of cant phrases, no vain repetition of theological formulas, no exclusive monopolistic interpretation of religion was this. To exclude religion from any department of human affairs was to maim and deform it. Human fellowship, cooperation, and service were at the heart of the Evangelical Revival.[3] A saved soul was a social factor, for no man lives unto himself.

The foundations of the Methodist movement were ethical, practical, and experimental rather than doctrinal, theoretical, or metaphysical. Its ideal disciple, Wesley declares, loves every man as his own soul. As he has time and opportunity, he does good towards all men—"neighbors and strangers, friends and enemies—not only to their bodies by feeding the hungry, clothing the naked, visiting those that are sick or in prison, but much more does he labor to do good to their souls."[4] "Beware the sins of omission," he adds.[5]

In "An Earnest Appeal to Men of Reason and Religion" Wesley states the heart of his problem: "We see (and who does not?) the numberless follies and miseries of our fellow creatures. We see on every side either men of no religion at all or men of a lifeless, formal religion. We are grieved at the sight, and should greatly rejoice if by any means we might convince some that there is a better religion to be attained—a religion worthy of God that gave it. And this we conceive to be no other than love, the love of God and of all mankind.

"This love we believe to be the medicine of life, the never-failing remedy for all the evils of a disordered world, for all the miseries and vices of men. Wherever this is, there are virtue and happiness going hand in hand. There is humbleness of mind, gentleness, long suffering, the whole image of God, and at the same time a peace that passeth all understanding and joy unspeakable and full of glory.

"This religion we long to see established in the world, a religion of love, and joy, and peace, having its seat in the inmost soul, but ever showing itself by its fruits continually springing forth, not only in all innocence (for love worketh no ill to his neighbor) but likewise in every kind of beneficence, spreading virtue and happiness all around it."[6]

In the preface to his sermons he remarks: "We may die without the knowledge of many truths and yet be carried into Abraham's bosom. But if we die without love, what will knowledge avail?"[7] True religion does not consist in meat and drink or in any ritual observances, nor indeed in any outward thing whatever, in anything exterior to the heart. Only one condition exists: "All things are possible to him that believeth."[8]

"Very excellent things are spoken of love; it is the essence, the spirit, the life of all virtue. It is not only the first and great command, but it is all the commandments in one. . . . Not that this forbids us to love anything besides God; it implies that we love our brother also."[9]

No one could be a good Methodist without engaging in social activities. The rules demanded it. The existence of social distress was held to impose a special obligation upon Methodists. Good works themselves were quite meritless. It was the habitual disposition that was basic. "Without this all is of no value," it was affirmed.[10] Methodists were requested to abstain from "fighting, quarreling, brawling, brother going to law with brother, returning evil for evil." [11] The necessary fruit of temper was manifested in the "hungering and thirsting to do good in every possible kind." [12] No note of condescension was to be tolerated. "Give none that asks relief either an ill word or an ill look. Do not hurt them." (When Wesley relieved poor people in the street he always removed his hat when they thanked him.)[13] No credit was to be sought—"Do it in as secret a manner as is possible." [14] Wesleyans were enjoined to constant vigilance in their attention to distress within the societies, but they were warned they must not allow their "love or beneficence [to] be confined to Methodists." [15]

Members manifested an aggressive interest in distress about them. Mutual helpfulness and spontaneous friendliness rather than a calculating apportionment of alms were the dominant tone. The sheer felt imperative to give was so strong that self denial was no burden.

Wesley made it possible for the poorest of the poor to make contributions to social well being. Classes were so organized to make social obligations inescapable. Paying their pennies every week, they were contributing in some degree to the support of the sick, the distressed, the poor, and the friendless. "The burdens of others were on the hearts of all." [16]

Insistence upon right conduct, moral duty, moral responsibility led Methodists out from a merely personal conception of religion. It exchanged a sense of human impotence for unlimited strength. Its religious psychology rejected human moral weakness as unnatural and acquired disability. Its effect on the population rooted in servility was revolutionary.[17] A man might be born into the laboring section of society, but he might gain a higher rank if he showed unusual abilities. Wesley hewed out a new status for the individual as a civic personality.

Were people brought into erroneous opinions by this concept of religion? "It matters not a straw whether they are or no (I speak of such opinions as do not touch the foundation); it is scarce worth while to spend ten words about it." Wesley was sick of opinions; he was weary to hear them; he loathed this frothy food. "Whether they embrace this religious opinion or that is no more concern to me than whether they embrace this or that system of astronomy. Are they brought to holy tempers and holy lives? . . . Are they brought to the love of God and the love of their neighbor? Pure religion undefiled is this. How long will you darken counsel by words without knowledge? The plain religion now propagated is Love. And can you oppose this without being an enemy to mankind?"[18]

This did not mean indifference to truth, but when men persecuted Methodists because they disliked their opinions, Wesley said, "Remove your emphasis, gentlemen. Ask not what are our opinions, but what are our lives? Do we make the world better? If so do not oppose us so bitterly."[19]

2.

Ignorance, cruelty, vice, misery, and poverty were rampant among the teeming multitudes of men. Wesley had unflagging faith that Christ would redeem them and that he was the humble and active instrument in the work of redemption. He was to make men vitally conscious of God. "Rest not till you enjoy the privilege of humanity, the knowledge and love of God. Lift up your heads, ye creatures capable of God! Lift up your hearts to the source of your being."[20]

His great sermon on Free Grace, a vigorous attack on Calvinism which aroused the ire of Toplady and his followers, contains trenchant passages: "This is the blasphemy clearly contained in the horrible decree of predestination! And here I fix my foot. On this I join issue with every assertor of it. You represent God as worse than the devil, more false, more cruel, more unjust. But you say you will prove it by Scripture. Hold! what will you prove by Scripture? That God is worse than the devil? It cannot be. Whatever that Scripture proves, it never can prove this; whatever its true meaning be, this cannot be its true meaning. . . . It cannot mean, whatever it means besides, that the God of truth is a liar. Let it mean what it will, it cannot mean that the judge of all the world is unjust. No Scripture can mean that God is not love, or that his mercy is not over all his works; that is, whatever it proves beside, no Scripture can prove predestination." [21]

In a fiery outburst Wesley goes on: "Call it therefore by whatever name you please, election, preterition, predestination, or reprobation it comes in the end to the same thing. . . . The sense of all is plainly this: by virtue of an eternal, unchangeable, irresistible decree of God, one part of mankind are infallibly saved and the rest infallibly damned, it being impossible that any of the former should be damned or that any of the latter should be saved.

"Oh, how would the enemy of God and man rejoice to hear these things were so! How would he cry aloud and spare not! How would he lift up his voice and say, 'To your tents, O Israel!' Flee from the face of this God or ye shall utterly perish! But whither will ye flee? Into heaven? He is there. Down to hell? He is there also. Ye cannot flee from an omnipotent, almighty tyrant. And whether ye flee or stay, I call heaven his throne and earth his footstool to witness against you. Ye shall perish, ye shall die eternally. Sing, oh hell, and rejoice ye that are under the earth, for God, even the mighty God, hath spoken, and devoted to death thousands of souls, from the rising of the sun unto the going down thereof! Here, oh death, is thy sting! They shall not, cannot escape, for the mouth of the Lord hath spoken it. Here, oh grave, is thy victory! Nations yet unborn, or ever they have done good or evil, are doomed never to see the light of life, but thou shalt gnaw upon them forever and ever. Let all those morning stars sing together who fell with Lucifer, son of the morning! Let all the sons of hell shout for joy! For the decree is past and who can disannul it?"[22]

Charles Wesley summed up the matter in a memorable epigram—

> "To damn for falling short,
> Of what they could not do,
> For not believing the report
> Of that which was not true."[23]

There were no hedging this-or-else clauses. This was the gist: "To believe is to walk in the light of eternity."[24]

Yet misery was overspreading the land as a flood and daily increasing. The believer must buttress his faith by social well doing. "Behold the day of the Lord is come. He is again visiting and redeeming his people. Having eyes, see ye not? Having ears, do ye not hear, neither understand with your hearts? At this hour the Lord is rolling away our reproach. Already his standard is set up. His spirit is poured forth on the outcasts of men and his love shed abroad in their hearts. Love of all mankind, meekness, gentleness, humbleness of mind, holy and heavenly affections, do take place of hate, anger, pride, revenge, and vile or vain affections. . . . And those who thus show their love of God, show they love their neighbors also, by being careful to maintain good works, by doing all manner of good, as they have time, to all men. They are likewise careful to abstain from all evil. Cursing, sabbath breaking, drunkenness, with all other (however fashionable) works of the devil are not once named among them. All this is plain demonstrable fact. For this also is not done in a corner. Now do you acknowledge the day of your visitation? Do you bless God and rejoice therein?"[25]

Was this enthusiasm? Wesley's religion was rational as well as Scriptural. "It is as pure from enthusiasm as from superstition. . . . Who will prove that it is enthusiasm to love God, even though we love Him with all our heart?" [26]

He refused to be called a mystic. "It is best to drop the quietists and mystics altogether and at all hazards keep to the plain, practical written word of God." [27] Yet we can tax him with boundless credulity. In every incident great or small that turned out well he saw like Bunyan a special providence. "He who governed the world before I was born shall take care of it likewise when I am dead." [28] And a mystic grace and glow brighten this passage on the infiniteness of God. "Suppose there are more worlds than there are sands on the seashore, is not the universe finite still? It must be, unless it be God. And if it be finite, it can still bear no proportion to Him that is infinite—no more than this ball of earth does. How large so ever it be, still, compared to Him, it is as nothing as the small dust of the balance. Do you ask then, what is this spot to the great God? Why, as much as the millions of systems. Great and little have place with regard to us, but before Him, they vanish away. Enlarge the bounds of creation as much as you please; still it is as but a drop to the Creator.

"And still the power of His Almighty hand
Can form another world from every sand." [29]

"Yet were this done," he adds, "there would be no more proportion than there is now between Him and His creatures. In this respect, one world and millions of worlds are just the same thing. Is the earth a cypher, a nothing, to the infinitely great, glorious, wise, and powerful God? So is any number of worlds which can be conceived: so is all finite being to the infinite." [30]

3.

The true Christian does all possible good of every possible kind to all men.[31] When giving a definition of an "altogether Christian," he affirmed "it means among other things the love of our neighbor." And lest anybody should be in doubt as to "who is my neighbor," he adds, "Every man in the world." [32]

"I reverence these ancient Christians (with all their failings) the more because I see so few Christians now, because I read so little in the writings of later times and hear so little of genuine Christianity." [33]

But Wesley and his followers never stinted their Christianity. He gave them rules to be polite, honest, gentle, loving, kind, and courteous to all men.[34]

Who is a Christian indeed? What does the term imply? "He is full of love to his neighbor, of universal love, not confined to one sect or party, not restrained to those who agree with him in opinions, or in outward modes of worship, or to those who are allied to him by blood or recommended by nearness of place. Neither does he love those only that love him or that are endeared to him by intimacy of acquaintance. But his love resembles that of Him whose mercy is over all His works. It soars above all these scanty bounds, embracing neighbors and strangers, friends and enemies, yea not only the good and gentle, but also the forward, the evil, and unthankful. For he loves every soul that God has made, every child of man, of whatever place or nation. . . . And this universal, disinterested love is productive of all right affections. It is fruitful of gentleness, tenderness, sweetness, of humanity, courtesy, and affability." [35]

Constant in emphasis that Christianity is not a solitary religion, that love of God leads to social and spiritual redemption, that a true Christian advances peace and good will among his fellow creatures, promotes the happiness of mankind, what then is a Methodist?

"The distinguishing marks of a Methodist are not his opinions of any sort. His assenting to this or that scheme of religion, his embracing any particular set of notions, his espousing the judgment of one man or of another are all quite wide of the point. Whosoever, therefore, imagines that a Methodist is a man of such or such an opinion, is grossly ignorant of the whole affair; he mistakes the truth totally.

"What then is the mark? Who is a Methodist according to your own account? I answer: A Methodist is one who has the love of God shed abroad in his heart and has this commandment written in his heart: that he who loveth God loves his brother also. Loves not only God but loves his neighbor as himself, and does good unto all men, neighbors and strangers, friends and enemies.

"These are the principles and practises of our sect; these are the marks of a true Methodist. If any man say, 'Why, these are only the common fundamental principles of Christianity!' Thou hast said; so I mean. This is the very truth. I know they are no other." [36]

CHAPTER NINE

THE EVIL OF RICHES

"Let the world be as corrupt as it will," challenged Wesley, "is gold or silver to blame?" To which the obvious answer was, "The fault does not lie in the money, but in them that use it." "It may be used ill, and what may not? But it may likewise be used well. It is full as applicable to the best as to the worst uses." [1]

Wesley not only extolled the economic virtues, but he endowed his followers with a special capacity for successful economic enterprise. With unhesitant terseness Methodists were exhorted: Gain all you can. Work was a condition of happiness. A persistent industriousness was the mark of moral character. "Fervent in spirit, not slothful in business" had acquired the force of law. "Every man that has any pretence to be a Christian will not fail to school himself rigorously to the business of his calling, seeing it is impossible that an idle man can be a good man"—sloth being inconsistent with religion.[2] "Without industry we are neither fit for this world or the world to come." [3] To be "patterns of diligence, frugality, and cleanliness" summed up one standard of conduct in temporal affairs. When Methodists at Bristol protested to the Mayor and Corporation against a proposed playhouse, it was not the evil of literary pleasures upon which opposition was founded, but a practical consideration, for it was pointed out, it would be "peculiarly hurtful to a trading city . . . directly opposite to the spirit of industry and close application to business."[4]

The Wesleyan movement almost invariably addressed itself to practical problems. Utilitarian considerations, not theological argument, made the strongest appeal to its temper. A man's business and refreshments as well as his prayers "all served the one great end." [5]

Of the ruin that came to honest men through the execrable bill trade, Wesley speaks with a good deal of feeling, backed up with forceful action—he expelled from the society those who endorsed notes without means to pay —"It is no wonder that a young man should be ruined who connected himself with that execrable bill trade. In London I expel everyone out of our society who has anything to do with it. Whoever endorses a bill (that is, promises to pay) for more than he is worth is either a fool or a knave." [6]

Deceit or sharp practice in commercial transactions was not to be tolerated. "Never think of being religious unless you are honest. What has a thief to do with religion?" [7] The insistence upon business integrity was uncompromising. "We cannot consistent with brotherly love," it was pointed out, "sell our goods below the market price. We cannot study to ruin our neighbor's trade in order to advance our own." [8] Owe nothing, keep expenses within income, and deal fairly.[9]

The labor relationship was an ethical one. One group acted as workers, the other as masters. A total denial was given to the mood of exploitation. Since the authority of a master was due simply to the function entrusted to him and not to his inherent superiority over other men, he had no excuse for despising them, though they be poor, mean, weak, or aged. The poorest and weakest have the same place and authority which the richest and strongest have.[10] To masters: "Your servants of whatever kind," they were told, "you are to look upon as a kind of secondary children. These, likewise, God has committed to your charge." [11] The right of the laborer to claim enough to live, not on a mere subsistence level, but sufficient for an active if frugal life, was upheld. No one excoriated the "bawling mob" and the "beasts of the people" more fiercely than did Wesley, yet he added a terse moral approval of a huge multitude of tinners in Truro who "on being nearly starved, were come to beg or demand an increase of their wages without which they could not live." [12]

Wesley and his associates thought in terms of personal responsibility, fair prices, and just wages in a day when those conceptions were rapidly losing all their meaning. The pursuit of economic ends even though conditioned by the strictest moral standard was a divinely sanctioned calling.[13]

2.

"The church," cried St. Bernard in the twelfth century, as he gazed at the wonders of Gothic architecture, "is resplendent in her walls, beggarly in her poor. She clothes her stones in gold and leaves her sons naked." [14]

Wesley six centuries later was to protest against the extravagances of wealth. The cardinal article of his creed was the divine proprietorship of all wealth and the responsible stewardship of man. All talents of whatever nature were to Wesley a temporary trust from God. The acid test of economic life was the query, "To what purpose do the wheels go round?" And unless they moved for the common good, they obviously were out of gear. All snatching to hoard and hoarding to snatch was stupid and mad. "In seeking happiness from riches, you are only striving to drink out of empty cups. And let them be painted and gilded ever so finely, they are empty still." [15]

The idea of a frugal and strictly self-disciplined moral life was defined not as the virtue of any one class but an indispensable test of all men whatever their social status. Although riches were not in themselves held to be evil, and it is no more sinful to be rich than to be poor, yet "it is dangerous beyond expression" because of its effect upon the life of the possessor.[16] The reason was obvious. Riches cannot give happiness when happiness is defined in spiritual terms. Riches seduce men to concentrate upon material satisfactions. The idea of moral character is a life of serious purpose, austerity in manners, frugality, instead of self indulgence. Riches divert men to "the love of the world, desire of pleasure, of ease, of getting money. It makes Methodists unwilling to do hard things, to toil and to sacrifice. It nurtures self indulgence and pride." [17] Furthermore it raises a consciousness of inequality among men. How hard it is for the rich, exclaimed Wesley, "not to think themselves better than the poor, base, uneducated herd of men!" [18] Then secondly by spending for luxuries and not being "content with what plain nature requires," the rich divert to their own luxury what would serve to supply the necessities of the community." [19] "I apprehend by a rich man here is meant not only a man that has immense treasures, one that heaped up gold as dust, and silver as the sands of the sea, but any one that possesses more than the necessaries and conveniences of life." [20]

God was working out a moral purpose in social institutions which only faulty human will at points thwarted. Man had no exclusive control of possessions. "As to yourself," wrote Wesley to a man of property, "you are not the proprietor of anything, no, not of one shilling in the world. You are only a steward of what another entrusts you with, to be laid out, not according to your will, but his." [21]

The worthiness of Wesley's doctrine does not lie in its originality but in the thoroughness and sincerity with which it was set forth as a fresh and imperative requirement. The essence of stewardship was defined to be not control for personally chosen ends, but control for a definite moral purpose. Those who use property in any form for any other purpose than that dictated by Christian ethic "are not only robbing God, continually embezzling and wasting their Lord's good and by that very means corrupting their own souls, but also violating the rights of the community. It is but like keeping money from the poor to buy poison for ourselves." [22] The moral use of money was the obligation of stewardship.

Was all money then to be thrown into the sea? Such an affirmation was mere empty rant, said Wesley. Gold and silver, he argued, is "an excellent gift of God, answering the noblest ends. In the hands of His children, it is food for the hungry, drink for the thirsty, raiment for the naked; it gives to the traveler and the stranger where to lay his head. By it we may supply the place of an husband to the widow and of a father to the fatherless. We may be a defence for the oppressed, a means of health to the sick, of ease to them that are in pain; it may be as eyes to the blind, as feet to the lame, yea, a lifter up from the gates of death. . . .

"We ought to gain all we can, without buying gold too dear, without paying more for it than it is worth." [23]

But the criterion of behavior remained: What would make one most useful? The first claim was economic dependence of the possessor. One must owe no man anything and one must provide for the necessities of oneself and one's dependents. Those necessities were carefully appraised in the light of what are "reasonable wants." They must be "plain necessities of life, not delicacies, not superfluities—just reasonable wants." [24] We are not forbidden "the providing for ourselves such things as are needful for the body; a sufficiency of plain wholesome food to eat and clean raiment to put on. Yea, it is our duty, so far as God puts it into our power to provide these things also." [25] But riches are not to be used for self indulgence such as high eating and drinking, fine clothes and fine houses, state and equipage, gay pleasures and diversions.[26]

The worst possible use is to accumulate money for posterity. Inherited wealth is a prime evil, for it will be certain to injure those who receive it. Having provided a basis for a self respecting and independent life there was no further justification for accumulating wealth. "Therefore I charge you," said Wesley, "do not increase your substance." [27]

In three plain rules in a sermon on the use of money the first great rule of Christian wisdom with respect to money was, "Gain all you can. Gain all you can by honest industry. Use all possible diligence in your calling. Lose no time. . . . Never leave anything till tomorrow which you can do today. And do it as well as possible. Do not sleep or yawn over it; put your whole strength to the work. Spare no pains . . . Gain all you can by common sense, by using in your business all the understanding which God has given you." It is equally imperative that one live without ease and luxury. "2. Having gained all you can by honest wisdom and unwearied diligence, the second rule of Christian prudence is, 'Save all you can.' Do not throw the precious talent into the sea; leave that folly to heathen philosophers. . . . Expend no part of it merely to gratify the desire of the flesh, the desire of the eye, or the pride of life. . . . 3. But let not any man imagine that he has done anything barely by going thus far, by 'gaining and saving all he can' if he were to stop here." It is mandatory that all the remainder, after providing for the necessities of life, be devoted to satisfy the needs of the community. "All who observe the first two rules, 'to gain and to save,' without the third, to give all they have will be twofold more the children of hell than ever they were before." [28]

"No more sloth . . . no more waste . . . no more covetousness! But employ whatever God has intrusted you with in doing good, all possible good, in every possible kind and degree, to the household of faith, to all men! This is no small part of the wisdom of the just." [29]

No alternative is offered. "We ought not to forbid people to be diligent and frugal. We must exhort all Christians to gain all they can, that is, in effect to grow rich," said Wesley.[30] But this is to undermine and destroy the religious experience itself and to defeat God's purpose. "How then is it possible that Methodism, that is, the religion of the heart, though it flourishes now as a green bay tree, should continue in this state?" [31] Wealth and religion are opposed to each other. Yet diligence and frugality must in the natural course of things beget riches. Riches beget pride, love of the world, and a spirit destructive of Christianity. Christianity thus saps its own foundations. Is there no way to prevent this? "There is one way," insisted Wesley, "and there is no other under heaven. If those who gain all they can, and save all they can, will likewise give all they can, then the more they gain the more they will grow in grace and the more treasure they will lay up in heaven. . . . Give all you can; otherwise I can have no more hope of your salvation than for that of Judas Iscariot. . . . 'Lay not up for thyself treasures on earth.' This is a flat, positive command, full as clear as 'Thou shalt not commit adultery.' " [32]

In "The Good Steward" Wesley describes a scene in which the Lord's steward is called upon to render his account. "The Lord of all will next inquire, 'In what manner didst thou employ that comprehensive talent money? . . . Not squandering it away in vain expenses the same as throwing it into the sea? Not hoarding it up to leave behind thee, the same as burying it in the earth. But first supplying thy own reasonable wants, together with those of thy family, then restoring the remainder to me, through the poor. . . . Wast thou accordingly a general benefactor to mankind? Feeding the hungry, clothing the naked, comforting the sick, assisting the stranger, relieving the afflicted. . . . Wast thou eyes to the blind and feet to the lame?" [33]

It was this radical and clearcut demand that one should give everything and possess nothing that makes the Wesleyan philanthropic outlook noteworthy. The moral use of property forbade great economic inequalities. Failure to adhere to the simplest of rules (after providing for necessities "one must give not a tenth, a half, no, nor three fourths, but all") [34] was held to be a threefold offense—against God, against the community, and against one's self. "Those who fail to do it," said Wesley, "are not only robbing God, continually embezzling and wasting their Lord's goods, and by that very means corrupting their own souls, but also robbing the poor, the hungry, the naked, wronging the widow and the fatherless, and making themselves accountable for all the want, affliction, and distress which they may but do not remove." [35]

Both in his theory and his own deliberate example of that theory, Wesley was at least as revolutionary as Owen and the radicals who later inspired the abhorrence of official Methodism. Wesley did not himself seem to realize just how revolutionary a position it was. But he insistently reiterated it.[36] He who gains and does not give that gain back is the "twofold son of hell." [37]

3.

"Does anyone who knows anything of me suppose that I would drudge for money? What is money to me? Dung and dross. I love it as I do the mire in the streets. But I find enough that want it, and among these I disperse it with both hands, being careful only to owe no man anything, to wind my bottom round the year." [38]

When Wesley had £30 a year, he lived on £28 and gave away 40 s. The next year receiving £60, he still lived on 28 and gave away 32. The third year he received £90 and gave away 62. The fourth year he received £120. Still he lived on 28 and gave to the poor all the rest. In this ratio he proceeded during the rest of his life.[39] Eighteen years preaching netted him together a debt of £1236.[40]

In 1776 he received a communication from the Commissioners of Excise saying they could not doubt but he had plate for which he had neglected to make any entry. Wesley's reply was succinct.

LONDON
September, 1776

Sir,—I have two silver teaspoons at London and two at Bristol. This is all the plate which I have at present and I shall not buy any more while so many round me want bread.

I am, sir,
Your most humble servant,
JOHN WESLEY.[41]

Wesley's income from the unprecedented sale of his tracts, pamphlets, books—between thirty and forty thousand pounds—made him a rich man, but never did he spend upon his personal needs more than £30 a year allotted him by the London circuit. In the country Methodists were occasionally paid their hostelry bill and other similar expenses incurred in traveling. According to Dr. Whitehead, in the course of fifty years Wesley gave away between twenty and thirty thousand pounds.[42] ("My wife used to tell me, 'My dear, you are too generous. You don't know the value of money.' "[43]) Besides he bequeathed his book business and books then on sale to the Methodist conference. When Robert Dall asked for money to build a preaching house, he replied, "This is no time of year for making collections. . . . I see no way but who will lend?" Adding a note of encouragement "I will be security for forty pounds more. Look up!"[44]

His example in matters of money influenced his followers. During the years 1770-1789 London Methodists gave away to the poor some £15,000.[45]

In 1743 Wesley wrote:"I will now simply tell you my sense of these matters, whether you will hear or whether you will forbear. Food and raiment I have—such food as I choose to eat and such raiment as I choose to put on. I have a place where to lay my head; I have what is needful for life and godliness, and I apprehend this is all the world can afford. The kings of the earth can give me no more. For as to gold and silver, I trample it under my feet. . . . I desire it not; I seek it not; I only fear lest any of it should cleave to me, and I should not be able to shake it off before my spirit returns to God. . . . I will take care (God being my helper) that none of the accursed thing shall be found in my tents when the Lord calleth me hence. And hear ye this all you who have discovered the treasures which I am to leave behind me: if I leave behind me ten pounds above my debts and my books, or what may happen to be due on account of them—you and all mankind bear witness against me that I lived and died a thief and a robber." [46]

Wesley kept his word. Shortly before his death he closed his cashbook with the following words written in a tremulous hand: "For upward of eighty-six years I have kept my accounts exactly; I will not attempt it any longer, being satisfied with the continual conviction that I save all I can and give all I can, that is, all I have." [47]

No eulogy was more appropriate than that printed in *The Monthly Review* and quoted by the *Leeds Intelligencer*: "Mr. Wesley's real worth is demonstrated by nothing more convincingly than by his dying worth nothing. It proves that the influence which he acquired and long preserved over a numerous sect was not employed to any sordid purpose. The poverty of such a man enriches his fame." [48]

CHAPTER TEN

THE EVILS OF POVERTY

Do ye hear the children weeping, O my brothers,
  Ere the sorrow comes with years?
They are leaning their young heads against their mothers,
  And *that* cannot stop their tears.
The young lambs are bleating in the meadows,
  The young birds are chirping in the nest,
The young fawns are playing with the shadows,
  The young flowers are blowing towards the west—
But the young, young children, O my brothers,
  They are weeping bitterly!
They are weeping in the playtime of the others,
  In the country of the free. . . .
    (ELIZABETH BARRETT BROWNING, *The Cry of the Children*)

"I aver," writes Wesley, "that in every part of England where I have been (and I have been east, west, north, and south within these two years), trade in general is exceedingly decayed and thousands of people are quite unemployed. Some I know to have perished for want of bread. . . .

"I have seen wretched creatures within little more than a hundred miles of London, standing in the streets with pale looks, hollow eyes, and meagre limbs, or creeping up and down like walking shadows. I have known families, who a few years ago lived in an easy genteel manner, reduced to just as much raiment as they had on, and as much food as they could gather in the field. To this one or other of them repaired once a day to pick up the turnips which the cattle had left, which they boiled, if they could get a few sticks, or otherwise ate them raw. Such is the want of food to which many of our countrymen are at this day reduced by want of business." [1]

"We may as well all be hanged as starved to death," was the common sentiment.[2] Laborers did not desire to see their childern "weep for bread and none to give them." "The distresses of the poor are melancholy beyond description," said *Lloyd's Evening Post.*[3] "Some measures will be taken," the Court of Aldermen in London hoped, "to stop the exportation of corn which if suffered to continue must inevitably finish the miseries of the poor." [4] It was "very shocking to humanity," commented one correspondent in the *London Chronicle,* to see people dying from want. The poor "reduced to the greatest extremities of want and distress" were obliged to rob, steal, or perish.[5]

Yet the administration, said Wesley, "have been assured from every part of the kingdom that trade was as plentiful and flourishing as ever and the people as well employed and as well satisfied." A more notorious falsehood could not have been palmed off upon them.[6]

From 1740-1800 discontent continually prevailed which flared up in frequent riots and serious disorders. Loads of meal and flour were stopped and taken; crowds of women cut the sacks and took away the grain. They resented attempts to export corn while people were starving. Colliers in 1740 unable to buy grain plundered from the granaries all that they required. Cornfactors kept up the price of grain and in addition closed their shops, preventing the sale of any grain. *The Country Journal or Craftsman,* February 16, 1740, speaks of the great numbers of poor wretches perishing with hunger and cold and the streets swarming with beggars.[7] At Bristol in January, 1740, the severe frost threw many out of work. They had no assistance from the parish and were in the last extremity. Wesley, deeply affected by their distress, made three collections in one week and was able to feed a hundred, sometimes a hundred and fifty a day.[8]

Food riots were frequent through 1750-60, but only a few scattered disturbances took place in the next decade. A fever of unrest, however, swept England in 1766. Flour mills were destroyed, and bags of corn seized or ripped open. Bakers were compelled to sell bread cheaper, farmers to sell corn at 5s a bushel. Riots broke out in many places. The mob objected to 9s, 6d a bushel for wheat. When butter or wheat dealers refused to lower their prices, their supplies were seized and sold at lower prices and the money given to the dealers. "Many thousands of people at Manchester, Birmingham, Leicester, and Nottingham will probably starve this year for want of work and money to buy food," remarked *Lloyd's Evening Post* of September 20-23, 1765.[9]

Wages rose between 1760 and 1813 by 60 percent and the price of wheat by 130 percent. The normal laborer even with constant employment was no longer solvent. Besides he lived under the capricious tyranny of the old law of settlement which froze him in his own parish. To seek employment elsewhere meant starvation.[10]

London escaped the fever of unrest in 1766 but not in 1768. Watermen, coalporters, laborers, and journeymen tailors paraded the streets and protested against high prices and low wages. Violence was more outrageous the following year, and a proclamation to suppress riots was issued.[11]

Disturbances were less numerous from 1770-80 apart from the year 1772 when food riots occurred. Once a miller was set on the table and put up for auction after which the rioters drove him through town, beating him with sacks. Long letters on the starved condition of the country were published in newspapers and magazines. Some entered into elaborate calculations, showing that in London alone during six winter months, twenty thousand sheep and two thousand oxen were used in making soup for taverns and tables of the great. When the king opened Parliament, he referred in his speech to the dearness of corn and recommended "My lords and gentlemen" to consider a scheme "for alleviating the distresses of the poor." This was done and a bill was passed.[12]

For the next few years disturbances were rare. That may have been due to severe sentences inflicted for trivial offences. The years 1790-1800 were the most critical and most turbulent in the last twenty years of the century. The year 1795 may be called the revolt of the housewives. That year was marked by a series of food riots all over England in which a conspicuous part was taken by women.[13] With the close of the century distress was rampant and anger threatened. Soaring prices created widespread unrest, more impatient, more impassioned. Injustices burned like fires in men's minds and hearts.

Yet despite the riots there was no evidence of disloyalty to the crown or disaffection towards the government. Even when an opportunity came in 1745 and again in 1789 to ally themselves with revolutionary movements, the people remained aloof. The suffering masses of the eighteenth century suffered dumbly—never tried to alter the constitution and never openly desired a change in the form of administration. What concerned them most was meeting their daily needs. When high prices and continued exports met them, they quickly lost patience and vented their rage in noisy demonstrations. Physical distress and anxiety were responsible for explosions of violence so frequent in the century.[14] Shelley's appeal—

> Rise like lions after slumber
> In unconquerable number;
> Shake your chains to earth like dew,
> Which in sleep had fallen on you,
> Ye are many—they are few,

was hardly known to the working classes.[15]

The poor were starved, stunted, and stifled. Richard Atkinson made it known to readers of *Lloyd's Evening Post* that colliers for the paltry sum of less than a penny an hour had to encounter numerous perils and endure a drudgery which the veriest slave in the plantations of America would regard as intolerable. They regularly worked sixteen to seventeen hours a day for the noble sum of 7s a week. When they were too old to work, they were "cast off to the wretchedness both of poverty and disease." [16] Children of five or six were forced to work in mills and factories twelve or thirteen hours on end, for a mere pittance. They entered the mill gates at five or six and left them at seven or eight, Saturday included. Cotton workers toiled in temperatures varying from 75 to 85 degrees, the flue choking their lungs. Boys and girls taken out of workhouses were farmed out to employers as labor fodder. Young women were employed in the depths of the earth to win coal. In a cruel sense the poor lived in legal chains—baffled, beaten, brutalized, finally defeated. The laws punishing them, the prisons confining them, the judges condemning them in every case were the creation of powers above them, of industry, commerce, and state.[17] "The evidence is irrefutable, indisputable, inescapable." [18]

In the year 1740 foodstuffs were meagre, prices rising, discontent raging, and the laboring class suffered a plague of human misery. Their patience was at a breaking point, their behavior surly, angry, and violent. There was no amelioration in the shape of cheaper and ampler supplies of the staff of life. Instead authorities called out the soldiers, armed the civilians, arrested most of the ring-leaders, and sent several to the gallows. Instead of punishing the cornfactors the authorities made war on the rioters. Trade unions and combinations of workers were visited by repressive measures.[19]

Judicial savagery went on unabated—three men suffered death for robbing 3s 6d and a penknife on the highway.

Crime grew and grew. Women were banished from the country at the first offence.

A frequent visitor bluntly asserted that England was the only country in Europe where the people were murdered by the law. At one old Bailey Sessions 24 unfortunates were sentenced to death mostly for theft and robbery; at two Sessions 65; at seven Sessions 150. The year 1785 was the blackest in English judicial history—nearly 500 were sentenced to death.[20] The crimes for which most of these sentences were inflicted would be regarded today as petty offences: For example, five were condemned for robbery to the value of 2s; two women for 3s 2d; two for 2s; two for 1s 10½d; two for a watch and 1s; two for three silver spoons; two for 4d, a handkerchief, and a knife; two for 2½ d; one for 1s; one for 10½d; one for 8¼d; and one for 6d.[21] Yet a correspondent to a London newspaper thought it was too merciful to let them "glide so gently out of the world." He preferred castration and slow torture and death.[22] The extremes to which judicial brutality could go is shown by the report of Thomas Taylor, a Methodist preacher. He attended a malefactor in prison and accompanied him to the place of execution. Before the final scene was enacted, "they chopped off his right hand with a great axe, just as a butcher would chop off a piece of beef with a cleaver." [23]

The gallows were busy and the prison ships in full sail; yet Lord Stormont contended that "Our constitution in its present form . . . was the most perfect, the most wise, and the most happy system of government that ever the wisdom of man framed; its basis was natural justice." [24]

The hungry sheep looked up and were sent to the slaughter. Reform in the social and economic life of the nation was urgent. All work and no play was the maxim imposed upon the laboring class. The sharp antithesis between sordid squalor and starvation on the one hand and plenty and abundance on the other did not disturb the minds of those in power. Little children could be sold into employment little less than slavery; small boys could be forced to squeeze themselves through hot, sooty, and suffocating flues of chimneys. Innocent lives were ruined by the insensitive wheels of industry. Misery was everywhere.[25]

Real justice was hard to come by. "Suppose a great man . . . oppress the needy; suppose the rich grind the face of the poor; what remedy against such oppression can he find in this Christian country? If the one is rich and the other poor, doth not justice stand afar off?"[26]

Wesley knew the poor better than any man of his age. "If you could see these things with your own eyes, could you lay out money on ornaments and superfluities?"[27] Something was "rotten in the state of Denmark." He never plumbed the depths out of which come such injustices and abuses. Neither the economics of labor problems nor sociology as such had been heard of in Wesley's days. But he saw the evils and he made Methodism the kind of religious movement that devoted itself to the removal of these evils,[28] even though the reform he most earnestly sought was a moral and religious one. He said to his preachers, "You have nothing to do but to save souls."[29]

He never accepted a law of indifference or drift. All economic problems were primarily ethical ones. Spiritual values were the only ultimate reality; hence those values he would cause to permeate and control every material relationship of man. Poverty and degradation sullied the face of this earth, destroyed the God in man. "Man's inhumanity to man made countless thousands mourn."

He was emphatically a constitutionalist and anti-revolutionist, but unless government and economic institutions strove sincerely, resolutely, and intelligently for the common good, he believed them a hollow mockery of Christian intent.[30]

Greatly distressed in the '70's because of the condition of the poor, he wrote a letter to *Lloyd's Evening Post*, later revised and enlarged and published as a pamphlet.

"I ask first, why are thousands of people starving, perishing for want in every part of England? The fact I know: I have seen it with my eyes in every corner of the land; I have known those who could only afford to eat a little coarse food every other day. I have known one picking up stinking sprats from a dunghill and carrying them home for herself and her children. I have known another gathering the bones which the dogs had left in the streets, and making broth of them to prolong a wretched life. Such is the case at this day, of multitudes of people in a land flowing, as it were, with milk and honey, abounding with all the necessities, the conveniences, the superfluities of life!

"Now, why is this? Why have all these nothing to eat? Because they have nothing to do. They have no meat, because they have no work.

"But why have they no work? Why are so many thousand people in London, in Bristol, in Norwich, in every country from one end of England to the other, utterly destitute of employment?

"Because the persons who used to employ them cannot afford to do it any longer. Many who employed fifty men now scarce employ ten. Those who employed twenty now employ one or none at all . . .

"But where is the remedy? Perhaps it exceeds all the wisdom of man to tell. But it may not be amiss to offer a few hints, even on this delicate subject.

"1. What remedy is there for this sore evil? Many thousand poor people are starving. Find them work and you will find them meat. They will then earn and eat their own bread.

"2. But how shall their masters give them work without ruining themselves? Procure vent for it, and it will not hurt their masters to give them as much work as they can do, and this will be done by sinking the price of provisions, for then people will have money to buy other things too.

"3. But how can the price of wheat be reduced? By prohibiting forever that bane of health, that destroyer of strength, of life, and of virtue, *distilling*.

"4. How can the price of oats be reduced? By reducing the number of horses. And may not this be effectually done (1) by laying a tax of ten pounds on every horse exported to France, (2) by laying an additional tax on gentlemen's carriages.

"5. How can the price of beef and mutton be reduced? By increasing the breed of sheep and horned cattle. And this would be increased sevenfold if the price of horses was reduced.

"6. How can the price of pork and poultry be reduced? First, by letting no farms of above an hundred pounds a year. Secondly, by repressing luxury, either by example, by laws, or both.

"7. How may the price of land be reduced? By all the methods above named, all which tend to lessen the expense of housekeeping, but especially the last, restraining luxury, which is the grand source of poverty.

"8. How may the taxes be reduced? By discharging half of the national debt, and so saving at least two millions a year.

"How this can be done the wisdom of the great council the land can best determine." [31]

CHAPTER ELEVEN

RELIEF OF THE POOR

Wesley led the way for Methodists to practise social duties. At his London headquarters he repeatedly provided for the poor. In 1763 great numbers of poor people had "pease and pottage and barley broth" given them at the Foundery "at the expense of Mr. Wesley," and on Sunday there was a collection for further supplying the necessities of the poor when upwards of £100 was collected.[1] On occasions in depression he and his followers were feeding from a hundred to a hundred and fifty persons a day in a single place. They raised money to clothe and relieve prisoners and to buy food, medicine, fuel, or tools for the stricken and unfortunate. In twenty years London Methodists gave to the poor about £15,000. This was remarkable when it is remembered that many members themselves were poor.[2]

On January 7, 1759, Wesley paid a visit to Bristol and told Methodists there he had come in order "to provide for the poor." He preached a sermon in their behalf and afterwards announced that the collection "was a great deal more than double what it used to be." [3] In March, 1765, the condition of unemployed weavers caused him anxiety. "I made a collection in our congregation for the poor weavers who are out of employment. It amounted to about forty pounds. In the evening our own Society met and contributed fourteen pounds more to relieve a few of their own distressed members." Twelve months later a legacy of £1000 was left to him by a Miss Lewen, and in less than one year "it had all been given away to the poor." [4] If an exceptional period of hardship was experienced, he organized special relief agencies as in 1740 and 1772.

Wesley's own pity and courtesy came out in his advice to the stewards. To guard against grieving the poor, he exhorted them to "give soft words if nothing else. Abstain from either sour looks or harsh words. Let them be glad to come, even though they should go empty away. Put yourself in the place of every poor man, and deal with him as you would God should deal with you." [5]

On Friday, November 2, 1750, he wrote in his diary: "I began taking an account of all in the Society that were in want, but I was soon discouraged, their number so increasing upon me, particularly about Moorfields, that I saw no possibility of relieving them." [6] In a letter to Ebenezer Blackwell he related how he had spent a gift of five guineas:

"To Eliz. Brooks expecting daily to have her goods seized for rent, £1, 1s;

"To Eliz. Room (a poor window) for rent, 5s;

"Towards clothing Mary Middleton and another poor woman almost naked, 10s;

"To John Edger, a poor weaver, out of work, 5s;

"To Lucy Jones, a poor orphan, 2s;

"To a poor family for food and fuel, 5s;

"To Christopher Brown, out of business, 2s 6d;

"To an ancient woman in great distress, 2s 6d;

"Distributed among several sick families, 10s." [7]

On Thursday, February 8, 1753, Wesley was again busy among the sick poor of London. "But such scenes who could see unmoved. There are none such to be found in a pagan country." On his visits he "found some in their cells underground; others in their garrets, half starved both with cold and hunger added to weakness and pain. But I found not one of them unemployed who was able to crawl about the room." A fortnight later he was visiting once more. Some of the sick upon whom he called were without fire "bitterly cold as it was." [8]

Again he was out begging money to relieve the distress of the destitute. "God's steward for the poor," he called himself.[9] No wonder such a man was popular and no wonder that his presence was a loadstone drawing the poor around him. At Norwich a whole host of poverty-stricken people flocked about his carriage. His purse was low, containing only what was necessary to take him back to London, and the clamor of the mendicant crowd for once disturbed his temper. Somewhat sharply he said, "I have nothing for you. Do you suppose I can support the poor in every place?" At the moment he was entering his carriage his foot slipped, and he fell upon the ground. Feeling as though God had rebuked him for his hasty words, he turned to his friend Joseph Bradford and with subdued emphasis remarked, "It is all right, Joseph; it is all right; it is only what I deserved, for if I had no other good to give, I ought at least to have given them good words." [10]

James Lackington says that in going the few yards from his study to the pulpit, Wesley generally distributed a handful of half crowns to the poor old people of his society.[11] Nor did Wesley confine himself to the care of his own societies. "Open your eyes, your heart, your hand," he writes to the societies at Bristol. "If this one rule was observed throughout England, we should need no other collection. It would soon form a stock sufficient to relieve all that want and to answer all occasions." [12]

The essential thing though in Wesley's philanthropic activities was the spirit or attitude in which he approached those whom he would help. Important as was the relief he gave, in itself more precious was the quality of his giving. Wesley never tried to be kind; he never patronized people. "If you cannot relieve, do not grieve the poor." [13]

Relief he felt is much more effective if carried instead of being sent. "I visited as many as I could of the sick.

How much better is it when it can be done to carry relief to the poor than to send it! and that both for our own sake and theirs. For theirs, as it is so much more comfortable to them, and as we may then assist them in spirituals as well as temporals, and for our own sake, as it is far more apt to soften our heart and to make us naturally care for each other." [14]

Stewards found great difficulty in visiting the sick. Wesley called together the entire membership of the society in London, then numbering 4,000, and asked, "Who among you is willing, as well as able, to supply this lack of service?" The next morning many willingly offered themselves. Wesley chose forty-six of the most "tender loving spirits," divided the town into twenty-three parts, and appointed two to visit the sick in each division. The business of each visitor was to see every sick person within his district three times a week—not only to inquire into the state of their souls but to advise them, to inquire into their disorders and procure advice for them, to relieve them if they were in want, to do anything for them which he (or she) could do. Individual members, preachers, leaders, as well as appointed visitors combined to make the service effective. It extended not only to members but others outside the societies. Visitors were enjoined to observe strictly four rules: "1. Be plain and open in dealing with souls. 2. Be mild, tender, patient. 3. Be cleanly in all you do for the sick. 4. Be not nice."[15]

"Together with the more important lessons which you endeavor to teach all the poor whom you visit, it would be a deed of charity to teach them two things more which they are generally little acquainted with: industry and cleanliness. It was said by a pious man, 'Cleanliness is next to Godliness.' Indeed the want of it is a scandal to all religion, causing the way of truth to be evil spoken of. And without industry we are neither fit for this world nor for the world to come." [16]

Wesley's desire to help the poor led him to form the

Christian community at the Foundery in 1772. Through this society he secured a body of workers who regularly visited the workhouses in several of the London parishes and sought to "improve and elevate the moral and social condition of the poor inmates." In addition he established at the Foundery a small poorhouse and in 1748 there were nine widows, one blind woman, two poor children, and two upper servants, a maid, and a man.[17] Without money in sight Wesley leased two houses "warm and clean" as a home for destitute widows who ate with him and the preachers at the family table in the Foundery. For children of the poor who were like "wild ass's colts" he opened his own house for a school of sixty children over six years of age, providing clothing for those who needed it and made the noted Silas Todd preacher. In seven years Todd trained three hundred boys "who were fitted for almost any trade."[18]

A melting pot indeed for all good things was the old Foundery—a home for Wesley and his preachers, a house of mercy for widows, a school for boys, a dispensary for the sick, a work shop and employment bureau, a loan office and savings bank, a bookroom, and a church.

Two experiments in the relief of economic distress were noteworthy. One attempted to provide employment. A small group of the poorest persons was set to work carding and spinning cotton in 1740, a scheme like our WPA, started by Thomas Firmin. The experiment was kept up for four months. On another occasion knitting was provided for women under the supervision of the society's visitors to the sick. An experiment of longer duration and greater success was the provision of 1746 of a loan fund from which deserving persons could borrow amounts up to 20s to be repaid in three months. The scheme worked—in less than a year 250 persons were assisted—and later was enlarged, the borrowing limit increased in 1772 to five pounds.[19] Among the beneficiaries was the cobbler James Lackington who in 1775 borrowed £5 with which to start a second hand bookshop in connection with his shoe shop. The new business grew more rapidly than his cobbling, and in the course of time he gave up the latter. The book business developed into the largest second hand bookshop in London, if not in the world. The year Wesley died, Lackington's profits amounted to £5,000.[20]

As a result of Wesley's teaching and example the Strangers' Friend Society was established and found enthusiastic and liberal support in him. "In the morning I met the Strangers' Society," he says, "instituted wholly for the relief, not of our society, but for poor, sick, friendless strangers. I do not know that I ever heard or read of such an institution till within a few years ago. So this also is one of the fruits of Methodism." [21] The idea behind the Strangers' Society spread rapidly among the Methodists, and by 1800 most of the large centers of population supported a similar enterprise. The Society not only saved souls but gave food and raiment as well. Thousands were relieved. In twelve years in Manchester alone £6,403 were expended on relief and over 60,000 assisted.[22]

In his efforts to help the sick poor and recognizing the inadequacy of provisions for public health, Wesley started the first free medical dispensary in England in 1746 which treated large numbers of people. He had for his assistants an apothecary and an experienced surgeon and sometimes Dr. Whitehead, a local preacher, who for many years had been his personal physician. He resolved at the start not to go beyond his depth "but to leave all difficult and complicated cases to such physicians as the patients should choose. "Medicines were to be provided. All such persons, whether they belonged to the society or not were invited by Wesley to come to him every Friday. About thirty people came December 5, 1746; in less than three months the number had risen to five hundred. The dispensary continued for several years, but the number of patients still increasing the expense was greater than Wesley could bear, and in 1754 the work was discontinued.[23]

Of still greater importance than the dispensary was Wesley's educational program in the matter of health. Wesley was a vital pioneer of the national health movement. In 1747 appeared the long despised *Primitive Physic or An Easy and Natural Method of Curing Most Diseases.* The booklet, easily slipped into the pocket, was immensely popular, running through twenty-three editions by 1828. No less than seven editions appeared in America between 1764 and 1839.[24] In addition Wesley published *Advices with Respect to Health Extracted from a Work of Dr. Tissot* in which he protested against the current fondness for bleeding patients.

"If it be said," Wesley remarked in *Primitive Physic,* " 'But what need is there of such attempt?' I answer, the greatest that can possibly be conceived. Is it not needful in the highest degree to rescue men from the jaws of destruction? from wasting their fortunes as thousands have done and continue to do daily? from pining away in sickness and pain either through the ignorance or dishonesty of physicians, yea, and many times throwing away their lives after their health, time, and substance?

"Is it inquired, 'But are there not books enough already on every part of the art of medicine?' Yes, too many ten times over, considering how little to the purpose the far greater part of them speak. But, beside this, they are too dear for poor men to buy, and too hard for plain men to understand. Do you say, 'But there are enough of these collections of receipts.' Where? I have not seen one yet, either in our own or any other tongue which contains only safe, and cheap, and easy medicines. In all that have yet fallen into my hand, I find many dear and many far-fetched medicines, besides many of so dangerous a kind as a prudent man would never meddle with. And against the greater part of these medicines there is a further objection. They consist of too many ingredients. Experience shows that one thing will cure most disorders, at least as well as twenty put together. Then why do you add the other nineteen? Only to swell the apothecary's bill, nay possibly on purpose to prolong the distemper, that the doctor and he may divide the spoil."[25]

Certainly *Primitive Physic* contained odd remedies. For approaching the infirmities of old age Wesley prescribed: "Take tar water every morning and evening . . . or a decoction of nettles . . . or be electrified. But remember! the only radical cure is wrought by *death.*"[26] Yet the treatment advocated (in clear and terse language) was eminently sensible: plain foods, abundance of fresh air, daily exercise, and contented spirits. Laugh as one will at the plums in *Primitive Physic,* the fact remains: wherever the spirit of Revival spread, there was spread the accompanying influence of temperance, cleanliness, and sanitation, sick visitation, domestic hygiene, and sociability. Between 1740 and 1820 the mortality of London children under five years of age dropped from 74.5 to 31.8.[27] How far Wesley was responsible for the decline in child mortality is impossible to ascertain, but his dynamic and widespread influence was thrown into the scale of public health and personal care.

The text of *Primitive Physic* consisted of paragraphs recommending treatment arranged under 289 headings in alphabetical order indicating diseases, symptoms, and accidental injuries. There are 829 numbered paragraphs, but as there are a few without numbers and as some paragraphs mention more than one form of treatment, the actual number of receipts is fairly large.[28]

Admirable as far as general principles go, it was a little wild in details. It might be inadvisable to swallow three pounds of quicksilver ounce by ounce as a cure for twisted guts, but whether wearing leaves of celandine, upon and under the feet, will cure jaundice is still conjectural. A considerable number of remedies recommended were nothing but charms—a little roll of white paper placed under the tongue was recommended for nose bleed. For consumption every morning cut a little turf of fresh earth and lying down breathe into the hole for a quarter of an hour. Canine appetite or "an insatiable desire of eating" can be removed by dipping small pieces of bread in wine and applying them to the nostrils. For baldness you are told to rub your scalp with honey and onions and to electrify daily; the cure for hoarseness: rub the soles of the feet before the fire with garlic and lard well beaten together.[29] Yet the belief was prevalent in Wesley's day that scrofula could be cured by the King's touch. Dr. Samuel Johnson was "touched" for scrofula in 1712.[30] A popular couplet expressed the opinion of current medical skill—

> The cannon shot and doctor's pill
> With equal aim are sure to kill.[31]

The sober therapeutic methods of Sydenham made hardly any impression until after Wesley's death. Sydenham was more talked about than read. The rank and file of the profession were almost wholly uninfluenced by his work.[32]

Wesley in many instances showed independence and good judgment. He objected to the common advice not to attempt to cure gout, saying he had cured himself many times. He held that madmen "may be conquered by binding only, without beating," anticipating the reform of Pinel by half a century. He warned against breathing near the face of the sick who have infectious fevers. He says he was bitten six times by a mad dog and cured himself by squeezing, bathing, and washing the wound for an hour with salt water—a pound to the quart—and binding salt on it for twelve hours. He warned against constipation and against catching cold after measles. But he adds with emphasis on the latter: "Immediately consult an honest physician." His suggestions about diet included such things as prunes for constipation (used by the Romans), whole wheat bread for the same, vegetables for obesity, the withholding of meat from children under two years old, and the drinking of milk.[33]

This statement is never too commonplace: "When the nerves perform their office languidly, good air is the first requisite." The fewer clothes anyone uses, by day or night, the hardier he will be.

"Exercise first should be always on an empty stomach; secondly should never be continued to weariness; thirdly after it we should take care to cool by degrees, otherwise we shall catch cold.

"Cold bathing is of great advantage to health. . . . Tender people should pour water upon the head before they go in, and walk swiftly. To jump in with the head foremost is too great a shock to nature." [34]

Wesley frequently recommended the use of water internally and externally. In the text he recommends cold baths no less than sixty times. He was aware of the doctrines of Floyer and others and preached them with energy. "Everyone that would preserve health should be as clean and sweet as possible in their houses, clothes, and furniture." He ascribed much of his good health to the scheme of life adopted from Cheyne. Cheyne condemned salt and seasonings, also pork, fish, or stall fed cattle and recommended for food eight ounces of animal and twelve ounces of vegetable food in twenty-four hours. For drink: "Water is the wholesomest of all drinks, quickens the appetite, and strengthens the digestion most." [35] Besides what Wesley learned from Cheyne and the popular medicine of Tissot, he laid stress on constant exercise and change of air, his never having "lost a night's sleep, sick or well, on land or sea"—having sleep at command so that he could call it and it came—"to having risen for more than sixty years at four a.m., preaching at five, and having so little pain or sorrow." [36]

His perception of the interdependence of mental and bodily conditions—the concept of psychosomatic medicine—was unusual for his time. "The passions have a greater influence on health than most people are aware of . . .

Till the passion, which caused the disease is calmed, medicine is applied in vain." A woman came to him who had been treated by doctors for a constant pain in her stomach. The doctor did not know the cause of her trouble, but gave every likely drug a chance. "Whence came this woman's pain?" asked Wesley. "From fretting for the death (which she would not have told had she never been questioned about it) of her son. Just what availed medicine while that fretting continued? Why then do not all physicians consider how bodily disorders are caused or influenced by the mind, and in these cases which are utterly out of their sphere call in the assistance of a minister, as ministers when they find the mind disordered by the body, call in the assistance of a physician?" [37] If we substitute the word psychiatrist for minister—whose duties now as then took on aspects of the psychological—this advice is modern.

Wesley was the child of his age—able to see the rational features in the practice of the best men of his time like Sydenham, Cheyne, Floyer, and Fothergill. But at the same time he was saturated with superstitions that go back to the earliest legends of medicine.[38] He did not pretend to special knowledge, but when we compare his methods with those of physicians, we find a good deal to admire or to excuse. As to treatment in general, Wesley's was much better than that of his contemporaries in the respect that his remedies were never likely to be habit forming, blood destroying, or in other ways distinctly harmful. The others devastated their patients with violent drugs, bled them to extremities, salivated them, and kept open sores running for weeks or months. Wesley's consumptive living on milk and breathing in the turf every day was infinitely better off than Morton's and the patients of many others with their bleeding, and gentle vomits, and purges.[39] Besides, thousands who would have relied solely on deadly drugs and superstitions culled sound advice from *Primitive Physic.*

A certain Dr. William Hawes wrote an unfavorable review for *Lloyd's Evening Post* in which he condemned *Primitive Physic* as the work of a dangerous quack. He received a letter from Wesley which must have angered him: "My bookseller informs me that since you published your remarks on the *Primitive Physic* . . . there has been a greater demand for it than ever. If, therefore, you would please to publish a few further remarks, you would confer a farther favor upon your humble servant.[40]

Wesley avidly examined the writings of Franklin, Priestley, and other authorities. In 1753 he read Franklin's letters on electricity and printed in his *Journal* a précis of some of the more striking parts, including the notion "that lightning is no other than electrical fire" and "that anything pointed, as a spire or tree, attracts the lightning just as a needle does the electrical fire." Wesley had, too, a practical interest in electricity. Convinced of its healing power, he forthwith established a free electrical treatment for the poor. He writes in 1756 that he appointed first some hours every week and afterwards an hour every day wherein any that desired electrical treatment might try "the virtue of this surprising medicine." Two or three years later patients were so numerous he was obliged to divide them. "So part we electrified in Southwark, part in the Foundery, others near St. Paul's, and the rest near the Seven Dials." "Perhaps," he records, "thousands received unparalleled good." [41]

"At all hazards," he writes to Ann Bolton, "get an electric machine. It is your bounden duty." [42] "Be electrified (if need be) eight or ten times," he urges Thomas Taylor.[43] He felt the subject was important enough to impress on his followers and in 1760 published his *The Desideratum or Electricity Made Plain and Useful. By a Lover of Mankind and of Common Sense* (five editions by 1781). It is written in two sections—the first telling of experiments and theories, and the second discussing the application of electricity to medicine. It is an admirable popular account of what was known about electricity up to the time of its publication. There is an interesting section "endeavoring to make electricity plain": one fluid theory, electrical fire, effluvia, "electricity per se," ingenious speculations, and accounts of electrical experiments, including Franklin's kite, and a discussion of the possibility of lightning rods (the use of which would involve no contravention of Divine Providence). But Wesley's major concern with electricity was its curative powers, and he devoted almost half of his book (a most amusing and charming part) to citations of the numerous disorders electricity could alleviate. The list was long and varied—from deafness and dropsy to toothache, gout, and palsy. "Indeed there cannot be in nature any such thing as an absolute *Panacea*: a medicine that will cure every disease incident to the human body. If there could, electricity would bid fairer for it than anything in the world. . . . It seems therefore to be the grand *Desideratum* in physic from which we may expect relief when all other relief fails. . . .

"How many may they (the doctors) relieve from racking pain or pining sickness by this inexpensive and speedy remedy, restoring them to ease, health, strength generally in a few minutes, frequently in a moment. . . . I doubt not but more nervous disorders would be cured in one year by this single remedy than the whole English *Materia Medica* will cure by the end of the century." [44]

CHAPTER TWELVE

EDUCATIONALIST, EDITOR AND AUTHOR

If education means character building, the ability to live usefully and cooperatively, Wesley was the greatest educationalist of the century. He and his preachers found many of the people in a semi-barbarous state, deeply sunk in ignorance and vice and almost lost in dirt and wretchedness, and transformed them.

Strictly speaking, Wesley's educational program revolved about three distinct sorts of agencies—schools for elementary instruction, Sunday schools, and dissemination of popular literature. The actual organization was left to local initiative, but the number of charity schools scattered throughout the societies were numerous.

Wesley's educational theory expressed a strong religious bias, but he did maintain that everyone should have the advantage of education, that teachers should interest children in things rather than words, and should proceed from the known to the unknown. Rousseau's *Émile* he found lighter than vanity, "the most empty, silly, injudicious thing that ever a self conceited infidel wrote. . . . Sure a more consummate coxcomb never saw the sun!" [1] But even the educators must not be mistaken with regard to the manner of instilling religion into children. They may lean to this or that extreme. "The leaning either to one extreme or the other (if they either use no punishment at all or more than is necessary) may frustrate all their endeavors. In the latter case it will not be strange if religion stink in the nostrils of those that were so educated. They will naturally look upon it as an austere, melancholy thing, and if they think it necessary to salvation, they will esteem it a necessary evil and so put it off as long as possible. As far as this [the teaching of religion] can be done by mildness, softness, and gentleness certainly it should be done." Unless religion be described as consisting in the love of God and our fellow men, "it is no wonder if those that are instructed therein are not better but worse than other men." For they think they have religion when indeed they have none at all and so add pride to all their other vices.[2]

Though Wesley confessed his indebtedness to Milton and Locke, most of his convictions came from his mother. The rules he drew up for his schools at Kingswood and Newcastle were narrow and shortsighted. The hour of rising was 4 a.m., and the time until 5 was to be spent in devotional exercises. On no day was any time allowed for play; children were never allowed to work alone—a master had to be present. The curriculum comprised not only the three R's, but also English, French, Latin, Greek, Hebrew, History, Geography, Chronology, Rhetoric, Logic, Ethics, Geometry, Algebra, Physics, and Music. (When Wesley made out such a list, he glowed with satisfaction.) He complained that the children took impish delight in breaking many rules.[3]

The ideas were antiquated and unworkable, but practice was often more tolerant than theory. Matthias Joyce, a Papist, went to hear Wesley in Dublin and afterwards said that what impressed him most was to see Wesley stoop down and kiss a little child that sat upon the pulpit stairs. Southey himself tells of the way he felt attracted to Wesley when he saw him kiss his little sister.[4]

A great impetus to education was given through the Methodist Sunday Schools. Wesley adopted Raikes' idea with enthusiasm and lost no opportunity in urging societies to adopt it. They needed little encouragement, for

Methodist Sunday Schools quickly multiplied. Before the end of the century a central Methodist Sunday School Society was formed to coordinate the work in London. In Raikes' schools the teachers were paid. The feature of the Methodist Schools was a voluntary teaching staff. The content of instruction varied, though religious and moral instruction was of course central. There was no condescension in teaching, no attempt to fit the poor for industrial life and keep them docile. The important point was to teach them how to read.[5]

The majority of the children had no other education than what they received at Sunday Schools. Pupils did learn to read and the more intelligent acquired a useful general knowledge. Wesley claimed that Sunday Schools restrained children from vice and taught them good manners. An interesting entry appears in the *Journal* for July 18, 1784. He preached in Bingley Church and before the service he stepped into the Sunday School which contained 240 children, taught every Sunday by several masters and superintended by the curate. "I find these schools springing up wherever I go. Perhaps God may have a deeper end therein than men are aware of. Who knows but some of these schools may become nurseries for Christians." [6]

If Sunday Schools were centers of instruction and breeding for children otherwise neglected, then John Wesley must be reckoned one of the leaders responsible for the growth of popular education.[7]

The schooling of the century was ridiculously inadequate. Before the institution of Sunday Schools, the lower classes were illiterate. Grammar schools were few in number and largely derelict. In 1734 there were no boys in the Birmingham School; sometimes in large centers of population only half a dozen boys were in attendance. For the poorer classes there was hardly any provision. The Charity School, started before Wesley's day in 1698, was greatly fostered by the activities of the Society for the

Propagation of Christian Knowledge. Education consisted largely of reading and writing; afterwards boys were put out to handicraft trades, and girls, with instruction in linen knitting and washing, put out to menial service. It was computed that by the middle of the century five thousand children had been thus educated, but later the influence of these schools dwindled.[8]

Excessive emphasis in Charity Schools was put on the difference of classes and the need for "due consideration in the lower orders." Education was coupled with the determination to reform them by the application of what Defoe aptly called "the great law of subordination."

"God bless the squire and his relations,
And keep us in our proper stations—"[9]

a sentiment which was socially repugnant to Wesley and his societies.

In addition to Charity Schools, whose greatest scope was in the metropolis, there were Dames' Schools scattered over the country. An unmarried woman, sometimes in genteel poverty, and sometimes in poverty not genteel, took some village children in order to eke out a livelihood. In almost all cases the Dame herself knew little and neither her teaching nor her control was effective. With the Industrial Revolution came Schools of Industry whereby pauper children were trained with a wage-earning object in view.[10]

Besides there were Methodist schools for elementary instruction. Wesley not only built Kingswood for the sons of his preachers, but made provision for children of the poor. At the Foundery, at the New Room in the Orphan House in Bristol, and in Newcastle children were taught and some housed. In each of the first great centers Wesley established schools for the instruction of children. Not that Wesley was alone in the wish to reach the poor, but that others were unknown and isolated. Wesley was famous and had behind him a powerful body. The schools in London, Bristol, and Newcastle were forerunners of a great number of lay schools which made Methodism in the last century rank with the Church of England as the greatest force for popular education in England.[11]

The service Wesley rendered was reinforced by the spiritual transformation effected. The desire of the Methodists to read their Bible and to improve their minds led to a restless search for knowledge and a profound reluctance to remain in ignorance.

2.

Wesley considered his ministry of writing as important as his ministry of teaching and preaching. He knew that books to be of value had to be read, and he knew too that people would read books for which they paid, however small the price. He perceived that ignorance and the Christian religion were incompatible and inimical to each other. He set out first to create an appetite for knowledge and then to satisfy it. Hence, heedless of waspish criticism he pushed and sold books wherever he went, and he prodded his preachers whose saddlebags were always packed with literature for sale to like efforts. "Be not ashamed. Be not weary. Leave no stone unturned." [12] Thus Wesley's cheap publications found their way into thousands of humble homes. Indeed evangelical conversion had as a sequel the overcoming of illiteracy in the individual.

Wesley's vivid, chaste, logical Saxon style was specially adopted to people's immediate needs. Most publications sold at a small price, but for those too poor to buy, funds were forthcoming to provide literature. In 1782 he formed the Religious Tract Society to distribute religious tracts among the poor. Men might not read the Bible, but a small tract might engage their attention for half an hour.[13]

Justice has not been done to Wesley both for the quantity and variety of his publications or for his pioneer educational work among the masses. It is Wesley who deserves the credit of having been the first in England to provide cheap popular literature of a useful kind. The starved and uninstructed minds of the workers in mines, fisheries, remote rural districts, and in unschooled and neglected areas were now stimulated and nourished by pamphlets, books, Scripture, and hymns, and cheap editions of some of the best books of the day. Wesley too was among the first to open a vast popular market, in turning literature from dedicating books to the rich to making its appeal to millions.* No man in the eighteenth century, says John Telford of Wesley in the *Encyclopedia Britannica,* "did so much to create a taste for good reading and to supply it with books at the lowest prices." [14]

In a sermon written in 1780 Wesley naively remarks: "Two and forty years ago, having a desire to furnish poor people with cheaper, shorter, and plainer books than any I had seen, I wrote many small tracts, generally a penny apiece, and afterwards several larger. Some of these had such a sale as I never thought of and by this means, I unawares became rich." [15]

The campaign through a central office called the Book Room was a deliberate cultivation of a taste for reading. Its success was unparalleled. The bookseller Lackington reported: "There are thousands in this society who will never read anything besides the Bible and the books published by Mr. Wesley." [16]

"The work of grace," Wesley said, "would die out in one generation if the Methodists were not a reading people." [17] Wesley helped to democratize learning.

3.

The greatest popularizer of the age, against diffuseness in writing, Wesley leveled the most industrious abridging pen before the *Reader's Digest.* This open air preacher

*A two hundred years precursor of Pocket Books, Inc.

to ignorant mobs became also an "historian, a biographer, a magazine editor, a writer of medical treatises, a producer of novels, a lexicographer, a translator of poems, a music critic, a philologist, a grammarian in half a dozen languages" (for the Kingswood School he wrote an English, a Latin, a Greek, a Hebrew, and a French grammar), "a writer in natural philosophy, a poetry anthologist, a writer on logic, a political controversialist, an economist, an ecclesiastical historian, a Bible commentator, and one of the most thorough literary dictators in history," Jack of all trades to many people, a universal genius. From such extremes as George Eliot and the Brontës, the singers of American Negro spirituals, and the great poets of English Romanticism come voices modified by his.[18]

Richard Green in his Wesley Bibliography has 420 publications for John and Charles. Some of these publications ran into as many as twenty editions. Listed are 233 original works for John, more than 100 abridged, edited, or revised by him, 8 for which he wrote the preface or notes, 20 by Charles Wesley alone, and 30 in their joint names.[19]

John Wesley's work was divided into four sections: 1) Books and pamphlets explaining what Methodism was; 2) Rules and regulations for his followers; 3) Tracts, short publications, printed in thousands to be sold cheaply or given away. These include pamphlets addressed to the inhabitants of England and Ireland in times of special emergency, such as the earthquake scare of 1755 and at the time of the fear of French invasion, and tracts on political matters such as smuggling, shortage of food, slave trade, American rebellion, etc.; 4) Lastly, sermons. They all remain, says Leslie Stephen, on the level of terse, vigorous sense. The actual amount of theoretical speculation was small.[20]

Wesley read the best books on a subject, then extracted the more important passages and summarized their arguments. He never doubted his ability to abridge any book in the world. His method was to mark the important parts, join up extracts, alter a few of the hard words, append notes taken from various authorities, add a preface, and publish it. He seized on the most important points of any book he read. Their many editions prove they were popular.[21]

He had a horror of large books. Everything he wrote had a practical end in view and he knew that those to whom he appealed had neither much money nor much time to spend upon bulky books. He often said to his friend Henry Moore, "Ah, Henry, if angels were authors, we should have but few folios!" [22] In his *Journal* of February 17, 1769, he remarks: "I abridged Doctor Watt's pretty *Treatise on the Passions*. His hundred and seventy-seven pages will make a useful tract of four and twenty. Why do persons who treat the same subjects with me, write so much larger books? Of many reasons is not this the chief? We do not write with the same view. Their principal end is to get money; my only one to do good." [23]

Wesley admired Goldsmith's *An History of the Earth and Animated Nature* published in 1774 and "almost repented of having written anything on the subject." His own *A Survey of the Wisdom of God in the Creation: or A Compendium of Natural Philosophy* in two volumes had been published in 1763 and enlarged to five volumes in 1777 (third edition).[24] His intention was "to make men think and assist them in thinking." No sentences were spun out with an abundance of unnecessary words. The preface explains his aim:

"I have long desired to see such a compendium of natural philosophy as was 1) not too diffuse, not expressed in many words, but comprised in so moderate a compass as not to require any large expense, either of time or money.

"2) Not maimed or imperfect but containing the heads of whatever (after all our discoveries) is known with any degree of certainty, either with regard to the earth or heavens. And this I wanted to see.

"3) In the plainest dress, simply and nakedly expressed,

in the most clear, easy, and intelligible manner that the nature of the things would allow, particularly free from all the jargon of mathematics which is mere heathen Greek to common readers. At the same time I wished to see this short, full, plain account of the visible creation directed to its right end, not barely to entertain an idle, barren curiosity, but to display the invisible things of God, his power, wisdom, and goodness.

"I had finished the addition before I saw Dr. Goldsmith's *History of the Earth and Animated Nature*. I had not read over the first volume of this when I almost repented of having wrote anything on the head. It seemed to me that had he published his but a few years sooner, my design would have been quite superseded. . . . It cannot be denied he is a fine wrter. He was a person of strong judgment, of a lively imagination, and a master of language both of the beauty and strength of the English tongue.

"Yet I could not altogether approve of this, that it seemed to be the design of the author to say all he could upon every article, rather than all he should say. Hence arose his numerous and large digressions . . . useful only to the bookseller by swelling the bulk and consequently the price of his book.

"Indeed, this, the price of it, must ever remain a weighty objection to many readers. They cannot afford to purchase eight volumes at six or seven shillings a volume. Ten or fifteen shillings they may possibly afford for five or six smaller volumes, especially when they contain all that is curious or useful in the far more costly work."

A Survey of the Wisdom of God in the Creation is a book to be read for a picture of eighteenth century popular ideas of science: sound is caused by motion of air; heat is a mode of motion; light is a material substance, and there exists "some matter in the air much finer than the air itself." The biological theories of preformation are discussed. The opinion that "all brutes are mere machines" may be agreeable enough to the pride of man, but is not agreeable to daily observation. The treatment of magnetism and electricity are, as might be expected, very good. The Copernican system is generally accepted. But the significant lack in Wesley's knowledge of science may be due to his attitude towards mathematics, experimentation, and theory. Repeatedly he emphasized his belief that the importance of science was its immediate practical value to man and its power to demonstrate the existence and goodness of God. "The measure of prosecuting learning is its usefulness to good life, and, consequently, all prosecution of it beyond or beside this end is impertinent and immoderate."

Yet one virtue *A Survey of the Wisdom of God in the Creation* did eminently possess: There were at that time numerous books giving better treatments of the special branches of science contained within the *Compendium:* astronomy, mechanics, electricity, chemistry, biology. But, as one scientist, Robert E. Schofield suggests, were better treatments of these subjects combined in one work and sold as cheaply and as conveniently? It would not be easy to find them.

In 1753 Wesley brought out his *The Complete English Dictionary explaining most of those hard words which are found in the best English writers, By a Lover of Good English and Common Sense,* with a second edition in 1764. To this he added several hundred words from Dr. Johnson's *Dictionary* which appeared in 1755. Wesley's dictionary was a little book intended for the pocket and giving simple explanations of hard words. It consisted of only 144 pages with a vocabulary of about 4600 words. Wesley's dictionary had this advantage over Dr. Johnson's dictionary—shortness and cheapness. Definitions rarely exceed a line, but for their modest purpose they are adequate. Wesley is not concerned with elegance; he is thinking only of comprehension. He drew up his word list independently. Conspicuous are terms dealing with religion, medicine, music, and French words or phrases such as might be found in ordinary reading *(Belles Lettres, Billet-Doux, Carte-Blanche, Valet de Chambre, etc.)*. Two historians of the art of lexicography, Starnes and Noyes, remark of *The Complete English Dictionary:* "It lacks all the departments which had been developed in the course of a century and a half of experimentation in lexicography. . . . On further examination, however, it becomes apparent that this little work possesses real individuality and that its retrogressive character is purposeful." [25]

Wesley's preface, though humorous, is concise and militant:

"The author assures you he thinks this is the best English Dictionary in the world.

"As incredible as it may appear, I must allow that this Dictionary is not published to get money, but to assist persons of common sense and no learning to understand the best English authors and that with as little expense of either time or money as the nature of the thing will allow.

"To this end it contains not a heap of Greek and Latin words just tagged with English terminations (for no good English writer, none but vain and senseless pedants, give these any place in their writings), not a scroll of barbarous law expressions, which are neither Greek, Latin, nor good English, not a crowd of technical terms, the meaning whereof is to be sought in books expressly wrote on the subjects to which they belong, not such English words as *and, of, but,* which stand so gravely in Mr. Bailey's, Pardon's, and Martin's Dictionaries, but most of those hard words which are found in the best English writers. . . . And this I have done in order to make this Dictionary as short and cheap as possible.

"I should add no more but that I have so often observed the only way, according to the modern taste, for any author to procure commendation to his book, is vehemently to commend it himself. . . . In compliance therefore, with the taste of the age, I add that this little Dictionary is not only the shortest and cheapest, but likewise by many degrees, the most correct which is extant at this day." [26]

A few random definitions acidly contrast Dr. Johnson of polysyllabism, Wesley of perspicuity.

Wesley	*Dr. Johnson*
aba'ndon—to give up, resign, forsake.	*abandon*—47 lines.
aba'se—to bring low.	*abase*—22 lines with quotes.
a'bbot—the chief of a convent.	*abbot*—15 lines.
ze'phyrus—the west wind.	*zephyrus*—11 lines.
zone—a girdle anciently worn by virgins.	*zone*—43 lines.
aba'sh—to make ashamed.	*abash*—v.a. [See Bashful. Perhaps from *abaisser*, French]

1. To put into confusion; to make ashamed. It generally implies a sudden impression of shame. [Quote from Milton's *Paradise Lost* and Dryden's *Fables.*]
2. The passive admits the particle *at;* sometimes *of,* before the causal noun. [Quotes.] [28 lines with quotes.]

Here is a consecutive list of Wesley's definitions under *G.*

The Galaxy, the milky way.
A Galeon, a large ship.
A Galley, a ship with oars.
A Gallicism, a way of speaking peculiar to the French tongue.
To Gambol, to dance, skip, frisk.
The Gamut, the scale of music.
A Gangrene, the beginning of mortification.
A Gantlet, an iron glove.
A Garner, a store-house.

To Garnish, to furnish, to adorn.
Garrulity, talkativeness.
A Garth, a yard.
A Gasconade, a bravado, cracking, boasting.
A Garb, a dress.

Finally, Starnes and Noyes remark of *The Complete English Dictionary*. "It is perhaps the most eloquent proof of the practical value of this work that its users wore out their copies and left us so few to study."[27]

At the request of the Countess of Huntingdon Wesley compiled an anthology of poetry, *A Collection of Moral and Sacred Poems* in three volumes. Spenser's works were omitted because they were "scarce intelligible to the generality of modern readers." [28] George Herbert was included in the anthology, and Walton's Life of *Herbert* was put in *The Christian Library.*[29] It was Wesley who kept alive the appreciation of Herbert in the eighteenth century. In the anthology he followed his bad habit of not naming most of the authors of the poems.

But Wesley overstepped himself when publishing his anthology. He included ten pages of Young's *Night Thoughts,* which had been published two years before. Dodsley owned the copyright of this and of Mrs. Paine's poems, and action was brought against Wesley. He received a Chancery bill, "a foul monster . . . a scroll of forty-two pages in large folio to tell a story which needed not to have taken up forty lines." [30] (This increased his hatred of lawyers and legal forms.) The matter was finally settled for £50.[31]

John Pomfret in *The Choice* expressed a sentiment of which Wesley could heartily approve—

"I'd be concerned in no litigious jars. . . .
Lawsuits I'd shun, with as much studious care
As I would dens where hungry lions are;
And rather put up injuries than be,
A plague to him who'd be a plague to me.[32]

Dodsley died in 1764 and Young in 1765. Thus anyone could then print the poems, and in 1768 Wesley read over Young's *Night Thoughts,* corrected lines, explained hard words and left out indifferent lines. In 1770 he published *An Extract from Dr. Young's Night Thoughts on Life, Death, and Immortality.* "My design in the following extract is: 1) To leave out all the lines which seem to me either to contain childish conceits, to sink into prosaic flatness, to rise into the turgid, the false sublime, or to be invariably obscure to common readers. 2) To explain the words which are obscure not in themselves, but only to unlearned readers. 3) To point out, especially to these, by a single or double mark, what appears to me to be the sublimest strokes of poetry and the most pathetic strokes of nature and passion." [33]

Night Thoughts was reissued several times. Wesley's passion for reissuing books which he admired was only equalled by his belief in his ability to select their best parts. One of his followers remarked: "It is a wonder Mr. Wesley does not abridge the Gospel According to St. John." [34]

Wesley's *Paradise Lost* came out in 1763. His sympathies were with the multitude and he labored to bring this inimitable work "within the reach of all," the immense learning which he [Milton] has everywhere crowded together, making it quite obscure to persons of a common education." Wesley omitted passages considered too difficult, appended notes on minor difficulties, and marked with asterisks passages of peculiar excellence. Roughly one-fifth of the book was marked as "peculiarly excellent." "These I believe it would be worth while to read over and over or even to commit to memory." [35] Long practice in abridging had made Wesley adept in converting long, involved sentences into short ones. A few examples will show something of his method.[36] Words in brackets are deleted:

. . . Sulphurous and Nitrous Foam They found, they mingl'd, and with [subtle] Art, [Concocted and adusted they] reduc'd To blackest grain, and into store convey'd: (VI, 512-15)	. . . sulphurous and nitrous foam They found, they mingled, and with art reduc'd To blackest grain, and into store convey'd: (ll. 483-85)
Till Night, then in the East [her turn she] shines, [Revolv'd on Heav'n's great Axle,] and her Reign. [With thousand lesser lights dividual holds,] With thousand thousand Stars, that then appear'd Spangling the Hemisphere: . . . (VII, 380-84)	Till night, then in the east shines, and her reign With thousand thousand stars, that then appear'd Spangling the hemisphere: . . . (ll. 311-313)
Him after long debate, [irresolute Of thoughts revolv'd,] his final sentence chose IX, 87-88)	Him after long debate his sentence chose (1.34)
Meanwhile in Paradise the hellish pair Too soon arriv'd, *Sin* [there in power before. Once actual, now in body] and [to dwell behind her *Death* Habitual habitant;] behind her *Death* (X, 585-88)	Mean while in Paradise the hellish pair Too soon arriv'd, Sin and behind her Death (ll. 433-34)

Mere abbreviation was no part of Wesley's purpose. In the whole work less than two thousand lines were struck out. Strange proper names were omitted; long similes were converted into short ones. The deletions left the poem more universally understandable. Wesley took care to preserve the general integrity of Milton's line. Notes were short and consisted of glossorial definitions of unusual or archaic words, or words that might seem difficult to his readers, or identification of names of men or places retained in the text. Less frequently they contained supplementary information. For the unlearned, the edition was epochal. It brought them one of the greatest poems cleared of the thorns which had discouraged them.[37]

Soon Wesley was writing to his Book Room: "O Matthew, how is this? There is not one Milton here, nor one set of the *Philosophy*. Pray send immediately twelve sets of the *Philosophy* and twenty Miltons." [38]

Pilgrim's Progress, published in 1743, suffered a drastic abridgment, but the people whom Wesley wanted to reach were distressingly poor. The price was scaled down to 4d, but the leisurely charm of Bunyan's style disappeared. Where Bunyan was vigorous and straightforward, Wesley's abbreviated sentences became almost staccato, the manner of delivery swift, direct, curt. He deliberately altered the material, adding new sentences and paragraphs of his own. Wesley's abridgment was vastly inferior to the original, and yet the little paperbound booklet was immediately popular. Seven editions were printed during Wesley's lifetime.[39]

The Fool of Quality, published in 1766 by Henry Brooke, was issued in 1781 as *The History of Henry, Earl of Morland* in two volumes. Wesley's abridgment was popular, running into seven editions. The tedious digressions were omitted. Here Wesley's methods were seen at their best. He pruned, erased, and altered as he wished.[40]

A Concise History of England, compounded chiefly of Goldsmith, Rapin, and Smollett, "only with various corrections and additions," attempted to see God in all things—the one great cause, God pervading the moral as well as the natural world. "Let there be one Christian History of what is still called a Christian country." [41]

"The grand objection," his preface reads, "which every thinking man naturally makes to most of the histories that are extant and to the histories of England in particular is that they are unimportant, that they are well nigh filled with incidents, the knowledge of which brings the reader neither profit nor pleasure. For instance, it no more concerns us to know nine parts in ten of what is contained in Rapin's History than to know that on such a day a bird dropped a feather on one of the Pyrenean mountains.

"A contrary objection may nevertheless be made to the generality of our historians. Although they are far too prolix on most occasions, yet on others they are too concise. They do not in any wise copy after Tacitus (although some of them profess to do it) who lightly passes over a thousand circumstances which less judicious writers would have related at large while he gives a very minute detail of those striking incidents which have a tendency either to improve the understanding or to amend the heart.

"But a greater fault is partiality. And how very few are free from it! Accordingly some violently attach themselves to the cause of King Charles the First, others with equal violence defend and extol the long parliament or Oliver Cromwell. Many suppose the whole family of the Stuarts to have been good men and excellent princes; others paint them as the worst of men and the vilest of tyrants.

"There is yet another objection which may be made to all the histories of England which I have seen, that is, they seem calculated only for atheists, for there is nothing of God in them." [42]

Ten thousand dull passages, Wesley again insisted, should have been omitted which were inserted for no other purpose than to enlarge the volume and consequently the price, to oblige the bookseller rather than the reader.[43]

In 1778 Wesley began *The Arminian Magazine, consisting of Extracts and Original Treatises on Universal Redemption.*[44] The magazine gave Wesley a chance to republish many of his sermons and to reproduce some of his books that had not secured great sales owing to their price. It influenced the Brontës and George Eliot. Each issue consisted of four parts: 1) a defense of the doctrine: "God willeth all men to be saved and to come to the knowledge of the truth," 2) an extract from the life of some holy man, 3) accounts and letters containing the experience of pious persons, and 4) verses. The magazine frequently reported on scientific subjects too and printed extracts from scientific books. The number of Arminian Magazines printed at the period of Wesley's death was 7,000. The circulation continued to increase to the number of 24,000 and then receded to 13,500.[45]

To a friend who complained that the magazine was too short, he replied by quoting Prior's Epistle to F. Shephard on Tonson the publisher—

> Tonson, who is himself a wit,
> Weighs writers' merits by the sheet—

and added: "So do thousands besides, but I do not write for these. I write for those who judge of books not by the quantity but by the quality of them, who ask not how long, but how good they are. I spare both my reader's time and my own by couching my sense in as few words as I can. Those who prefer the dealers in many words may find them on every side."[46]

A Christian Library was begun in 1749 and completed in 1755. A prodigious number of books was read. Some were abridged on horseback and others at wayside inns and houses where Wesley tarried for a night. His effort was to make the masses acquainted with the galaxy of noblest men in the Christian world. The Library comprised abridgments or extracts of the choicest pieces of practical divinity published in the English tongue. He began with the Epistles of St. Clement and summarized or made extracts of the works of Fox, Bunyan, Baxter as well as a host of seventeenth and eighteenth century divines. He followed his usual method when he found blemishes, circumlocutions, and repetitions.[47]

Fifty volumes of the *Christian Library* suggest the breadth of this spiritual nourishment. Wesley's labors in the project brought him no personal gain despite charges of his opponents. He himself confessed he lost money on the volumes. A *Journal* entry notes his preparation of "the rest of the books for the *Christian Library,* a work by which I have lost about two hundred pounds. Perhaps the next generation may know the value of it." [48]

4.

"Let me make a nation's songs," says Carlyle on Burns, "and you shall make its laws." [49] With his brother Charles, Wesley caused the masses to break out into song. Together they published 56 hymn books besides several tune books. The tunes were those in the classical style of the ancients. A collection of psalms and hymns issued in 1737 was probably the first hymn book for use in the Church of England. In the famous preface to the hymn book of 1779 he says:

"As but a small part of these hymns is of my own composing, I do not think it inconsistent with modesty to declare that I am persuaded no such hymn book as this has yet been published in the English language.

"May I be permitted to add a few words with regard to the poetry. 1) In these hymns there is no doggerel, no botches, nothing put in to patch up the rhyme, no feeble expletives. 2) Here is nothing turgid or bombastic on the one hand or low and creeping on the other. 3) Here are no cant expressions, no words without meaning. Those who impute this to us know not what they say. We talk common sense, whether they understand it or not, both in verse and prose, and use no word but in a fixed and determinate sense. 4) Here are, allow me to say, both the purity, the strength, and the elegance of the English language, and at the same time the utmost simplicity and plainness, suited to every capacity. Lastly I desire men of taste to judge (these are the only competent judges) whether there be not in some of the following hymns the true spirit of poetry, such as cannot be acquired by art and labor, but must be the gift of nature. By labor a man may become a tolerable imitator of Spenser, Shakespeare, or Milton, and may heap together pretty compound epithets as pale-eyed, meek-eyed, and the like, but unless he be born a poet, he will never attain the genuine spirit of poetry.

"And here I beg leave to mention a thought which has been long upon my mind, and which I should long ago have inserted in the public papers, had I not been unwilling to stir up a nest of hornets. Many gentlemen have done my brother and me (though without naming us) the honor to reprint many of our hymns. Now they are perfectly welcome so to do, provided they print them just as they are. But I desire they would not attempt to mend them, for they really are notable. None of them is able to mend either the sense or the verse. Therefore I must beg of them one of these two favors: either to let them stand as they are, to take them for better or worse, or to add the true reading in the margin, or at the bottom of the page, that we may no longer be accountable either for the nonsense or for the doggerel of other men." [50]

In *A Pocket Hymn Book for the Use of Christians of all Denominations*, 1787, Wesley goes on bluntly to say: "Out of two hundred and thirty-two hymns I have omitted seven and thirty. These I did not dare to palm upon the world, because fourteen of them appeared to me very flat and dull, fourteen more, mere prose, tagged with rhyme, and nine more to be grievous doggerel. But a friend tells me, 'Some of these, especially those two that are doggerel double-distilled, namely, "The despised Nazarene," and that which begins, "A Christ I have; O what a Christ have I" are hugely admired and continually echoed from Berwick-upon-Tweed to London.' If they are, I am sorry, for it will bring a deep reproach upon the judgment of the Methodists. But I dare not increase that reproach by countenancing in any degree such an insult both on religion and common sense. . . .

"Whereas in the other hymn book the hymns are strangely thrown out of their places and all jumbled together, they are here carefully methodized again and ranged in their proper order." [51]

John Wesley not only selected the tunes for the hymns but taught Methodists how to sing. He threatened to dismiss those preachers who sang more than two hymns at a service. Methodists sang lustily. Only a cold sinner could hear the great concourse of plain men and women rolling out, "Blow ye, the trumpet blow," or "O for a thousand tongues to sing," or "Soldiers of Christ, Arise" without being swept off his feet. *The Collection of Hymns for the Use of the People Called Methodists* sold by the millions.

Before 1736 the Church of England had no hymn book. The Psalms metrically rendered by Sternhold and Hopkins, or Tate and Brady, George Herbert's *Temple,* and Jeremy Taylor's *Golden Grove* were in circulation together with devotional books in which hymns were included, but there were no hymn books. Consequently congregational singing which Wesley had learned from the Moravians appealed to people with the attractiveness of novelty. By expression of their religious experiences, they were led to a clearer definition of their doctrine. At the same time emotion was intensified by its expression.[52]

The number of hymns Charles Wesley wrote was amazing—over 6,000 of them. Although they expressed too many times the same ideas, they were often rapturous, virile, romantic, vivid. Penetrating analysis was combined with spaciousness.

> The fullness of my great reward
> A blest eternity shall be,
> But hast Thou not on earth prepared
> Some better thing than this for me?
> What, but one drop?
> One transient sight!
> I want a sun, a sea of light.

As Courthope says, religious feelings were chastened and controlled in expression by the masculine taste of a scholar and gentleman. "A combination of impulse and judgment" makes Charles Wesley the most admirable devotional lyric poet in the English language.[53]

"The Methodists in general," said one carping critic, "have very little taste for any poems but those of a religious or a moral kind." [54] But it was a sincere taste for poetry, and Wesleyan hymns were religiously superb and lyrically excellent.

5.

"I doubt you had a dunce for a tutor at Cambridge," writes Wesley to preacher Samuel Furly, "and so set out wrong. Did he never tell you that of all men living, a clergyman should talk with the vulgar? Yea, and write imitating the language of the common people throughout so far as consists with purity and propriety of speech?" [55]

Wesley's letter writing was carried on in moments snatched from other engagements. Dr. Johnson felt "the cool of leisure, the stillness of solitude" necessary to the production of his letters. Wesley's note to Furly on July 15, 1764, throws an interesting light on his method of composition. "I never think of my style at all, but just set down the words that come first. Only when I transcribe anything for the press, then I think it my duty to see that every phrase be clear, pure, and proper. Conciseness (which is now, as it were, natural to me) brings *quantum sufficit* of strength. If, after all, I observe any stiff expression, I throw it out neck and shoulders." [56] Adding in another letter, "I scarce ever yet repented of saying too little, but frequently of saying too much." [57]

In truth Wesley showed remarkable literary power—at times writing with the fire and moving earnestness of a prophet, more often adopting a businesslike tone—direct, helpful, sympathetic, vigorous, dynamic, to the point. For example, this to Samuel Bardsley: "Dear Sammy,—I suppose John Atlay has paid the money. He is cautious to an extreme. I hear what angry men say or write, but I do not often regard it. Lemonade will cure any disorder of the bowels (whether it be with or without purging) in a day or two. You do well to spread the prayer meetings up and down. They seldom are in vain. Honest Andrew Dunlop [the Assistant at Limerick] writes me word that the book money is stolen. Pray desire him to take care that the knave does not steal his teeth." [58] Or this to John White: "John White, whoever is wrong, you are not right." [59]

"It would be difficult," says Leslie Stephen, "to find any letters more direct, forcible, and pithy in expression. He goes straight to the mark, without one superfluous flourish. He writes as a man confined within the narrowest limits of time and space. . . . The compression gives emphasis and never causes confusion. The letters, in other words, are the work of one who for more than half a century was accustomed to turn to account every minute of his eighteen working hours." [60]

Wesley could speak plainly but not brutally. He tells Thomas Wride on February 24, 1775: "Beware of your own spirit! You bite like a bull dog. When you seize, you never let go." More sharply a few months later after an outburst in one of Wride's letters which had given great offense to the preachers in Ireland: "Such base language is too bad for the fishwives of Billingsgate. It is such as an archangel would not use to the devil! You must have done with it for ever if you desire to have any further fellowship with John Wesley." [61]

Wesley did not write for fame. His object was to instruct and benefit people. He used no trappings to please or to gain applause. The distinguishing character of his style is brevity and clarity. Never did he lose sight of the rule which Horace gives:

> Concise your diction, let your sense be clear,
> Nor with a weight of words fatigue the ear.[62]

He was not at ease when Whitefield preached, being constantly reminded of his "luscious" method of speaking. Wesley himself had the simplicity and clarity of Defoe, used the same homely illustrations, and gave the same exact detail of events in a colloquial manner. His preachers were also trained and almost drilled in his methods of writing and speaking plainly and without any flourishes and affectation.[63] All fit into his standard: "What is it that constitutes a good style? Perspicuity and purity, propriety, strength, and easiness joined together. Where any of these is wanting, it is not a good style. Dr. Middleton's style wants easiness; it is stiff to a high degree. And stiffness in writing is full as great a fault as stiffness in behavior. It is a blemish hardly to be excused, much less to be imitated. He is *pedantic*. 'It is pedantry,' says the great Lord Boyle, 'to use an hard word where an easier will serve.' Now, this the Doctor continually does, and that of set purpose. It is abundantly too artificial. *Artis est celare artem* (It is the perfection of art to conceal itself), but his art glares in every sentence. He continually says, 'Observe how fine I speak!' Whereas a good speaker seems to forget he speaks at all. . . .

"Clearness in particular is necessary for you and me because we are to instruct people of the lowest understanding." [64]

CHAPTER THIRTEEN

AGITATION FOR REFORM

"Go always not to those who want you," said Wesley, "but to those who want you most." [1]

No social evil before Howard, Romilly, and Bentham was more glaring than England's inept criminal jurisprudence and prison administration. The unique service of Wesleyanism consisted of the humane attitude it generated in the community. Its record in the relief of prisoners included three kinds of activity—visitation, publicity regarding prison conditions, and approval of reform movements. The official rules of the society which were standard after 1743 established "visiting or helping them that are . . . in prison" as one of the conditions of membership.[2] In 1778 the conference asked: "Is it not advisable for us to visit all the jails we can?" and answered, "By all means. There cannot be a greater charity." [3] In one period of nine months Wesley preached at least sixty-seven times in various gaols. The members of societies seemed to possess "a peculiar talent for that benevolent work."[4] The true motive for the universal practice of visiting gaols was mainly religious, but material needs were often relieved.

A simple constructive service was rendered in giving publicity to existing conditions. In January, 1761, Wesley wrote to the *London Chronicle* criticizing the degrading conditions at Newgate and pointing to a reformed Bristol Newgate administered by a Methodist gaoler as an example worthy of emulation by other prisons. "Of all the seats of woe this side hell few, I suppose, exceed or even equal Newgate. If any region of horror could exceed it a few years ago, Newgate in Bristol did, so great was the filth, the stench, the misery, and wickedness which shocked all who had a spark of humanity left."[5] And again: "You may easily be convinced of this by going into either Ludgate or Newgate. What a scene appears as soon as you enter! The very place strikes terror into your soul. How dark and dreary! How unhealthy and unclean! How void of all that might minister comfort!"[6]

Gaoler Dagge, converted by Whitefield, had instituted many changes at Bristol Newgate. Cleanliness was present everywhere, fighting and brawling put down, any prisoner wronging another punished. Drunkenness and whoredom were quite stopped while idleness was prevented as far as possible. The whole prison had a new face. "Nothing offends the eye or ear, and the whole has the appearance of a quiet, serious family."[7]

On May 13, 1739, Wesley writes: "Every morning I read prayers and preached at Newgate."[8] On September 3, 1742, he went to visit a murderer and was surprised to find the doors open to him. "I exhorted the sick malefactor to cry unto God with all his might. . . . It was not long before the rest of the felons flocked around."[9] On Sunday, August 28, 1743, he was preaching in the Castle at Exeter and half the grown persons in the city "had gathered for the service." It was an awful sight "to see so many people within the solemn prison walls."[10] In October, 1761, he gave them another discourse.[11] At the gaol in Whitley, he preached to the malefactors and was asked to go on and at Yorkshire, he preached to the prisoners at six o'clock on the morning of April 28, 1779. The ground was covered with snow, but so many people attended that the service was held in the prison court. The snow continued to fall and the north wind to whistle round them.[12]

The hardened criminal, the malefactor, the transgressor, reiterated Wesley, could be justified by faith.

"My God is reconciled,
His pardoning voice I hear,
He owns me for his child,
I can no longer fear." [13]

Those in disease ridden, pestilential prison holes, numbers chained like beasts in dens, heard the message of grace and forgiveness and were comforted and uplifted in spirit.

"Sunday, December 26, 1784. I preached the condemned criminals' sermon in Newgate. Forty-seven were under sentence of death. While they were coming in, there was something very awful in the clink of their chains, but no sound was heard, either from them or the crowded audience, after the text was named: 'There is joy in heaven over one sinner that repenteth more than over ninety and nine just persons that need not repentence.' The power of the Lord was eminently present, and most of the prisoners were in tears. A few days after twenty of them died at once, five of whom died in peace . . .

"Friday, 31. We had a solemn watch-night and ushered in the new year with the voice of praise and thanksgiving." [14]

Was what Wesley preached an opiate and drug? Suppose the prisoners had raged in their last moments or acted out a grotesquely comic spectacle before the thousands lined like rotten oranges at the windows and rooftops near Tyburn. What would have been gained? Had Wesley come before their crime, perhaps he would not afterwards have needed to come at all. Never did he blink or rationalize the fact that poverty leads to viciousness and crime, not vice versa. The prisoners were grateful that a kind and sincere person had shown concern for them, who brought tidings of a heavenly as well as human concern. Exulting voices rose like psalms from dungeons and gallows: "This is the happiest day I ever saw in my life," "Who can express the joy and peace I now feel," "Death has no sting for me," "Welcome halter," "Welcome gallows," "I have peace within." Of certain criminals, all received their punishment with perfect calm, "appeared like giants refreshed with new wine." [15]

What direct relation did Wesley bear to the organized prison reform movement? Howard himself testified that Wesley was a source of inspiration to him and Wesley reciprocated by declaring: "Mr. Howard is really an extraordinary man. God has raised him up to be a blessing to many nations." [16]

On Oct. 15, 1759, Wesley walked to Knowle, a mile from Bristol, to see the French prisoners. He found they had only a few foul thin rags to clothe them. Eighteen pounds were collected and next day it was made up to £24. Clothes were bought and carefully distributed to the most needy. "I was much affected and preached in the evening on Exodus XXXII,9: 'Also thou shalt not oppress a stranger, for ye know the heart of a stranger, seeing ye were strangers in the land of Egypt.' " [17]

2.

Four abuses Wesley did help directly to abolish. He contended for a lifetime against bribery and corruption in politics, against the Press Gang, against the plundering of wrecked vessels, and against smuggling.

"Act as if the whole election depended on your vote," he remarked in *A Word to a Freeholder*.[16] In a letter to the Societies of Bristol he was emphatic on the subject. "Beware of bribery. On no account take money or money's worth. Keep yourselves pure. Give, not sell your vote." [19] He came to St. Ives, Cornwall, on the evening of an important election and took the opportunity of speaking to all his society who had votes. To his great satisfaction he found not one of them would consent to eat or drink at the expense of him for whom he intended to vote. One of them had received a bribe of five guineas, but straightway returned it. Another not only refused to be bribed, but when he heard his mother had accepted money privately, persuaded her to give it to him and then returned it without delay. In the *Journal* entry of Oct. 6, 1774, he advised voters, 1) to vote without fee or reward for the person they judged most worthy, 2) to speak no evil of the person they voted against, and 3) to take care their spirits were not sharpened against those that voted on the other side.[20] One thing was certain: Methodists became known as the most incorruptible voters in the realm.

The second abuse Wesley fought against was the Press Gang. Once when he was in the middle of a sermon, the Press Gang took off one of his hearers. Wesley made the comment, thrice bitter: "Ye learned in the Law, what becomes of Magna Charta and of English liberty and property? Are not these mere sounds while on any pretense there is such a thing as a Press Gang suffered in the land?" [21]

Many magistrates found this a convenient method of getting rid of Methodists and especially Methodist preachers. Unfortunately the protest was not at first effective because the close of the century brought with it a struggle which made the Press Gangs invaluable to the government.[22]

The third evil which Wesley tackled was mainly confined to the Cornish coast. People plundered vessels wrecked on the rocks of their coast. The offence was made more heinous by a deliberate attempt to decoy vessels to their doom. When Wesley preached there in 1743 he was in danger of his life. When he paid his last visit in 1789 he was received as a monarch and estimated the crowd which thronged to hear him at "two or three and twenty thousand." Happily his life work had born fruit.[23]

Wesley waged unremitting war against the fourth evil—smuggling and "smuggling villains." In 1784 Pitt calculated that thirteen million pounds of tea were consumed in the kingdom of which only five and one half millions had paid duty.[24] Parson Woodforde, a truly good as well as "respectable" man, wrote on March 29, 1777: "Andrews the smuggler brought me this night about 11 o'clock a bagg of Hyson Tea 6 pound weight. He frightened us a little by whistling under the parlour window just as we were going to bed. I gave him some Geneva and paid him for the tea at 10/6 per pound."[25] The inhabitants of this inland rectory thought and spoke of Andrews the smuggler just as one might speak of Andrews the grocer.

In Methodism the most effective opposition to smuggling appeared. From the very beginning smuggling was banned by the same discipline which forbade the consumption of or traffic in spirits. The Conference of 1767 asked how smuggling could be abolished and the answer it supplied was: 1) speak tenderly and frequently of it in every society near the coast; 2) carefully disperse the *Word to a Smuggler;* 3) expel all who will not leave it off; 4) silence every local preacher that defends it. To reinforce the spoken word Wesley wrote *A Word to a Smuggler* in 1767. The pamphlet was circulated in Cornwall and around the south coast where smuggling was notorious and where even strict and religious people were inclined not to ask questions when buying wines and lace.[26] Thousands of copies of *A Word to a Smuggler* were sold.

Wesley was trenchant. "Open smugglers are worse than common highwaymen and private smugglers are worse than common pickpockets, for it is a general robbery; it is, in effect, not only robbing the king, but robbing every honest man in the nation. For the more a king's duties are diminished, the more the taxes must be increased. And these lie upon us all; they are the burden not of some, but of all the people of England. Therefore every smuggler is a thief general, who picks the pockets both of the king and all his fellow subjects. He wrongs them all and above all the honest traders, many of whom he deprives of their maintenance, constraining them either not to sell their goods at all or to sell them to no profit."[27]

Using the method of short pointed questions and answers he concludes:

" 'But I only buy a little brandy or tea now and then just for my own use?' That is, I only steal a little. God says, 'Steal not at all.'

" 'Why, I should not meddle with it, but I am forced by my parent, husband, or master.' If you are forced by your father or mother to rob, you will be hanged nevertheless. This may lessen but does not take away the fault, for you ought to suffer rather than sin.

" 'But I do not know that it was run.' No! Did he not that sold it tell you it was? If he sold it under the common price, he did. The naming the price was telling you, 'This is run.' "[28]

Wesley won the battle before statesmen won theirs. The gradual extirpation of smuggling from Methodist Societies in itself was a considerable contribution to the creation of a public conscience in the matter.

3.

What contribution did Wesley, the outstanding man of the century, make to the abolition of human servitude? Wesley's opposition to slavery was lifelong and bitter, if the latter term could be applied to one so full of kindness. It is probable that the determined attitude of Oglethorpe, the founder of Georgia, who declared that the trustees of the colony refused "to make a law permitting such a horrid crime" because "it is against the Gospel as well as against the fundamental law of England" was in part due to Wesley's influence.[29] Even "the prince of pulpit orators," George Whitefield, condoned slavery. Whitefield could speak in terms of the highest indignation against slave owners who treated their dogs better than their slaves and made their horses work less hard than the human cattle they possessed. Yet Whitefield not only approved of slavery upon the ground of scriptural authority and expediency, but had fifty slaves in his Orphan House at Georgia and at the time of his death bequeathed them to the Countess of Huntingdon.[30]

Before 1778, Negroes had been brought to England and kept as slaves. Already 14,000 or 15,000 were in the country and open slave sales had taken place in England. A growing protest crystallized and began to assume the proportions of a popular movement. In this atmosphere Wesley read an indictment of the slave trade by the Quaker Anthony Benezet.[31] It focused all of Wesley's energies in opposition to "that execrable sum of all villainies, commonly called the slave trade." [32] Two years later in 1774 he published *Thoughts Upon Slavery,* a tract for popular consumption, phrased incisively and with fiery clarity. No more severe arraignment of slavery than this was ever written. It condemned slavery not only on religious grounds, but on grounds of human sympathy, political right, and economic expediency. True, the only proposal was a personal appeal to individuals engaged in the traffic or who owned slaves. The use of organized political measures was rejected as useless. But the pamphlet was broadcast within and without the societies and given the widest circulation for many years.[33]

A direct outcome was that the American Methodists' Conference in 1780 declared (before King Cotton rolled like a juggernaut to crush out libertarian doctrine): Every person holding slaves was acting contrary to the laws of God and man.[34]

Thoughts Upon Slavery discussed the whole question. Wesley quoted from official French reports to prove that in Africa itself the black man lived happily and healthily, was well behaved, peaceable, and religious, though this picture of idyllic life is overdrawn.[35] Slave traders argued they removed Negroes from Africa for their own good. Generally Wesley maintained a cool logical account of happenings, but towards the close the sweet Samaritan spoke with rapt Isaiah's seraphic fire.

In what numbers and in what manner were the slaves

carried to America? "Mr. Anderson in his *History of Trade and Commerce* observes: 'England supplies her American colonies with Negro slaves, amounting in number to about a hundred thousand every year,' that is, so many are taken on board our ships, but at least ten thousand of them die in the voyage, about a fourth part more die at the different islands in what is called the seasoning. So that at an average, in the passage and seasoning together thirty thousand die, that is, properly are murdered. O earth, O sea, cover not thou their blood!

"I would inquire whether these things can be defended on the principles of even heathen honesty, whether they can be reconciled (setting the Bible out of question) with any degree of either justice or mercy.

"The grand plea is, 'They are authorized by law.' But can law, human law, change the nature of things? Can it turn darkness into light or evil into good? By no means. Notwithstanding ten thousand laws, right is right, and wrong is wrong still. There must still remain an essential between justice and injustice, cruelty and mercy. So that I still ask, who can reconcile this treatment of the Negroes first and last, with either mercy or justice? . . . Yea, where is the justice of taking away the lives of innocent, inoffensive men, murdering thousands of them in their own land, by the hands of their own countrymen, many thousands year after year on shipboard, and then casting them like dung into the sea and tens of thousands in that cruel slavery to which they are so unjustly reduced?

"When they are brought down to the shore in order to be sold, our surgeons thoroughly examine them, and that quite naked, women and men, without any distinction; those that are approved are set on one side. In the meantime a burning iron, with the arms or name of the company lies in the fire with which they are marked on the breast. Before they are put into the ships, their masters strip them of all they have on their backs, so that they come on board stark naked, women as well as men. It is common for several hundred of them to be put on board one vessel where they are stowed together in as little room as it is possible for them to be crowded. It is easy to suppose what a condition they must soon be in between heat, thirst, and stench of various kinds. So that it is no wonder so many should die in the passage, but rather that any survive it.

"When the vessels arrive at their destined port, the Negroes are again exposed naked to the eyes of all that flock together for the examination of their purchasers. Then they are separated to the plantations of their several masters to see each other no more. Here you may see mothers hanging over their daughters bedewing their naked breasts with tears, and daughters clinging to their parents, till the whipper soon obliges them to part. And what can be more wretched than the condition they then enter upon? Banished from their country, from their friends and relations forever, from every comfort of life, they are reduced to a state scarce any way preferable to that of beasts of burden.

"But if this manner of procuring and treating Negroes is not consistent either with mercy or justice, yet there is a plea for it which every man of business will acknowledge to be quite sufficient. Fifty years ago, one meeting an eminent statesman in the lobby of the House of Commons, said, 'You have been long talking about justice and equity. Pray, which is this bill, equity or justice?' He answered very short and plain, 'D—n justice, it is necessity.' . . .

"I answer you stumble at the threshold. I deny that villainy is ever necessary. It is impossible that it should ever be necessary for any reasonable creature to violate all the laws of justice, mercy, and truth. No circumstances can make it necessary for a man to burst in sunder all the ties of humanity. It can never be necessary for a rational being to sink himself below a brute. A man can be under no necessity of degrading himself into a wolf. The absurdity of the supposition is so glaring that one would wonder anyone can help seeing it.

" 'But the furnishing us with slaves is necessary for the trade, and wealth, and glory of our nation.' Here are several mistakes. For first wealth is not necessary to the glory of any nation, but wisdom, virtue, justice, mercy, generosity, public spirit, love of our country. These are necessary to the real glory of a nation, but abundance of wealth is not. . . . But, secondly, it is not clear that we should have either less money or trade (only less of that detestable trade of man—stealing), if there was not a Negro in all our islands or in all English America. It is demonstrable, white men inured to it by degrees can work as well as they, and they would do it, were Negroes out of the way, and proper encouragement given them. However, thirdly, I come back to the same point. Better no trade than trade procured by villainy. It is far better to have no wealth than to gain wealth at the expense of virtue. Better is honest poverty than all the riches bought by the tears, and sweat, and blood of our fellow creatures. . .

"You kept them stupid and wicked by cutting them off from all opportunities of improving either in knowledge or virtue. And now you assign their want of wisdom and goodness as the reason for using them worse than brute beasts." [36]

To the sea captains employed Wesley pleaded: "Quit the horrid trade; at all events be honest men." To the merchant: "Have no part in this detestable business. Men buyers are exactly on a level with men stealers. . . . Give liberty to whom liberty is due, that is, to every child of man, to every partaker of human nature. Let none serve you but by his own act and deed, by his own voluntary choice. Away with all whips, all chains, all compulsion. Be gentle toward all men." [37]

It was obvious that if Wesley wrote against slavery, he would preach against it. He delivered a sermon at Bristol, "the dark den of slave traders." Two days' notice was given of his intention. At the hour of meeting the hall was jammed. The next day was given to fasting and prayer that the "poor outcasts" might find a way of escape and "their chains be broken in sunder." [38]

Methodists were not hesitant in cooperating with non-Wesleyan groups in the anti-slavery cause. "Whatever assistance I can give those generous men who join to oppose that execrable trade, I certainly shall give," wrote Wesley.[39] He expressed to Granville Sharp his "perfect destestation of the horrid slave trade." [40] Wilberforce placed so high a value upon the cooperation of Wesley and his followers that he sent anti-slavery literature to all Methodist preachers. The Methodist Conference as early as 1780 passed a resolution condemning the trade. Days of fasting and prayers were observed that God would remember the slaves. Through the agency of Methodist preachers the effort to boycott slave-produced articles spread. The *Arminian Magazine* reminded Methodists to ponder "how many backs have sweated for the sweet your cane affords"—it was "a drug composed of the slave dealer's sin and the slave's misery." [41]

How thoroughly the members of the societies complied, how influential was their support is indicated by statistics of anti-slavery petitions. While twenty-one other non-conforming bodies including Roman Catholics secured 122,978 signatures, Wesleyans forwarded 229,426 names.[42]

If one gives the credit of abolition to the Evangelicals, then one makes Wesley father of the whole movement, for he made possible the Evangelical party and he remained the guide, counsellor, and friend of its first leaders. Far more than that, he was the inspirer and friend of those in the van of Negro abolition. Hardly any name was more important. When Wilberforce, Clarkson, and Granville Sharp are mentioned, the name of John Wesley must also be included. He was a pioneer in the movement against slavery.[43]

"I would to God," Wesley thundered again in *A Serious*

Address to the People of England "that we may never more steal and sell our brethren like beasts, never murder them by thousands and tens of thousands! O may this worse than Mohammedan, worse than Pagan abomination be removed from us forever." [44]

On his deathbed he had read aloud to him passages from Gustavus Vasa, the autobiography of a black slave. And it was fitting that the last important letter he wrote (February 24, 1791) should have been to young William Wilberforce.

"Dear Sir,—Unless the divine power has raised you up to be as *Athanasius contra mundum* I see not how you can go through your glorious enterprise in opposing that execrable villainy, which is the scandal of religion, of England, and of human nature. Unless God has raised you up for this very thing, you will be worn out by the opposition of men and devils. But if God be for you, who can be against you? Are all of them together stronger than God? O be not weary of well doing! Go on, in the name of God, and in the power of His might, till even American slavery (the vilest that ever saw the sun) shall vanish away before it. . . .

Your affectionate servant,
JOHN WESLEY." [45]

On April 20, 1791, the Commons rejected Wilberforce's motion for the abolition of the slave trade by 163 votes to 88, though Pitt, Fox, and Burke spoke in its favor, and it was not till 1807 that the great victory was won.

The next rampart was carried in 1833: abolition of slavery in the West Indies. A major share in the agitation was taken by Methodists.

CHAPTER FOURTEEN

THE NEW JERUSALEM

John Wesley was a Church of England clergyman who constantly professed his allegiance to both church and state. As the church was considered by him an integral part of the state, love for one meant affection for the other. In politics he was wholeheartedly monarchial. That Methodism was allied to liberty or that his project was a fresh enterprise in contemporary society, he never realized. In politics as in so many other spheres, he was both realist and opportunist. He needed protection against the senseless violence of mobs and this protection had to come from the state. Had Methodism sided with political parties, the same fate would have come to it as came to them. Government never ceased to be hostile.

Cobblers, tinkers, porters, and hackney coachmen, wrote Wesley during the excitement about John Wilkes, thought themselves wise enough to instruct both king and council.[1] He concluded a eulogium on the throne with: "If the best of kings, the most virtuous of queens, and the most perfect constitution could make any nation happy, the people of this country had every reason to think themselves so." [2] Yet as Wesley quite forgot, it was he more than the first three that rescued the common people from moral and social paralysis and transformed them into useful, happy individuals and citizens. The seeds of radicalism and reaction lay together in Wesleyanism. Nevertheless inherently democratic influences of the movement made it impossible ever to extirpate those sympathies.[3]

Wesley was not the man to mistake the institution of monarchy for the action of monarchs. He denounced Charles I because "he persecuted godly men" although he blamed his ministers. Queen Mary, and Elizabeth after her, he branded as persecutors of religious people. James I permitted the most atrocious cruelties to be practised on the Puritans and Charles II was guilty of causing thousands of men, guiltless of any crime, to be "stripped of all they had . . . and driven to beg for bread . . . because they did not dare to worship God according to other men's consciences." [4] George III was regarded by Wesley as a man of understanding and good moral character (which he was).[5]

The appeal to popular will uninformed by social purpose, said Wesley, could result only in unhinging all government and plunging society into chaos. The end of the state was ethical. Extend political power to that many-headed beast, the ignorant people, and society instituted for men's welfare would be overturned.[6] The idea that the people were the origin of power was abhorrent to him. To refute it he used two arguments continually. The first was on historic grounds. He affirmed that there was but one instance in history when the people gave the sovereign power to one man. That was in the case of Massaniello of Naples.[7] The second was on the grounds of impracticability. Once you say people have power to appoint rulers, you affirm the right belongs to every man and woman and child, which, added Wesley, nobody in his century really believed.[8] Probably the clear-brained, single-minded Wesley's detached attitude towards politics was that so long as man, "the highest product of creation is rotten, the whole structure must be proportionately infirm, but make him sound and the surrounding elements will partake of the perfection embodied in their loftiest manifestation." [9]

He had a naive view of the delegates of government—they should be "men of sound judgment . . . lovers of mankind, lovers of their country, and lovers of their king, men attached to no party, but simply pursuing the general good of the nation." [10] Existing evils of civil society arose from a denial of the moral responsibility of individuals and groups. Individuals were to feel free to work out their economic and social salvation in an orderly society. Civil power originates in Providence, but liberty of conscience and freedom of experience must be guaranteed—they are inseparable from humanity.[11]

All tracts show Wesley's exhortations for loyalty and obedience to the crown. In 1775 he published *A Calm Address to Our American Colonies,* based on Dr. Johnson's *Taxation No Tyranny*. He not only pruned but altered and put Johnson's pamphlet in conversational style. *Taxation No Tyranny* is a general essay; *A Calm Address* is a direct appeal. Wesley's tract was rapid in tempo, easier to read. Copies sent to America were never distributed. Friends foreseeing the danger destroyed them. Wesley's little pamphlet consisting of four pages and selling for 1d probably reached a hundred readers where Johnson's labored and magisterial discussion reached one. Perhaps 100,000 were circulated in England.

The government offered a reward, but the only reward Wesley agreed to accept was £50 from the privy purse to devote to charity. Why did he write the *Calm Address?* "I seriously answer not to get money . . . not to get preferment . . . not to please any man living, high or low; least of all did I write with a view to inflame any, just the contrary." [12]

Dissenters, most bitter, accused Wesley of being a turncoat and of stealing the tract of Johnson without publishing his name. Wesley was extremely careless about adding authors' names to the books he published. A month or so later he presented Dr. Johnson with a copy of his *Notes on the New Testament*. Dr. Johnson replied and thanked him for the book and for his support over the American question, closing with a magnificent compliment: "To have gained such a mind as yours may justly confirm me in my own opinion. The lecturer was surely in the right who though he saw his audience slinking away, refused to quit the chair while Plato stayed." [13]

If the pamphlet had considerable influence in forming public opinion hostile to all concession, Wesley shares a grave responsibility. Without support the Tory government might have hesitated to persevere in armed conflict.[14]

Wesley was not an out and out pacifist, but war to him was the foulest curse men knew—a rebellion against humanity and God. "War is a horrid reproach to the Christian name, yea, to the name of man, to all reason and humanity. . . . In all the judgments of God the inhabitants of the earth learn righteousness. When a land is visited with famine or plague or earthquake the people commonly see and acknowledge the hand of God. But whenever war breaks out, God is forgotten if He be not set at open defiance."[15] *A Calm Address* tried to prevent the American Revolution. But when war came, Wesley, adhering to his political tenets, supported the government.

The author managed with perfect honesty to get on the wrong side every time. Yet he was against slavery and ironically spread that doctrine which the American Revolution helped to disseminate—freedom and opportunity for all. The spirit he awoke in England motivated reforms of the next century.

Was England saved from Revolution by the Methodist Revival? Did Wesley forget "the new Manchester in the New Jerusalem?" [16] The miracle of modern England, says Halévy, was that it was anarchistic but orderly, practical and businesslike, but religious and even pietist. It was definitely on the side of king and government. Though great unrest prevailed—several factors favored an upheaval: the Jacobites, disturbances consequent upon the American War, the high price of food and economic distress in 1756-57 and later after 1770, and some sympathy with the French Revolution—a number of factors were working in the opposite direction. Amongst these were loyalty taught on religious grounds by all or almost all religious bodies, the memory of past political upheavals, and a general disinclination of the people to revolt. Mobs existed but not for any doctrinaire purpose. The commonest cause of mob action in the eighteenth century was the high cost of provisions—bread riots in times of scarcity and unemployment or protest as in the Wilkes riots. These movements had little or no political complexion. What radicalism did exist, was among the skilled artisans. Mobs were loyalist and not Jacobin and far more liable to demonstrate against Popery or Jacobinism than against an iniquitous government.[17]

The leaders of the factory acts movement—Richard Oastler, Michael Sadler, Lord Shaftesbury, Joseph R. Stephens—were all influenced by Methodism. Oastler and Sadler were brought up in it and spent their early lives as local preachers. Lord Shaftesbury admitted he owed his spiritual life to a Methodist servant. Fielden was a Wesleyan Sunday School teacher, and Stephens at one time was a Wesleyan minister.[18] "Only men who made a conscience of what they did could secure the Factory Acts: Methodism gave them that conscience." [19] William Lovett, one of the ablest of the Chartist leaders, was brought up a Wesleyan; Thomas Cooper was a Wesleyan local preacher; Samuel Bamford, "the radical," owed his inspiration to Methodism; the six Dorchester martyrs were Methodists.[20] In fact Wesley earned as much as Shaftesbury the right to be known as Friend of the Poor.

Did Wesley teach patience and resignation to industrial wrong and divert energy from the struggle of the employed? "The whole spirit of its mission," say the Hammonds in an amazing contention, "was unfavorable to the democratic movement and the growth of the Trade Union spirit. . . . Amidst the groans and tears of the poor, a new industrial world arose. . . . Methodism naturally engrossed in her work of the spiritual regeneration of the individual . . . hardly had eyes or heart for what was happening . . .

her mood was ecstatic and transcendental." [21]

But the Hammonds quote from political documents and no one ever claimed that Wesley was other than most conservative politically. Charged with Jacobitism, Catholicism, Lollardry, and other forms of subversive thought and action, he was kept constantly on the defensive in regard to his loyalty. Had he spoken outright rebellion, he would not have been mobbed but murdered. And his doctrine with him shut up in a handful of dust. England was not ripe for rebellion. To think so is to read the facts incorrectly. The English working classes in the centers of new industry were conservative, insular, Philistine when the French Revolution broke out. Manchester, like Birmingham, was predominantly church and king. The working classes as a body in the North and Midlands were profoundly indifferent to ideas or causes. No general revolt against the established order in 1790 was ever contemplated.[22]

The Methodist movement, add the Hammonds, "was a call not for citizens but for saints." [23] But elsewhere the authors remark that it is significant that this religion spread most quickly among the workers living in the deepest gloom. Perhaps the very dangers of their employment prompted them to see this special and miraculous sense of protection. Could it be too that when Wesley said to the brutish poor, "You too can be saved as well as the rich. God loves all," they willingly responded? And the Hammonds admit that Methodism did not ignore man's duty to his neighbor. They go on to say: Methodism was in a very real sense a school, and when men and women go to school, they may learn more lessons than those taught on the blackboard. Moreover, the early Methodists had the credit of introducing the teaching of writing in Sunday Schools. Again it is significant that the speakers at miners' meetings were Methodists. Finally the Hammonds admit Methodism made men better citizens and some even better rebels.[24]

What Bentham says of slavery may be said of Wesley's contribution: "If to be an anti-slavist is to be a saint, saintship for me. I am a saint." [25]

The revolution for 1789 powerfully attracted three classes in England—poets, reformers, and republicans, the last most noisy and least important. For the rest of England it created no more than broad ripples on the surface of their emotions. The Reign of Terror disillusioned the idealists, alienated the reformers. Republicans might grow jubilant at the triumph of liberty in 1793, but to the English that was no reason for overturning their system. Again England already possessed what the French were seeking to gain—constitutional rule, and absolutism an impossibility. France wished to uproot monarchial government; England wished to reform it. The English looked on the French Revolution as spectators.[26]

If there was no danger of an English Revolution, a volume of discontent and agitation did exist. Numerous Corresponding Societies were united only in their dissatisfaction with the existing order. But by far most wanted constitutional reform and sought it by pacific methods. As early as 1780 a committee of Wstminster electors drew up a scheme for constitutional reform which anticipated every demand of the Chartists and demanded that all men regardless of property should have a share in government. In the same year the Society for Promoting Constitutional Information was formed, and members drank the toasts of "Magna Charta," "The Majesty of the People," and "America in Our Arms, Despotism at Our Feet." [27] But beyond the pleasant thrill of drinking to Liberty, Constitutional Reform Societies had little to justify their existence. Even the leading one languished for lack of funds and backing. Other societies existed under the name of "Friends of the People," but they too failed to interest the great mass of people outside.

More radical still was the London Revolutionary Society guided by the energetic Dr. Price. But the much vaunted London Corresponding Society in 1792 had no more than three thousand names on its books. Some members spoke of physical force and even made a pathetically feeble attempt to arm themselves, but their efforts were ludicrous in effect.[28]

More important than the societies were the individuals who fomented agitation. The Dukes of Norfolk and Richmond, and Lords Lansdowne and Stanhope were openly sympathetic with the cause of the people. As fiery an orator as Dr. Price and as brilliant a scholar as Dr. Priestley took part in the agitation. Thomas Paine's books had a remarkable circulation. They were distributed not only in the Metropolis and larger towns but in obscure villages and isolated hamlets. Piggott's revelation of daring, *Warning to Tyrants, The Voice of the People, Political Dictionary*—scurrilous writings—and movement publications like *Politics of the People* and *The Philanthropist* had their vogue among the poorer classes. But if there was a flood of revolutionary and democratic pamphlets, yet the writings of those friendly to the government, Burke and Hannah More, were equally well distributed. The latter's *Village Politics*, elementary and homely, was distributed by the hundreds of thousands. England was not disturbed greatly by the French Revolution. Such unrest as there was expressed itself through pamphlets and societies of reform.[29]

Wesley effected his great work in towns springing up which would have become centers of agitation. But political discontent then could not have been channeled into revolutionary turbulence.

Pitt's stern repressive legislation against the Corresponding Societies was successful because England was in sympathy with his views. The country was greatly excited but never roused to frenzy or kindled to revolutionary pitch. Wesley did not avert a revolution in England, for whether he lived or not, that would never have happened.

The points of agreement with Benthamism were many. Wesley was at one with the Benthamites in his appeal to the principle of utility. The call to find happiness in this life and avoid eternal misery in the next was fundamentally the same appeal which Paley was making in theology and Bentham in legislation. As Dicey remarks, Benthamism and Evangelicism represented the development of the same fundamental principle in widely different spheres—the principle of individualism. The appeal of the Evangelicals to personal religion corresponded with the appeal of Benthamite liberals to individual energy. Indifference to the authority of the church was the counterpart of indifference to the authoritative teaching or guidance of the state. A low estimate of ecclesiastical tradition and historical criticism of the Bible bore a close resemblance to Bentham's contempt for legal antiquarianism. The theology which insisted upon personal responsibility and treated each man as himself bound to work out his own salvation had an obvious affinity to the political philosophy which regarded men almost exclusively as separate individuals, and made it the aim of law to secure for every person freedom to work out his own happiness.[30]

It is not surprising that a similarity of theory produced a similarity of aims to effect humanitarian reforms. Insistence on the value of human personality is a powerful argument against exploitation of the people. Yet that insistence confronts government with a challenge when people are unemployed and starving and when questions vital to general welfare are concerned.

2.

What was the later Methodist attitude towards working

class movements? The Methodist Conference of 1812 declared: "Our societies are uncontaminated with that spirit of insubordination, violence, and cruelty which had caused so much distress and misery. . . . We proclaim loudly and earnestly, 'Fear the Lord and the King, and meddle not with them that are given to change. Avoid them, come not near them.' "[31] Succeeding conferences continued the same attitude. Again the descendants of John Wesley regarded themselves as privileged people. Protection of property, freedom of their worship, formation of their societies, establishment of their organization were evidently reckoned as privileges and not as the rights of ordinary citizens. In reality the privileges were part of the rights of common citizens. The idea of privilege left no doubt about Methodist duty towards the rulers of the land. Methodist loyalty also had a prudential basis. For a religious minority to seek the reform of the nation would have been a dangerous task; with the Bible and common prudence behind them the Wesleys left no doubt about their loyalty. Through their devotion to this ideal they created a working class bourgeoisie from which the established order had nothing to fear.[32]

Methodist implications were evidenced in the Manchester outrages. That so many wild and unlearned people should have been kept quiet and submissive in the days of intense suffering and agitation was one of the marvels of English social life. No ministers enforced the duties of patriotism and loyalty more than the Methodist preachers and no people were more observant of these duties than the Methodist people. Methodists were urged not to become party politicians and to keep aloof from all party spirit.[33]

But to balance the ledger—a half truth is worse than a total lie—the democratic elements in Methodism were always more potent than the autocratic. The Wesleyan Conference was autocratic. By its pronouncements on politics it rightly earned the name of reactionary and conservative. But it did not always speak for the whole of Methodism. Even when official pressure was brought to bear upon outstanding individuals, many private members retained their liberal views. Lay Wesleyanism was more democratic than its conservative ministry and its richer members.[34]

In fact from the ranks came a large number of Trade Union leaders. As early as 1831 they began to make their presence felt. The religion of these men evidently gave them tenacity, patience and tranquillity. Trade Unions learned from Methodism "the method of organizing men and the art of public speaking." [35] "The educated people or the Methodists" were put forward to be the spokesmen on occasions of dispute with their masters and were hardest to deal with, for they showed great skill.[36]

The attitude of Methodism was neutral to Industrial Trade Unions, neither hostile nor sympathetic, unlike its active participation in Miners' Trade Unions. As T. R. Threlfall, Secretary of the Labor Electrical Association, said: "No one can read the detailed history of the great strikes in the mining world without observing how many of the leaders are connected with some branch of the Methodist Church. Take the first great Northumberland strike in 1831 as an instance. Name after name of those who organized it, guided it, and were imprisoned for it, are those of local preachers. Nor was this feature confined to Northumberland and Durham; it is a feature of all the mining struggles in Yorkshire and Wales, in Cornwall and Derbyshire." [37] These men learned other things from their connection with Methodism than training as speakers. They had obtained an education in the art of organization and this they put to good use. The result was that no workmen were so well organized as the miners.[38]

Methodist kinship with reformers became more pronounced in the Chartist period. The pathway from Methodist passion to reforming zeal was not a difficult one. As a religious democracy practically the whole of its technique was taken over by political societies. Its division into districts, circuits and societies, its propaganda methods of itinerant preaching and Sunday open air meetings, its society class and weekly penny subscription were all copied by political reformers.

In many districts Methodist people supported the Chartist principles and opened their chapels for Chartist meetings. A number of Methodist ministers were closely associated with Chartist agitation between 1839-48. According to one historian, the Chartists derived from Methodism "that sense of right, that love of justice, and that feeling of pity and compassion which, with religious conviction, turned some of them into never-to-be-forgotten social reformers." [39]

Weekly class and Sunday open-air meetings were the most important parts of Methodist organization copied by the working class political societies. Among local newspapers, the Home Office records, and government reports, numerous references are to be found of Methodist paternity. When Chartists desired to organize themselves more thoroughly in 1839, they decided at a conference in Rochdale "that the country should be formed into districts, and that the system of classes pursued by the Methodists should be adopted by the Chartists in every district." [40]

Local preachers and class leaders were to be appointed and camp meetings for political purposes were recommended. From 1839-50 Chartist camp meetings in imitation of the Methodists were held in the summer months. Following the custom of Methodists, hymns and prayers often served as an introduction to the speech. To provide suitable singing for such meetings the Wesleyan Hymn Book was sometimes used. Had Methodism been a cross current to political radicalism such plagiarism would have been well nigh impossible. It is nearer the mark to say that the two movements were supplementary to each other. Methodism was a kind of radicalism in the religious world, while radicalism was a sort of Methodism in the political sphere.[41]

CHAPTER FIFTEEN

CONTRIBUTION

Wesley brought about a moral enthusiasm which was healthy in its social tone. The real achievement of his movement was in the sphere of philanthropy—the creation of a mood, a habit, a state of mind which proceeded not from condescension but from a spontaneous impulse of social friendliness and mutual help. Wesley created a permanent aura of goodness. Methodists felt personally responsible to relieve social need.

Religion was shown to have a concern for the temporal as well as the spiritual interests of man. Methodism became through its disciples the friend of the prisoner, the champion of the oppressed, and the liberator of the slave.[1] It is not surprising that John Richard Green in his *History of the English People* says: "The Methodists themselves were the least result of the Methodist revival. . . . A yet nobler result of the religious revival was the steady attempt which has never ceased from that day to this to remedy the guilt, the ignorance, the physical suffering, the social degradation of the profligate and poor." [2]

Wesley undermined the foundation of old standards and made new values of spirit and personality supreme. The root of old values had been the economic helplessness and political impotence of the masses. Wesley's movement depended upon that class of inarticulate and neglected citizens commonly regarded as the dregs of society. Wesley offered them unlimited social opportunity, fostered aggressive initiative and self respect, provided discipline, incentive, guidance. A practical equality was promised. He was the most powerful and active understanding friend the working classes had during the eighteenth century. He proved dominantly and conclusively that the masses were not servile and impotent as believed.

Wesley worked with a multitude of other forces to make a new community, a new set of social values. His contribution, too, lay in its friendliness to contemporary trends. His liberalism was unlabeled and therein lay its power, for unperceived it spread a germinating influence. Priestley, the radical, gauged accurately what but few others saw when he predicted that Wesley's Methodism would accomplish far more than its leaders could foresee even while clothed in its conservative disguise.[3]

In short Wesley stirred the conscience of England and touched its finer feeling that leading men sought to abolish existing evils and to promote social well being. But he himself had no such primary intention. The Wesleyan movement was essentially a religious movement, its purpose reclamation of the souls of men. That it did not go the whole way and provide a long range program for reform is beside the point. It never attempted to do so—that was not the gist of its purpose, though the well being of man was bound up inextricably with it. That it did so much in social and personal advancement is a tribute to its greatness and significance. As Maldwyn Edwards has pointed out, Wesley believed so implicity that a changed man would change his environment that he never considered whether a changed environment might not help to change a man.[4] Anyway under Wesley's leadership the Methodist group achieved a breadth of social sympathy, a depth of religious motive, a sense and habit of wholehearted cooperation in welfare projects, a feeling of individual responsibility that became the expression of the group.

2.

What vital message does Wesley's voice bring us to-day? It is a simple but potent and magical one. We have spoken enough of rights; let us now speak of duties to our fellow men. Man must transform himself to transform his universe. It is not science that is at fault—science has been mangled and misused—but it is the wickedness and greed, the deceit and violence of man that aim to destroy the happiness of humanity. Wesley's message implies a dedication not only of aspiring minds, but of all minds, all hearts, and all impulses to absoute worthiness of purpose. It does not mean that we should be saints—Wesley knew too well the naked fact: dross or flood, if you will, of imperfection that flesh is heir to—but that we should strive honestly, strenuously, generously, in every act of our lives to be better and worthier men and women. Then like veins the healthful flow of purposeful good will course from every segment to the larger heart of government, there to be swiftly sent by arteries of action to nourish and sustain the source. Or like myriad streams mingle in a larger ocean of endeavor until that sea knows no national shore.

The turmoil that besets us, the harmony we wish to gain are premised on a proclamation of the sovereignty of moral law—justice—and the constant practice of doing good to our fellow men everywhere. The religions of the race of men may differ, but moral law—the brotherhood of all men—is an altar at which we can all worship. And not till the meaning of that law beats at the core will the smoke from the smokestacks have disappeared and our eyes see the stars silently shine again.

CHAPTER SIXTEEN

THE BEST OF ALL

"No single figure influenced so many minds," says Augustine Birrell of Wesley, "no single voice touched so many hearts. No other man did such a life's work for England. . . . You cannot cut him out of the national life." [1] His genius for government, remarks Macaulay, was not inferior to that of Richelieu.[2] Leslie Stephen calls him the greatest captain of men of his time; again, Lecky says that Wesley's work meant more for Britain than all the splendid victories by land and sea under Pitt.[3]

> Of these three hundred grant but three
> To make a new Thermopylae.

The prophecy of his sarcastic biographer, Robert Southey, has come true. "There may come a time when the name Wesley will be more generally known in remoter regions of the globe than those of Frederic and Catherine. For the works of such men [as Luther, Loyola, Wesley] survive them and continue to operate when nothing remains of worldly ambition but the memory of its vanity and its guilt." [4]

The epitaph on Shelley can well be applied to Wesley—*Cor Cordium*—Lift up your hearts.

2.

Old and worn, yet Wesley preached. He continued till "the weary springs of life stood still at last." [5] A lion heart rather than leather lungs kept him working at full speed until a few days before his death. Here is the record of a week's work at the age of eighty-four. He started out for Birmingham on Sunday at midnight and traveled nineteen hours. On Tuesday he rose at four a.m., on Wednesday at two, on Thursday at three, and on Friday at four. He was traveling continually. After traveling about 240 miles in eighty hours he went off "with a gentleman to hear a famous musician that plays upon the glasses." [6] He set down his route for the latter part of March, 1790, when he was eighty-seven years old:

Monday, 22, Wednesbury; 23, Dudley and Wolverhampton; 24 and 25, Madeley; 26, Salop; 27, Newcastle-under-Lyme; 28, Love-End and Burslem, and so on.[7]

Charles Wesley had died on March 29, 1788. His brother was away at the time and the letter announcing his death was misdirected and did not reach John Wesley until April 4. A fortnight after Charles's death, John Wesley was preaching at Bolton. He climbed slowly into the pulpit and began to give out the first verse of his brother's greatest hymn, "Wrestling Jacob"—

> "Come O thou traveler unknown
> Whom still I feel but cannot see,"

but when he came to the next two lines—

> "My company before is gone, ,
> And I am left alone with thee,"

his voice faltered, his eyes filled with tears, and he sat down in the pulpit and hid his face in his hands. The singing ceased, the congregation was silent. After a time he recovered his composure and finished the service.

His strength was exhausted in May, 1790. When he attempted to preach, few could hear him. His sight was likewise decayed so that he could neither read the hymn or text. In August he appeared very feeble, yet his voice was strong and his spirit remarkably lively and the powers of his mind as bright and as ardent as ever.

But his work was done. In February, 1791, he proposed to leave London for a long journey to the north. He actually sent his chaise and horses before him to Bristol and took places for himself and his friends in the Bath coach. But almost on the day he purposed to begin afresh his long journey, on March 2, he died, as he wished, without a groan.

There was no disease, but simply a breaking up of nature. When he left his parish, which was the world, he had enlisted and inspired a great host of kindred spirits on both sides of the Atlantic who shared his purposes and who were still able to join in his deathbed cry, "The best of all is, God is with us." [8]

He had made all his preparations temporal and spiritual. His little bequests—they were very littles ones, for he had saved absolutely nothing—were carefully considered. He gave "£6 to be divided among the six poor men named by the assistant who shall carry my body to the grave, for I particularly desire there may be no hearse, no coach, no escutcheon, no pomp, except the tears of those that loved me, and are following me to Abraham's bosom." His wishes were, of course, attended to and the tears not wanting. But when the officiating clergyman said, "Our dear father departed," instead of "brother," the multitude broke out into loud sobs.[9]

To prevent crowds the funeral was held at 5 o'clock, but a great throng followed him to his resting place. Each of the hundreds who gathered at the funeral was handed an envelope of paper in which was a biscuit beautifully stamped with an effigy of John Wesley arrayed in canonicals and adorned with a halo and a crown.[10]

NOTES

I wish to thank Mr. Robert F. Beach, former librarian of Garrett Biblical Institute, for sending me a microfilm of Wesley's edition of *Paradise Lost,* and Professor Charles Kenneth Eves of The City College of New York for making many suggestions as to references during the progress of this work.

Chapter 1

1. John Wesley, *The Letters of John Wesley,* ed. by Rev. John Telford, 8 vols. (London, 1931), VIII, 179.
2. George Berkeley, *Works,* ed. by Alexander C. Fraser, 4 vols. (Oxford, 1901), IV, 505-6; J. Wesley Bready, *England Before and After Wesley* (London, 1938), p. 19.
3. Berkeley, op. cit., IV, 505-6; Bready, op. cit., p. 19. See also Rev. Luke Tyerman, *The Life and Times of John Wesley,* 3 vols. (New York 1872), I, 61; John H. Overton, *The Evangelical Revival in the Eighteenth Century* (London 1886), pp. 1-7.
4. Bishop Joseph Butler, *A Charge Delivered to the Clergy of Durham, Works,* 2 vols., ed. by W. E. Gladstone (Oxford, 1896), II, 397; William C. Sydney, *England and the English in the Eighteenth Century,* 2 vols. (Edinburgh, 1913), II, 325.
5. Joseph Addison, *Works,* 6 vols. (London, 1877), V, 34.
6. Maldwyn Edwards, *John Wesley and the Eighteenth Century* (London, 1933), p. 170.
7. Montesquieu, *Oeuvres Complètes,* ed. par Laboulaye (Paris, 1879), VII, 195; John C. Collins, *Voltaire, Montesquieu, and Rousseau in England* (London, 1908), p. 143.
8. George R. Balleine, *A History of the Evangelical Party in the Church of England* (New York, 1911), p. 127; Bready, p. 60.
9. Bready, *op. cit.,* p. 94.
10. W. M. Thackeray, *The Four Georges, Works* (London, 1886), XIX, 46.
11. Aldred W. Rowden, *The Primates of the Four Georges* (New York, 1916), p. 378.
12. William Wake (1716-37) and Thomas Secker (1758-68).
13. Chas. J. Abbey and John H. Overton, *The English Church in the*

Eighteenth Century, 2 vols. (London, 1878), II, 30-31.
14. Rowden, *op. cit.*, p. 167; Bready, *op. cit.*, p. 45.
15. Rowden, *op. cit.*, p. 378.
16. *Ibid.*, pp. 311-12, 330-31, 336, 345.
17. John L. Campbell, *Lives of the Lord Chancellors*, 10 vols. (London, 1857), VII, 314-15; Abby and Overton, *op. cit.*, II, 23.
18. Rowden, *op. cit.*, p. 75.
19. Richard Watson, *Anecdotes of the Life of Richard Watson, Bishop of Landaff*, 2 vols. (London, 1818), I, 307, 388-89, II, 169, 263-64, 348-49; Sydney, op. cit., II, 335-37; Abbey and Overton, *op. cit.*, II, 12.
20. Thomas Newton, *The Works of the Right Reverend Thomas Newton*, 3 vols. (London, 1782), I, 95-96; Sydney, *op. cit.*, II, 342.
21. Newton, *op. cit.*, I, 96; Sydney, *op. cit.*, II, 342.
22. John Nichols, *Literary Anecdotes of the Eighteenth Century*, 6 vols. (London, 1812), III, 53; G. M. Trevelyan, *English Social History* (London, 1943), p. 359.
23. James Boswell, *Life of Samuel Johnson*, ed. by G. B. Hill (Oxford, 1887), II, 352, V, 80.
24. R. H. Tawney, *Religion and the Rise of Capitalism* (New York, 1926), pp. 188-90.
25. Abbey and Overton, *op. cit.*, II, 23, note.
26. Jonathan Swift, *An Essay on the Fates of Clergymen, Works*, ed. by Sir Walter Scott (London, 1883), VIII, 225-28; Bready, *op. cit.*, p. 56.
27. Bishop Gilbert Burnet, *History of His Own Time*, 6 vols. (Oxford, 1823), VI, 179; Abbey and Overton, *op. cit.*, II, 35.
28. John Wesley, *Sermons on Several Occasions*, 3 vols. (New York, 1831), III, 273.
29. Robert Southey, *Life and Correspondence*, 6 vols. (London, 1849), I, 177. See also pages 170, 172-73.
30. Mark Pattison, *Memoirs* (London, 1885), p. 203; Charles J. Abbey, *The English Church and Its Bishops*, 2 vols. (London, 1887), I, 325.
31. Abbey, *op. cit.*, I, 325.
32. *Ibid.*, I, 325-28.
33. Southey, *Life and Correspondence*, I, 176.
34. Edward Gibbon, *Autobiography, The Works of Edward Gibbon* (New York, 1907), pp. 57, 63-67, 69.
35. *Ibid.*, p. 233; Trevelyan, *op. cit.*, p. 359.
36. Edwards, *op. cit.*, pp. 175-77.
37. William Massey, *A History of England during the Reign of George the Third* (London, 1865), II, 31-32; Sydney, *op. cit.*, II, 331, 343-45; Bready, *op. cit.*, p. 55.
38. Oliver Goldsmith, *The Deserted Village, The Miscellaneous Works of Oliver Goldsmith* (London, 1919), p. 584; Tyerman, *op. cit.*, I, 17.

39. Henry Fielding, *Joseph Andrews*, 2 vols. (Oxford, 1926), Book I, Chapter 3.
40. Trevelyan, *op. cit.*, p. 359; Sydney, *op. cit.*, II, 331; Abbey and Overton, *op. cit.*, II, 13-14, 16; Massey, *op. cit.*, II, 32.
41. W. Tooke, *Life of Churchill* in *The Poetical Works of Charles Churchill* (London 1844), I, xxv, note; Abbey, *op. cit.*, I, 319.
42. Thomas Stackhouse, *The Miseries and Great Hardships of the Inferior Clergy in and about London* (London, 1722), pp. 120-21 and *passim;* Abbey and Overton, II, 17.
43. Parson James Woodforde, *The Diary of a Country Parson* (London, 1824), I, 187, 193.
44. M. Dorothy Georye, *England in Johnson's Day* (London, 1928), pp. 24-32; H. de B. Gibbins, *English Social Reformers* (London, 1892), pp. 71-72.
45. T. B. Macaulay, *The History of England*, 3 vols. (London, 1915), Chapter III, I, 255-56.
46. J. L. Hammond and Barbara Hammond, *The Village Labourer* (London, 1911), pp. 221-22.
47. James Thomson, *The Works of James Thomson* (Edinburgh, 1774), I, ii; Abbey, *op. cit.*, I, 314; Sydney, *op. cit.*, II, 343.
48. Tyerman, *op. cit.*, I, 64.
49. Arthur Young, *An Enquiry into the State of the Public Mind among the Lower Classes* (Dublin, 1798), p. 27; Hammonds, *The Village Labourer*, p. 221.
50. Sydney, *op. cit.*, II, 345.
51. Percy Fitzgerald, *The Life of Laurence Sterne*, 2 vols. (London, 1864), II, 26.
52. *Ibid.*, II, 26-27.
53. Wilbur Cross, Introduction to *Tristram Shandy* in *The Complete Works of Laurence Sterne* (New York and London, 1904), I, xxxvii.
54. Fitzgerald, *op. cit.*, II, 29.
55. Tobias Smollett, *Roderick Random, The Works of Tobias Smollett* (London, 1925), Vol. I, chap. ix.
56. Henry Fielding, *The History of Tom Jones*, 4 vols. (London, 1926), Book IV, chap. 10.
57. Goldsmith, *The Citizen of the World*, no. lviii, *op. cit.*, pp. 180-82.
58. *The Connoisseur* (London, 1757), Vol. IV, no. cv, Jan. 29, 1756.
59. Arthur Young, *Travels in France during the Years 1787, 1788, 1789* (London, 1924), pp. 327-28; Sydney, *op. cit.*, II, 347.
60. John Forster, *The Life and Times of Oliver Goldsmith*, 2 vols. (London, 1871), I, 256 n.; Sydney, *op. cit.*, II, 347-48.
61. Wilbur Cross, *op. cit.*, Intro., p. xxxviii.
62. Dr. Alexander Carlyle, *Autobiography* (Edinburgh and London, 1861), p. 441.
63. Vicesimus Knox, *Essays, Moral and Literary*, 2 vols. (London, 1827) , I, 19; Sydney, *op. cit.*, II, 349.
64. William Cowper, *The Task, The Poetical Works of William Cow-*

per (London, 1926), Bk II, ll. 378-83, 409-13.
65. George Crabbe, *The Village*, *Works*, 5 vols. (London, 1823), I, 16.
66. Sydney, *op. cit.*, II, 351.
67. Boswell, *op. cit.*, III, 304.
68. Gibbins, *op. cit.*, p. 70.
69. Thackeray, *The Four Georges*, *op. cit.*, XIX, 47.
70. Gibbins, *op. cit.*, pp. 70-71; John, Lord Hervey, *Memoirs of the Reign of George the Second*, 2 vols. (London, 1848), I, 425-26, 500-2 and *passim*.
71. Gibbins, *op. cit.*, p. 72; Hervey, *op. cit.*, II, 35-36, 174-90.
72. John Wesley, "A Further Appeal to Men of Reason and Religion," Part III, *The Works of John Wesley*, 7 vols. (New York, 1831), V, 142.
73. *The Spectator*, ed. by G. Aitken (London, 1898), Nos. 20, 50, 53, 242, 460, 503. See also Swift, "Sleeping in Church," *op. cit.*, VIII, 17-27.
74. *The Spectator*, nos. 158, 259.
75. *Ibid.*, no. 380.
76. *Ibid.*, no. 630; Abbey and Overton, II, 458-59.
77. Swift, "Baucis and Philemon," *op. cit.*, XIV, 83; "On Sleeping in Church," VIII, 19-20, 23-24.
78. *Joseph Andrews*, Book IV, Chap. 1. See Hogarth's Sleeping Congregation, 1736.
79. Balleine, *op. cit.*, p. 129.
80. Bready, *op. cit.*, pp. 67-73; White Kennett, *A Compassionate Inquiry into the Causes of the Civil War*, 1703/4 (London, 1704), pp. 1, 24, 27; White Kennett, *Sermon Preached before the House of Commons*, January 30, 1705/6 (London, 1706), p. 26; Bishop of St. David, *Sermon before the House of Lords*, January 30, 1727/8 (London, 1728). There is a host of Memorial Sermons preached on the anniversary of King Charles's death.
81. Bready, *op. cit.*, pp. 70-71.
82. W. E. H. Lecky, *A History of England in the Eighteenth Century* (London, 1891), I, 65.
83. Bishop William Warburton, Sermon 19, January 30, 1760, in *Works* (London, 1811), X, 18; Bready, *op. cit.*, pp. 71-72, 83.
84. Swift, Sermon 6, *op. cit.*, p. 72.
85. Bready, *op. cit.*, p. 72.
86. Leslie Stephen, *History of English Thought in the Eighteenth Century*, 2 vols. (London, 1927), I, 227.
87. Thomas Newton, *op. cit.*, *passim;* Abbey and Overton, *op. cit.*, II, 11; Bready, *op. cit.*, p. 73.
88. Lecky, *op. cit.*, I, 64-67.
89. See Gardiner, Ranke, Hallam, Macaulay, Carlyle. G. M. Trevelyan says that Charles I "was by temperament incapable of coming to an honest agreement and abiding by it." *History of England* (London, 1937), p. 419.
90. John Richard Green, *A Short History of the English People*

(London, 1893), III, 1285, 1278; Bready, *op. cit.*, p. 76.

91. [Richard Allestree], *The Whole Duty of Man* (London, 1842), pp. 223-25; Bready, *op. cit.*, pp. 87-88.
92. Balleine, *op. cit.*, pp. 52-53.
93. Abbey and Overton, *op. cit.*, II, 37-38; J. C. Ryle, *The Priest, the Puritan, and the Preacher* (New York, 1855), pp. 169-75.
94. Rev. Jos. Trapp, *The Nature, Folly, Sin, and Danger of Being Righteous Over-much* (London, 1758), pp. 3, 26-27, 38-39, 56-57, 62-63; Lecky, *op. cit.*, I, 467; Abbey and Overton, *op. cit.*, II, 38-39.
95. Albert D. Belden, *George Whitefield* (Nashville, Tenn., 1930), pp. 55-56; Bready, *op. cit.*, p. 91.
96. Abraham Lipsky, *John Wesley* (New York, 1928), p. 2.
97. Abbey and Overton, *op. cit.*, II, 39; Boswell, *op. cit.*, III, 248.
98. John Wesley, *Journal*, Everyman Edition, 4 vols. (London and New York, 1930), II, 138.
99. Bready, *op. cit.*, pp. 95-96.

Chapter 2

1. *Gentleman's Magazine* (March, 1791), LXI, 283; C. E. Vulliamy, *John Wesley* (London, 1931).
2. *Gentleman's Magazine* (September, 1735), V, 557-58; Alexander Andrews, *The Eighteenth Century* (London, 1856), pp. 276-77.
3. See articles by author: "Pilgrim's Progress: John Howard and and His Famous Book," and "Crime and Punishment in England of the Eighteenth Century," *The American Journal of Economics and Sociology* (Jan., 1945 and Jan., 1946).
4. Boswell, *op. cit.*, V, 59-60.
5. George I was always reckoned vile, still viler George II, says Landor. Hervey, *op. cit.*, *passim;* Justin McCarthy, *A History of the Four Georges* (New York, 1885), I, 273, II, 48-49, 304-5.
6. J. H. Whiteley, *Wesley's England* (London, 1938), p. 64; Arthur Young, *A Six Weeks Tour* (London, 1769), pp. 305-6.
7. Wesley, *Works*, V, 520.
8. *Ibid.*, II, 358-59.
9. *Ibid.*, V, 513, 514, 515-17, 520, 511-13. It is Swift rather than St. Augustine on whom Wesley leans for quotations in *The Doctrine of Original Sin.* His unflattering view of man is the view of classical or Christian tradition. If all were in perfect health, why need Christianity? "Take away the Scriptural doctrine of redemption—and in what is Christianity better than Heathenism?" Wesley, *Works*, V, 669; see also T. O. Wedel, "On the Philosophical Background of *Gulliver's Travels*," *Studies in Philology* (Chapel Hill, 1926), XXIII, 435, 450.
10. Wesley, *Works*, V, 520, 521.

Chapter 3

1. D. D. Thompson, *John Wesley as a Social Reformer* (New York, 1898), pp. 24-25; Robert F. Wearmouth, *Methodism and the Common People of the Eighteenth Century* (London, 1945), pp. 187-90; Wellman J. Warner, *The Wesleyan Movement in the Industrial Revolution* (London, 1930), pp. 266-67.
2. Robert F. Wearmouth, *Methodism and the Working Class Movements of England, 1800-1850* (London, 1937), pp. 21-25, 271-73.
3. Cf. Humphrey Clinker, the coachman and groom, in Smollett's novel.
4. Warner, *op. cit.*, pp. 258-59; 262-63, 264-65; Wearmouth, II, 203.
5. Wearmouth, II, 22-23, I, 220-30; Richard M. Cameron, *The Rise of Methodism* (New York, 1954), pp. 300-1.
6. Wearmouth, I, 222, 265; Kathleen W. MacArthur, *The Economic Ethics of John Wesley* (New York, 1936), pp. 131-32; Wearmouth, II, 230, 263-64.
7. Lipsky, *op. cit.*, pp. 285-86; see also Tyerman, *op. cit.*, III, 616.
8. *Proceedings of the Wesley Historical Society* (Burnley, 1926), XV, 139-40.
9. Sidney Webb, *The Story of the Durham Miners (1662-1921)* (London, 1921), pp. 23-24.
10. J. D. Chambers, *Nottinghamshire in the Eighteenth Century* (London, 1932), pp. 328-30; Wearmouth, *op. cit.*, II, 13; Ernest R. Taylor, *Methodism and Politics, 1791-1851* (Cambridge, 1935), pp. 59, 61-63; Warner, *op. cit.*, pp. 165-66.
11. Wearmouth, *op. cit*, II, 262.
12. Arnold Toynbee, *Lectures on the Industrial Revolution of the Eighteenth Century in England* (London, 1913), pp. 11-12, 7-10, 68.

    In 1685 Birmingham had a population of 4,000, in Macaulay's day, 200,000; Liverpool in 1685 a population of 4,000, in the 1840's a population of 300,000. Macaulay, *op. cit.*, Chap. 3, I, 259-67.

    In 1700 the five most populous counties were believed to have been Middlesex, Somerset, Gloucester, Wiltshire, and Northampton. In 1800 they were Middlesex, Lancashire, the West Riding of Yorkshire, Staffordshire, and Warwickshire. J. L. and Barbara Hammond, *The Town Labourer* (London, 1917), pp. 4-5.

    Sydney G. Dimond, *The Psychology of the Methodist Revival* (Oxford, 1926), pp. 36-37.
13. John R. Green, *op. cit.*, IV 1610; Dimond, *op. cit.*, pp. 39-40.
14. "Appendix to Report on Act for Building Churches," *Parliamentary Papers* (1821), X, 16-23.
15. Wesley, *Letters*, II, 271-72.
16. Warner, *op. cit.*, pp. 10-11, 17-20; Edmund Burke, *Reflections on the Revolution in France, The Writings and Speeches of Edmund Burke*, 12 vols. (Boston, 1901), III, 557-58. See also V, 134-35, 467; Samuel Johnson, "London: a Poem," in Cecil A. Moore,

English Poetry of the Eighteenth Century (New York, 1947), p. 563.

17. Warner, *op. cit.*, p. 11.
18. James E. Thorold Rogers, *Six Centuries of Work and Wages*, 2 vols. (London, 1884), p. 398.
19. Taylor, *op. cit.*, pp. 61-63, *Gentleman's Magazine* (1800), II, 1077.
20. Aaron C. H. Seymour, *The Life and Times of Selina, Countess of Huntingdon* (1844), I, 27; Lecky, *op. cit.*, II, 617.
21. Trevelyan, *History of England*, p. 531; Taylor, *op. cit.*, pp. 55-59.
22. Hugh Price Hughes, *The Heart of Wesley's Journals* (London and Edinburgh, n. d.), Intro., p. x.
23. Wearmouth, *op. cit.*, II, 224-25; "First Report of Commissioners on the Employment of Children in Mines," *Parliamentary Papers* (1842), XV, 9-35, 37-39, 46-65, 255-59. If such shocking conditions existed in 1842, we can well imagine what had existed years before.
24. Mac Arthur, *op. cit.*, p. 133; Wearmouth, *op. cit.*, II, 226-27.
25. Wesley, *Journal*, II, 12.
26. *Ibid.*, III, 270, 419, 514; IV, 86, 111, 137, 194, 220, 240, 409, 410.
27. Bready, *op. cit.*, p. 136.
    Sir Walter Besant pronounced the London Mob "brutal beyond all power of words to describe or imagination to understand, so bestial that one is induced to think there has never been in any town or in any age a population which could compare with them." Besant, *London in the Eighteenth Century* (London, 1902), preface, p. viii.
28. Wesley, *Letters*, V, 10.

Chapter 4

1. Wesley, *Journal*, II, 246.
2. *Ibid.*, III, 311, 313; Warner, *op. cit.*, p. 163.
3. Warner, *op. cit.*, pp. 162-63.
4. Wesley, *Letters*, V, 317.
5. Mac Arthur, *op. cit.*, pp. 78-79, 82; Warner, *op. cit.*, pp. 168-69.
6. Wesley, *Letters*, II, 94.
7. Sidney Webb, *op. cit.*, p. 20.
8. Edward Wellbourne, *The Miners' Unions of Northumberland and Durham* (Cambridge, 1923), pp. 56-59.
9. Wesley, *Letters*, II, 290.
10. Warner, *op. cit.*, pp. 174-75; Mac Arthur, *op. cit.*, pp. 124-27, 129, 131.
11. Wesley, *Works*, V, 336.
12. Wesley, *Letters*, V, 121.
13. Quoted in Warner, *op. cit.*, p. 175.
14. *Ibid.*, p. 175.
15. *Ibid.*, pp. 176-77.
16. *Ibid.*, pp. 177-78.

17. *Ibid.*, pp. 178-79
18. Tyerman, *op. cit.*, III, 499.
19. Wesley, *Journal*, II, 290.
20. Warner, *op. cit.*, pp. 185-86.
21. Wesley, *Works*, I, 229.
22. Warner, *op. cit.*, pp. 192-93.
23. *Wesleyan Bicentennial* (Wesleyan University, Middletown, Conn., 1904), p. 168.
24. Wesley, *Letters*, IV, 260; Tyerman, *op. cit.*, III, 3.
25. Bready, *op. cit.*, p. 263.
26. Wesley, *Journal*, IV, 199.
27. *Ibid.*, II, 382.
28. Wesley, *Journal*, I, 198-99.
29. E. D. Bebb, *Nonconformity and Social and Economic Life* (London, 1935), p. 53.
30. John and Charles Wesley, *The Poetical Works of John and Charles Wesley* (London, 1870), VIII, 479.
31. Wesley, *Letters*, III, 229, VII 343-44.
32. Wesley, *Works*, II, 182-83.
33. *Ibid.*, II, 193-94.
34. Wesley, *Letters*, V, 181.
35. Wesley, *Works*, II, 397.

Chapter 5

1. Wesley, *Letters*, VI, 61-62. "Rashness," says R. H. Tawney, "is a more agreeable failing than cowardice, and when to speak is unpopular, it is less pardonable to be silent than to say too much. Posterity has, perhaps, as much to learn from the whirlwind eloquence with which Latimer scourged injustice and oppression as from the sober respectability of the judicious Paley—who himself, since there are depths below depths, was regarded as a dangerous revolutionary by George III." Tawney, *op. cit.*, p. 287.
2. Tyerman, *op. cit.*, I, 239.
3. Wesley, *Letters*, V, 55.
4. *Ibid.*, VIII, 139-43.
5. Arnold Lunn, *John Wesley* (New York, 1929), pp. 164-65; Robert Southey, *The Life of Wesley*, 2 vols. (New York, 1925), II, 204-7. But Toplady never attained the heights of invective which distinguished the great Genevese. There was nothing in Toplady's *Gospel Magazine* quite so trenchant as this: "The villainous cur though refuted by obvious argument did but wipe his nozzle and say, 'There is no harm done here. Let us go on!' " Lunn, *op. cit.*, p. 164.
6. Southey, *op. cit.*, I, 205-6. The wise and gentle Tillotson has observed that we shall have two wonders in heaven: the one, how many came to be absent whom we expected to find there; the other, how many are there whom we had no hope of meeting.
7. Wesley, *Works*, V, 79-80. "How delicate a thing it is to reprove!

To do it well requires more than human wisdom." *Journal,* III, 354.

8. Wesley, *Letters,* VII, 247.
9. Wesley, *Journal,* I, 410.
10. Smollett, *Humphrey Clinker, op. cit.,* I, 107, 197.
11. Horace Walpole, *The Letters of Horace Walpole,* ed. by Mrs. Paget Toynbee (Oxford, 1903), II, 367.
12. Seymour, *op. cit.,* I, 108; Walpole, op. cit., II, 336.
13. Tyerman, *op. cit.,* II, 190-91.
14. Wesley, *Letters,* VI, 61-62. Compare Swift's statement in Book II of *Gulliver's Travels:* "I cannot but conclude the bulk of your natives to be the most pernicious race of little odious vermin that nature ever suffered to crawl upon the surface of the earth." Swift, *op. cit.,* II, 162.
15. James J. Ellis, *John Wesley* (New York, 1891), p. 226; Lunn, *op. cit.,* pp. 198-238.
16. Wesley, *Journal,* I, 374-75; Lipsky, *op. cit.,* pp. 143-44.
17. Wesley, *Journal,* I, 378.
18. Southey, I, 330, 324-31.
19. Wesley, *Journal,* III, 415; John Telford, *The Life of John Wesley* (London, 1886), pp. 189-90.
20. Wesley, *Journal,* II, 354.
21. *Ibid.,* I, 318-19; G. Holden Pike, *Wesley and His Preachers* (London, 1903), p. 132.
22. Wesley, *Journal,* I, 364.
23. *Ibid.,* I, 544-45.
24. *Ibid.,* I, 558.
25. *Ibid.,* II, 128.
26. *Ibid.,* I, 499.
27. *Ibid.,* II, 249; Tyerman, *op. cit.,* II, 163.
28. Wesley, *Journal,* II, 223.
29. *Ibid.,* I, 416.
30. *Ibid.,* II, 77-78, 128, III, 268, 350, IV, 136; Bonamy Dobrée, *John Wesley* (New York, 1933) p. 103.
31. Wesley *Journal,* I, 422.
32. *Ibid.,* II, 74-75.
33. *Ibid.,* I, 423.
34. *Ibid.,* III, 237.
35. *Ibid.,* III, 287.
36. *Ibid.,* III, 139.
37. Lunn, p. 205.
38. Lunn, pp. 211-14.
39. *Ibid.,* pp. 212-13. Once Wesley administered the Lord's Supper to nearly two hundred communicants. As a considerable part were Dissenters, Wesley desired everyone to use what posture he judged best. "Had I required them to kneel, probably half would have sat; now all but one kneeled down." *Journal,* II, 438.
40. *Ibid.,* I 508-10; Tyerman, *op. cit.,* I, 471.
41. Telford, *op. cit.,* p. 190; *Journal,* II, 224.

42. Wesley, *Journal*, I, 198; Tyerman, *op. cit.*, I, 238.
43. Wesley, *Journal*, I, 439-42; Lipsky, *op. cit.*, pp. 163-66; Tyerman, *op. cit.*, I, 410-12.
44. Wesley, *Journal*, I, 399.
45. Tyerman, *op. cit.*, II, 274; Wesley, *Journal*, II, 374.
46. Wesley, *Journal*, II, 465-66, 451; Tyerman, *op. cit.*, II, 274-75.
47. Wesley, *Journal*, II, 379-80; Tyerman, op. cit., II, 276.
48. Tyerman, *op. cit.*, III, 27.
49. *Ibid.*, III, 28.
50. Wesley, *Letters*, VIII, 142.
51. Wesley, *Journal*, II, 293.
52. *Ibid.*, II, 18.
53. *Ibid.*, II, 18-19.
54. *Ibid.*, II, 24.
55. *Ibid.*, II, 226. IV, 132. He had also high regard for the Irish: "Indeed so civil a people as the Irish in general, I never saw either in Europe or America." *Journal*, II, 53.
56. Wesley, *Journal*, IV, 240; Tyerman, *op. cit.*, III, 384.
57. Wesley, *Journal*, II, 353; Tyerman, *op. cit.*, II, 259.
58. Wesley, *Journal*, II, 460; Lunn, *op. cit.*, p. 169; Cameron, pp. 226-27.
59. Wesley, *Letters*, V, 23.
60. Wesley, *Works*, V, 80-81.

Chapter 6

1. *Wesleyan Bicentennial*, p. 169.
2. Bonamy Dobrée, *op. cit.*, pp. 98-99.
3. Leslie Stephen, *op. cit.*, II 423.
4. Wesley, *Journal*, II, 5.
5. *Ibid.*, II, 426.
6. *Ibid.*, II, 94, 487; III, 60.
7. *Ibid.*, IV, 1.
8. *Ibid.*, II, 274-75, 353, IV, 18.
9. Wesley, *Letters*, VIII, 97.
10. Wesley, *Journal*, I, 488-89.
11. *Ibid.*, II, 5.
12. *Ibid.*, IV, 50-51.
13. *Ibid.*, IV, 329.
14. Tyerman, *op. cit.*, III, 471-72; Wesley, *Journal*, IV, 336.
15. Wesley, *Journal*, III, 401.
16. *Ibid.*, II, 72.
17. *Ibid.*, III, 401.
18. Herbert, *op. cit.*, p. 3; Lunn, p. 223.
19. Tyerman, *op. cit.*, I, 418.
20. Wesley, *Letters*, III, 138-39.
21. Taylor, *op. cit.*, pp. 22-24; Bready, *op. cit.*, pp. 248-50; Tyerman, *op. cit.*, II, 513-14.
    Stanley Baldwin, commenting as Prime Minister on Wesley's

labors, said: "I am supposed to be a busy man, but by the side of Wesley, I join the ranks of the unemployed." Stanley Baldwin, *This Torch of Freedom* (London, 1936), p. 95.

22. Tyerman, *op. cit.*, III, 658.
23. *Ibid.*, III, 658.
24. Rev. Frank G. Porter, "Wesley, a Forerunner of Social Reform" *The Methodist Review* (New York, 1920), CIII, 5th series, XXXVI, 916.
25. Tyerman, *op. cit.*, III, 459-60.
26. *Ibid.*, III, 659-60.
27. Wesley, *Letters*, III, 97, I, 325-26.
28. Tyerman, *op. cit.*, I, 393-94; Dimond, *op. cit.*, p. 116.
29. Wesley, *Letters*, VII, 84; Tyerman, *op. cit.*, III, 410.
30. Wesley, *Journal*, IV, 80, 346; *Letters*, VIII, 320.
31. Wesley, *Letters*, VII, 266.
32. *Ibid.*, I, xxv-xxvi.
33. Wesley, *Journal*, II, 188-89.
34. Boswell, *op. cit.*, III, 230.
35. Wesley, *Letters*, VI, 292-93.
36. Wesley, *Journal*, IV, 80.
37. Wesley, *Letters*, VII, 74-76; *Works;* II, 295-99.
38. Quoted in Whiteley, *op. cit.*, p. 119.
39. *Ibid.*, p. 119.
40. Wesley, *Works*, VI, 577-79.
41. James J. Ellis, *John Wesley* (New York, 1891), pp. 96-97.
42. Lunn, *op. cit.*, pp. 184-86; Wesley, *Journal*, II, 169.
43. Wesley, *Letters*, VI, 81.
44. Tyerman, *op. cit.*, III, 318.
45. Wesley, *Letters*, V, 151.
46. *Ibid.*, VI, 292-93.
47. *Ibid.*, VII, 222.
48. *Ibid.*, VIII, 91.
49. Tyerman, *op. cit.*, III, 658, 226.
50. Wesley, *Letters*, I, 218-19.
51. Tyerman, *op. cit.*, III, 341-42.
52. Southey, *Wesley*, II, 344-49.
53. Tyerman, *op. cit.*, III, 341.
54. Wesley, *Letters*, I, 240.
55. *Ibid.*, I, 16.
56. *The Cambridge Modern History* (New York, 1934), VI, 82, 84.
57. Wesley, *Letters*, VIII, 104.
58. Lunn, *op. cit.*, p. 191.
59. Wesley, *Letters*, II, 34.
60. *Minutes of the Methodist Conferences* (London, 1812), pp. 60-61; Taylor, *op. cit.*, pp. 41, 45-47; Tyerman, *op. cit.*, II, 578-79. Mabel R. Brailsford, *A Tale of Two Brothers* (New York, 1954), pp. 244-45; 274, and *passim.*
61. Tyerman, *op. cit.*, II, 271; Brailsford, p. 273 and *passim.*

62. Wesley, *Letters,* VIII, 209; Abbey and Overton, *op. cit.,* II, 91-92.
63. Once Wesley was on the floor where his wife (Mrs. Vazeille) had been trailing him by the hair of his head.
64. Bready, *op. cit.,* pp. 256, 258, 277-78; Lipsky, *op. cit.,* p. 143; Lunn, *op. cit.,* pp. 335-36.
65. Porter, *op. cit.,* p. 912.
66. Wesley, *Journal,* IV, 483-84.
67. John S. Simon, *John Wesley, The Last Phase* (London, 1934), p. 318.

Chapter 7

1. Dobrée, *op. cit.,* pp. 76-77; T. B. Shepherd, *Methodism and the Literature of the Eighteenth Century* (London, 1940), p. 22; Telford, *op. cit.,* p. 317.
2. Overton, *Evangelical Revival,* pp. 99-100; Lipsky, *op. cit.,* pp. 144-45.
3. Wesley, *Works,* I, xviii pref.; Lipsky, *op. cit.,* pp. 145-46; Wesley, *Sermons on Several Occasions,* I, 3.
4. Wesley, *Works,* II, pref., iii—iv.
5. Leslie Stephen, *op. cit.,* III, 423.
6. Shepherd, *op. cit.,* pp. 78-79.
7. *Ibid.,* p. 79; Wesley, *Works,* Vols. I and II, *passim.*
8. Lipsky, *op. cit.,* p. 145.
9. *Ibid.,* p. 292.
10. Wesley, *Letters,* VI, 166-67.
11. Wesley, *Journal,* III, 69.
12. Lipsky, *op. cit.,* pp. 288-89.
13. Boswell, *op. cit.,* I, 458-59.
14. George Eliot, *Adam Bede* (Boston, 1887), Book I, Chap. 2, p. 23.
15. Lecky, *op. cit.,* II, 521.
16. Wesley, *Journal,* II, 452-56.
17. Wesley, *Journal,* I, 186.
18. *Ibid.,* I, 189.
19. Lipsky, *op. cit.,* pp. 148-49.
20. Wesley, *Journal,* II, 394.
21. *Ibid.,* II, 465.
22. *Ibid.,* III, 208.
23. *Ibid.,* I, 188.
24. *Ibid.,* I, 188-89.
25. *Ibid.,* I, 189.
26. Dimond, *op. cit.,* p. 117; James B. Pratt, *The Religious Consciousness* (New York, 1927), pp. 189-91.
27. Wesley, *Letters,* VIII, 266.
28. Herbert's *The Temple.* Read *body* for *person.* "The Church Porch," Stanza LXII in *The English Works of George Herbert* (Boston and New York, 1915), II, 57.
29. Wesley, *Letters,* V, 132-34.
30. Wesley, *Works,* V, 219.

31. Wesley, *Letters*, VII, 305.
32. Wesley, *Works*, V, 224-25.
33. Wesley, *Letters*, IV, 315, 240, VII, 90, 313; *Works*, V, 224-26.
34. Wesley, *Letters*, VI, 167.
35. Wesley, *Works*, VII, 487-93.
36. Wesley, *Letters*, IV, 231-32.
37. *Ibid.*, VI, 8.
38. Tyerman, *op. cit.*, II, 583.
39. Shepherd, *op. cit.*, p. 147.
40. Wesley, *Letters*, VII, 138, 139, 143.
41. Wesley, *Works*, V, 161, 226.
42. Wesley, *Letters*, VI, 3.
43. *Ibid.*, VII, 353-54.
44. *Ibid.*, VI, 41.
45. *Ibid.*, VI, 334.
46. *Ibid.*, VII, 243.
47. *Ibid.*, VII, 137.
48. *Ibid.*, VII, 281.
49. *Ibid.*, VIII, 49.
50. *Ibid.*, VIII, 86.
51. Bready, *op. cit.*, p. 218
52. Lunn, *op. cit.*, p. 186.
53. Warner, *op. cit*, pp. 248-61; Shepherd, *op. cit.*, pp. 144-47.
54. Shepherd, *op. cit.*, p. 147; Wesley, Letters, IV, 3.
55. Lipsky, *op. cit.*, pp. 193-94.
56. *Ibid.*, p. 199. Bebb, *op. cit.*, pp. 54-55; Wesley, *Letters*, VII, 245, Brailsford, pp. 235-37; Cameron, pp. 226-27.
57. Wesley, *Works*, V, 30.
58. Wesley, *Letters*, II, 146-49.
59. *Ibid.*, VI, 271-72.

Chapter 8

1. Wesley, *Works*, I, 211.
2. Warner, *op. cit.*, p. 211-12.
3. Bready, *op. cit.*, p. 202.
4. Wesley, *Works*, V, 190, 244-45.
5. Thompson, *op. cit.*, p. 27.
6. Wesley, *Works*, V, 5, 335.
7. *Ibid.*, I, pref., xx.
8. *Ibid.*, I, 61, 123.
9. *Ibid.*, I, 150.
10. *Ibid.*, V, 190-92; Warner, *op. cit.*, p. 212.
11. Wesley, *Works*, V, 191.
12. *Ibid.*, V, 244-45; Warner, op. cit., p. 213.
13. Wesley, *Journal*, II, 21; *Works*, II, 332; Warner, *op. cit.*, p. 213; Tyerman, *op. cit.*, III, 616; Thomas W. Herbert, *John Wesley as Editor and Author* (Princeton, 1940), p. 18.

14. Warner, *op. cit.*, p. 213.
15. *Ibid.*, pp. 213-14.
16. Wearmouth, *op. cit.*, I, 230.
17. Warner, *op. cit.*, p. 71.
18. Wesley, *Works*, V, 172-74.
19. Faulkner, *op. cit.*, pp. 54-55.
20. Wesley, *Works*, II, 57.
21. *Ibid.*, I, 488-89.
22. *Ibid.*, I, 483, 489.
23. Lunn, *op. cit.*, p. 157.
24. Wesley, *Works*, V, 757.
25. *Ibid.*, V, 32.
26. *Ibid.*, V, 146.
27. Shepherd, *op. cit.*, p. 28; Oliver Elton, *A Survey of English Literature, 1730-1780* (London, 1928), II, 220.
28. Wesley, *Letters*, II, 94.
29. "And yet the power of thy Almighty Hand
    Can build another world from every sand."
    "The Chapter of Ecclesiasticus," *The Poems of William Broome*, in Alexander Chalmers, *The Works of the English Poets* (London, 1810), XII, 31.
30. Wesley, *Letters*, IV, 286-87.
31. *Ibid.*, II, 378.
32. Wesley, *Works*, I, 23; *Letters*, II, 376-77.
33. Wesley, *Letters*, II, 388.
34. Wesley, *Works*, II, 347-49; *Letters*, II, 376-77.
35. Wesley, *Works*, V, 753.
36. *Ibid.*, V, 240-41, 245.

Chapter 9

1. Wesley, *Works*, I, 441.
2. Warner, *op. cit.*, pp. 138-40.
3. *Ibid.*, p. 141.
4. Wesley, *Letters*, IV, 279.
5. Warner, *op. cit.*, pp. 140-42.
6. Wesley, *Letters*, VIII, 26.
7. *Ibid.*, IV, 272.
8. Wesley, *Works*, I, 443. These injunctions carry the flavor of an outmoded economy.
9. Warner, *op. cit.*, p. 146.
10. *Ibid.*, pp. 147-49.
11. Wesley, *Works*, II, 302.
    "Wesleyanism through the teaching of its founder takes higher ground as an economic doctrine than any of the earlier Protestant sects." J. A. Hobson, *God and Mammon* (London, 1931), p. 33.
12. Wesley, *Journal*, IV, 483.
13. Warner, *op. cit.*, p. 151.

14. Bready, *op. cit.*, p. 234; G. G. Coulton, *A Medieval Garner* (London, 1910), pp. 71, 68-73; *Ten Medieval Studies* (Cambridge, 1930), pp. 56, 63.
15. Wesley, *Works*, II, 255; Bready, *op. cit.*, pp. 234-38.
16. Wesley, *Works*, II, 251-58, 401, 419, 251-58.
17. *Ibid.*, II, 252, 397-98; Warner, *op. cit.*, p. 153.
18. Wesley, *Works*, II, 397-98, 400; Warner, *op. cit.*, p. 153.
19. Wesley, *Works*, II, 399; Warner, *op. cit.*, pp. 153-54.
20. Wesley, *Works*, II, 397.
21. Wesley, *Works*, I, 449; Warner, *op. cit.*, pp. 154-55.
22. Wesley, *Works*, I, 448-57; Warner, *op. cit.*, p. 155.
23. Wesley, *Works*, I, 441-43.
24. *Ibid.*, I, 445-47; Warner, *op. cit.*, p. 157.
25. Wearmouth, *op. cit.*, II, 198.
26. Wesley, *Works*, I, 445; Tyerman, *op.cit.*, III, 639; Wearmouth, *op. cit.*, I, 240.
27. Wesley, *Works*, I, 445-46; Warner, *op. cit.*, pp. 157-58.
28. Wesley, *Works*, I, 444-48, 454-56; Thompson, *op. cit.*, pp. 81-86, 87.
29. Thompson *op. cit.*, pp. 90-91.
30. Wesley, *Works*, VII, 317.
31. *Ibid.*, VII, 317.
32. *Ibid.*, VII, 317; Lipsky, *op. cit.*, pp. 190-91; Tyerman, *op. cit.*, III, 638; *The Arminian Magazine* (London, 1787), X, 156.
33. Wesley, *Works*, I, 455-56; II, 455.
34. Warner, *op. cit.*, p. 210.
35. *Ibid.*, p. 210.
36. *Ibid.*, p. 195.
37. Wesley's violent theory was workable in the early stages of Methodism with its virile freshness of enthusiasm and the relative poverty of its members. Prosperous Methodists repudiated his doctrine by the judgment that in this respect Wesley was simply impracticable. The love of the world and of getting money became so prevalent that the Methodist character became adulterated. The rich withdrew or drifted from the societies or dominated them. Very few of the children of rich Methodists became members. And rich Methodists gained in prestige in the societies. The early Wesleyan theory was supplanted by a more comfortable doctrine. Theological literalism rose to take the place of an ethical theory of society. The uniqueness of the new movement as a program of social reform was adulterated into the pale hue of respectability. Warner, *op. cit.*, pp. 198-205, 273.
38. Wesley, *Letters*, V, 13-14; *Works*, II, 254.
39. Wesley, *Journal*, IV, 537.
40. *Ibid.*, II, 352.
41. Wesley, *Letters*, VI, 230.
42. Tyerman, *op. cit.*, III, 616.
43. Wesley, *Letters*, VIII, 76. In 1782 Wesley received £361, 19s from his book concern. Of this he spent £5, 19s for clothes. The balance

£356 he gave away. The same year the book steward by his directions gave a further sum of £237, 13s, making £593, 13s, for the year.
In 1783 he and the steward by his orders gave £832, 1s, 6d away; in 1784: £534, 17s, 6d; 1785: £851, 12s; 1786: £738, 5s; 1787: £961, 4s; 1788: £738, 4s; 1789: £826. (Tyerman, *op. cit.*, III, 615-16).

44. Wesley, *Letters*, VIII, 113.
45. Bebb, *op. cit.*, p. 143.
46. Wesley, *Works*, V, 31.
47. Thompson, p. 12.
48. *The Monthly Review* (London, 1791), p. 343.

Chapter 10

1. Wesley, *Letters*, VI, 175-76; *Works*, I, 516-21.
2. *London Chronicle* (Sept. 11, 1762), quoted in Wearmouth, *op. cit.*, I, 60.
3. Quoted in Wearmouth, *op. cit.*, I, 61.
4. *Lloyd's Evening Post* (Sept. 22-24, 1766), quoted in Wearmouth, I, 61.
5. *Lloyd's Evening Post* (Oct. 6-8, 1766), *London Chronicle* (Oct. 4-7, 1766), *Westminster Journal* (March 28, 1772), quoted in Wearmouth, I, 62-64.
6. Wesley, *Letters*, VI, 175-76.
7. Wearmouth, *op. cit.*, I, 19-22, 53, 54.
8. Wesley, *Journal*, I, 260.
9. Wearmouth, *op. cit.*, I, 60; *Gentleman's Magazine* (1766), pp. 386, 388; 436-37, 493-94; 1740, pp. 355, 356; 1756, pp. 544, 591; 1757, pp. 185, 234-35, 286-87, 430, 529.
10. J. L. and Barbara Hammond, *The Village Labourer* (London, 1911), p. 111. Arthur Young reports that the annual wage of a worker in Hertfordshire was £18 of which board, washing, and lodging amounted to £12. In Northamptonshire it was £17 a year. Colliers at Newcastle earned 15s a week, at Wakefield, 11s. Iron and cutlery workers received 10s at Rotherham and 13s 6d at Sheffield. In 1768 when Young began his tour, workers in porcelain at Liverpool, Burslem, and Worcester earned 8s 11d, 9s 6d, and 9s respectively, spinners and weavers, 8s 7d.
The average wage for women in textile manufactures was 4s 2½d, for boys 8s, 11¾d, for girls 2s 7d. (James E. Thorold Rogers, *Six Centuries of Work and Wages*, 2 vols. (London, 1884), pp. 404, 406-7).
11. *Westminster Journal* (April 30, May 14, 1768), quoted in Wearmouth, *op. cit.*, I, 36-37; *London Chronicle* (March 21-23, 1769), *ibid.*, 36-37.
12. *London Evening Post* (April 25-28, 1772), quoted in Wearmouth, I, 37-38; Tyerman, *op. cit.*, III, 130.

13. Hammond, *The Village Labourer*, pp. 120-22.
14. Wearmouth, *op. cit.*, I, 51.
15. Shelley, "The Mask of Anarchy," *The Complete Poetical Works of Percy Bysshe Shelley* (London, 1927), p. 337; Edward P. Cheyney, *Modern English Reform* (Phila., 1931), pp. 50-51.
16. *Lloyd's Evening Post* (Sept. 25-27, 1765), quoted in Wearmouth, I, 60-61.
17. Wearmouth, *op. cit.*, I, 76-78; Hammond's, *The Town Labourer*, pp. 157-58.
18. Wearmouth, *op. cit.*, I, 78.
19. *Ibid.*, I, 78-90.
20. *Ibid.*, I, 96, 105, 91-115.
21. Arthur Griffiths, *The Chronicles of Newgate* (London, 1884), I, 424 et seq. and II, *passim;* Wearmouth, *op. cit.*, I, 131-32.
22. *Gentleman's Magazine* (1750), p. 533; Wearmouth, *op. cit.*, I, 131-32.
23. Wearmouth, *op. cit.*, I, 133.
24. *Ibid.*, I, 111.
25. *Ibid.*, I, 113, 131.
26. Wesley, *Works*, V, 117.
27. Wesley, *Journal*, II, 246.
28. Faulkner, *op. cit.*, pp. 12, 18-19.
29. Wearmouth, *op. cit.*, I, 135
30 Bready, *op. cit.*, pp. 248-49.
31. Wesley, *Letters*, V, 350-54; Tyerman, *op cit.*, III, 130-34.

Chapter 11

1. Wesley, *Journal*, I, 260; Eric M. North, *Early Methodists Philanthropy* (New York, 1914), pp. 65-67.
2. North, *op. cit.*, p. 66.
3. Wesley, *Journal*, II, 435.
4. *Ibid.*, III, 208, 273; Wearmouth, *op. cit.*, I, 209.
5. Wesley, *Journal*, II, 21.
   Perhaps the Beveridge Report in our own day derives in some measure from the active and studious pity of John Wesley and his genius for organization.
6. Wesley, *Journal*, II, 176.
7. Wesley, *Letters*, III, 61.
8. Wesley, *Journal*, II, 246-47.
9. Wesley, *Letters*, V, 31.
10. Tyerman, *op. cit.*, III, 405.
11. James Lackington, *Autobiography* (London, 1830), p. 179.
12. Wesley, *Letters*, IV, 273.
13. Wesley, *Journal*, II, 21.
14. *Ibid.*, IV, 80; *Works*, II, 330-34.
15. Thompson, *op. cit.*, pp. 14-16; Wesley, *Works*, V, 186-87, II, 330-34; Wesley, *Letters*, II, 305-6.

16. Wesley, *Works*, II, 333.
17. Wearmouth, *op. cit.*, II, 200.
18. Porter, *op cit.*, pp. 910-11.
19. Warner, *op. cit.*, pp. 220-21
20. Lackington, *op. cit.*, pp. 133, 257.
21. Wesley, *Journal*, IV, 497; Wearmouth, *op. cit.*, I, 212-16.
22. Wearmouth, *op. cit.*, I, 214.
23. Wesley, *Journal*, II, 1, 21-22; Wearmouth, *op. cit.*, I, 207.
24. George Dock, M. D., "The Primitive Physic of Rev. John Wesley," *The Journal of the American Medical Association* (Chicago, Ill., Feb. 20, 1915), LXIV, no. 8, p. 629.
25. Wesley, *Works*, VII, 586.
26. John Wesley, *Primitive Physic: An Easy and Natural Method of Curing Most Diseases* (Phila., 1789, 21st edition).
27. Bready, *op. cit.*, pp. 321-22.
28. Dock, *op. cit.*, p. 631; *Primitive Physic, passim.*
29. *Primitive Physic*, pp. 161, 106, 43, 62, 38, 42, 105; Dock, *op. cit.*, pp. 631-32.
30. Boswell, *op. cit.*, I, 42.
In France other gifts of Louis XIV gave rise to a parody on the formula: "*Dieu te guerisse, le Roy te touche*—God save you, the King has kissed you."
In the treatment of ileus due to irritation Sydenham, the English Hippocrates, began with salts of wormwood in lemon juice night and morning, with sweetened mint water between, and a live puppy kept continually lying on the naked belly. Boerhaave, nearer to Wesley's time and in many respects more modern in treatment than Sydenham, used methods that make Wesley's look like sheer mental suggestion. For apoplexy he bled, used setons and fly blisters, bandages to the extremities, irritating powders to the nose and pharynx in order to "separate the pituita from the blood in the brain and set free the vital spirits," while internally he gave woodlice and cochineal. For epilepsy he described, though he did not recommend, the use of the blood of strangled gladiators or other men. Dock, pp. 633, 635.
31. Whiteley, *op. cit.*, p. 188.
32. Dock, *op. cit.*, p. 632.
33. *Primitive Physic*, pp. 99, 114-15, 116, 88, 53; Dock, *op. cit.*, p. 635.
34. *Primitive Physic*, pp. xiv-xix, 120, 179-82; *Works*, VII, 588; Dock, *op. cit.*, p. 635.
35. *Primitive Physic*, pp. xiv-xvi, 182; *Works*, VII, 587-88; Dock, *op. cit.*, pp. 635-37.
36. Dock, *op. cit.*, p. 636.
37. Robert E. Schofield, "John Wesley and Science in 18th Century England," *Isis*, XLIV, part 4, no. 138, (Dec. 1953), p. 335;
38. Dock, *op. cit.*, p.638.
Primitive Physic, p. x; Iipsky, *op. cit.*, pp. 267-68.
39. *Ibid.*, pp. 637-38.

40. Wesley, *Letters*, VI, 225-26.
41. Schofield, p. 335; Wesley, *Journal*, II, 355-56; Tyerman, *op. cit.*, I, 525.
42. Wesley, *Letters*, VI, 97.
43. *Ibid.*, VI, 185.
44. Wesley, *Works*, VII, 540; Schofield 335-36; Wesley, *Desideratum*, (London, 1760), pp. v, 43. According to the *Westminster Journal* of March 1-7, Wesley in 1772 was still using the electric machine. "Mr. Wesley says Electrifying in a proper manner cures St. Anthony's Fire, Gouts, Headache, Inflammations, Lameness, Palpitations of the Heart, Palsy, Rheumations, Sprain, Wen, Toothache, Sore Throat, and Swellings of all Sorts." Wearmouth, *op. cit.*, I, 209. *Desideratum* (pp. 42-43, 45) adds other disorders, including among others blindness, consumption, cramps, epilepsy, fits, King's Evil, leprosy, mortification, ringworms, surfeit, toe hurt.

Chapter 12

1. Wesley, *Journal*, III, 394; *Works*, VII, 458; Warner, *op. cit.*, pp. 225-26.
2. Wesley, *Works*, VII, 459.
3. *Ibid.*, VII 332-45; Edwards, *op. cit.*, pp. 129-33.
4. Edwards, *op. cit.*, p. 137.
5. Warner, *op. cit.*, pp. 225-29.
6. Wesley, *Journal*, IV, 292.
7. Edwards, *op. cit.*, p. 139.
8. *Ibid.*, pp. 140-41.
9. Trevelyan, *op. cit.*, p. 364.
10. Edwards, *op. cit.*, pp. 140-41.
11. *Ibid.*, pp. 141-43
12. Bready, *op. cit.*, p. 220; Bebb, *op. cit.*, pp. 172-73; Tyerman, II, 515-16, II, 359, 632.
13 Tyerman, *op. cit.*, III, 369.
14. *Encyclopedia Britannica* (14th Edition), XXIII, 518; Bebb, *op. cit.*, p. 173; Mac Arthur, *op. cit.*, pp. 129-30; Porter, *op. cit.*, p. 913.
15. Tyerman, *op. cit.*, I, 505.
16. Lackington, *op. cit.*, p. 78.
17. Wesley, *Letters*, I, XV.
18. Herbert, *op. cit.*, pp. v-vi, I am greatly indebted to Dr. Herbert's excellent study for material on Wesley's literary work. Mrs. G. Elsie Harrison holds the clue to the Brontë mystery in the Wesleyan influence as a result of the discovery that the home of Thomas Tighe, Patrick Brontë's patron, was the Mecca for Wesley's traveling preachers in Ireland. *The Clue to the Brontës*, (London, 1948).
19. Shepherd, *op. cit.*, p. 63; Richard Green, *The Works of John and Charles Wesley, A Bibliography* (London, 1896), p. 254.

20. Shepherd, *op. cit.*, pp. 63-64.
21. *Ibid.*, p. 95.
22. Frank W. Collier, *John Wesley among the Scientists* (New York, 1928), p. 90.
23. Wesley, *Journal*, III, 359.
24. Shepherd, *op. cit.*, p. 84; Richard Green, pp. 191-92.
25. Wesley, Works, VII, 578-80; Schofield, pp, 336-40; Tyerman, I, 368; De Witt T. Starnes and Gertrude E. Noyes, *The English Dictionary from Cawdrey to Johnson* (Chapel Hill, 1946), pp. 172, 175-77.
26. *Ibid.*, VII, 533-34; Shepherd, pp. 85-86.
27. The apostrophes within the words are Wesley's methods of indicating accent.
Samuel Johnson, *A Dictionary of the English Language*, 2 vols., 8th edition (London, 1799); Herbert, p. 120; Shepherd, p. 86. The authors could locate only one copy in the United States, a second edition in Stanford University Libraries at Stanford, California. (Starnes and Noyes, *op. cit., pp.* 177, 178.)
28. Shepherd, p. 87.
29. Later select parts of George Herbert were issued in book form. No reprint of Herbert appeared from 1709-1799. Herbert, *op. cit.*, p. 82.
30. Wesley, *Journal*, I, 482.
31. Wesley, *Letters*, II, 27-28.
32. John Pomfret, *The Choice*, in *The Works of the English Poets*, ed. by Alexander Chalmers (London, 1810), VIII, 308.
33. Wesley, *Works*, VII, 603.
34. Shepherd, *op. cit.*, pp. 89-90.
35. Wesley, *Works*, VII, 601; "To the Reader," *An Extract from Milton's Paradise Lost with Notes* (London, 1763). A second edition appeared in 1791 (*Green, Bibliography*, p. 126). Here are typical notes on Book I:

Ver. 4. *With loss of Eden.*—That is, of Paradise, which was in Eden . . .
Ver. 11. *Illumin.*—Enlighten . . .
Ver. 31. *Monarchy.*—Is Government by One.
Ver. 35. *Ruin.*—Falling with violence. *Combustion,*—Burning in a dreadful manner.
Ver. 37. *Adamantine.*—Firm like a diamond.
Ver. 45. *Balefull.*—Full of woe or mischief.
Ver. 48. *Ken.*—See, discern.
Ver. 52. *Darkness visible.*—A dark gloom . . .
Ver. 69. *Beelzebub.*—Our Lord terms him, Prince of the Devils; therefore signifies an enemy . . .
Ver. 76. A *myriad* is ten thousand . . .
Ver. 104. *Empyreal*—Fiery. Psalm. civ. 4.
Ver. 114. *Compeer.*—Equal and companion . . .
Ver. 154. *His minister of Vengeance.* To veil his shame, Satan as-

cribes his fall to the whole host of angels. But Raphael, Book VI, to the Messiah alone. Ver. 157. The *surge* is the swelling of the sea . . .

Ver. 181. A *rood* is two hundred and twenty yards . . .

Ver. 205. *Can make a Heaven of Hell.*—This is a fit rant for a Stoic or a Devil . . .

Ver. 238. *The Tuscan artist Galileo.*—a native of Tuscany . . .

Ver. 249. *Vallombrosa.*—This is, a shady valley, a valley in Tuscany, formerly called Hetruria.

Ver. 274. *Amram's son.*—Moses . . .

Ver. 290. *Erst.*—Formerly . . .

Ver. 325. *Chemos, Baalpeor, and Priapus* were the same, the Idol of Obscenity, worshipped with all manner of lewdness . . .

Ver. 456. *Amerced of Heav'n.*—Punished with the loss of it . . .

Ver. 558. —*Pandemonium.*—That is, the Palace of the Devils.

Ver. 576. *Demi-Gods.*—Little Gods.

36. I am using for comparison in the excerpts Professor Merritt J. Hughes's text of *Paradise Lost* (New York, 1935), based on Milton's second edition. See also Herbert, *op. cit.*, p. 78.
37. *Ibid.*, p. 79.
38. Wesley, *Letters*, IV, 246.
39. Herbert, *op. cit.*, pp. 86-88; Richard Green, p. 28.
40. Richard Green, p. 209; Herbert, *op. cit.*, pp. 90-97; Shepherd, *op. cit.*, pp. 90-91.
41. Wesley, *Works*, VII, 561.
42. *Ibid.*, VII, 559-60.
43. *Ibid.*, VII, 560.
44. Later the *Methodist Magazine.*
45. *Wesley Historical Society Proceedings* (1898), Part 3, I, 90-91; Schofield, p. 334.
46. Wesley, *Letters*, VI, 312.
47. Tyerman, *op. cit.*, II, 65-67; Shepherd, *op. cit.*, p. 94; Richard Green, p. 62.
48. Wesley, *Journal*, II, 244.
49. Thomas Carlyle, "Burns," *Critical and Miscellaneous Essays, Works* (London, n. d.), XXVI, 287.
50. Wesley, *Works*, VII, 605-6.
51. *Ibid.*, VII, 607.
52. Dimond, p. 120. As Charles Baudouin says: "The artist intensifies his own sentiment by the mere fact of expressing it." *Suggestion and Auto-Suggestion*, trans. by E. and C. Paul (New York, 1921), p. 81; see also James B. Pratt, *The Religious Consciousness* (New York, 1927), pp. 176-77, 179-80, 190-91.

    Wesley's hymn book was sometimes used at Chartist meetings.
53. W. J. Courthope, *A History of English Poetry* (London, 1905), V, 343-44.
54. Wesley, *Letters*, VIII, 107.
55. *Ibid.*, IV, 232.

56. *Ibid.*, IV, 257-58.
57. *Ibid.*, IV, 204.
58. *Ibid.*, VII, 347.
59. *Ibid.*, VII, 227.
60. Stephen, *op. cit.*, II, 409; Wesley, *Letters*, I, xv.
61. Wesley, *Letters*, VI, 141, 165.
62. Wesley, *Journal*, IV, 533.
63. Shepherd, pp. 45, 68, 127, 162.
64. Wesley, *Letters*, IV, 256-58.

Chapter 13

1. Wearmouth, *op. cit.*, I, 189.
2. Warner, *op. cit.*, p. 237.
3. *Wesley Historical Society Proceedings*, VIII, 118-19; Warner, *op. cit.*, p. 237.
4. *Ibid.*, p. 237.
5. Wesley, *Letters*, IV, 127; *Journal*, III, 33.
6. Wesley, *Works*, V, 122.
7. Wesley, *Journal*, III, 34-35; Bebb, p. 153.
8. Wesley, *Journal*, I, 192.
9. *Ibid.*, I, 397.
10. *Ibid.*, I, 430.
11. *Ibid.*, III, 74.
12. *Ibid.*, IV, 154.
13. Wearmouth, *op. cit.*, I, 219.
14. Wesley, *Journal*, IV, 303.
15. *Arminian Magazine* (1788), p. 349; 1796, pp. 496-97; 1799, pp. 14-16; *Gentleman's Magazine* (1752), p. 236; Wearmouth, *op. cit.*, I, 196-202.
16. Wesley, Works, VII, 86.
17. Wesley, *Journal*, II, 486.
18. Edwards, *op. cit.*, p. 158.
19. Wesley, *Letters*, IV, 271.
20. *Journal*, IV, 29.
21. *Ibid.*, I, 212.
22. Edwards, *op. cit.*, p. 160.
23. *Ibid.*, p. 161.
24. Wesley, *Letters*, VII, 235; Lecky, *op. cit.*, V, 29.
25. Woodforde, *op. cit.*, I, 201.
26. Bebb, *op. cit.*, pp. 149-50; Edwards, *op. cit.*, pp. 163-64; Shepherd, *op. cit.*, pp. 75-76.
27. Wesley, *Works*, III, 359-62.
28. *Ibid.*, III, 361-62.
29. Thompson, *op. cit.*, p. 42.
30. Edwards, *op. cit.*, p. 115; Warner, *op. cit.*, pp. 240-41.
31. Bready, *op. cit.*, pp. 104-5.
    Godwyn, an English clergyman, declared in 1680 his abhorrence of the slave traffic. Mrs. Aphra Behn made a Negro the hero of

her novel *Oroonoko.* Then came Defoe with his sympathetic study of Crusoe's man Friday. Such references argued a mild, compassionate interest in the slaves rather than a burning desire to mitigate their lot. Then Quaker Anthony Benezet in 1762 published his *Account of that Part of Africa Inhabited by Negroes.* Five years later he published his *Caution to Great Britain on the State of Negroes.* In 1767 came his *Account of Guinea,* the book which affected Clarkson so greatly. Benezet was important not only as a pioneer but because through his books Wesley was led to take an active interest in the fight to abolish the slave trade and if possible slavery itself.
In the Church Bishop Warburton deplored the evils of the traffic and outside the Church Richard Baxter and the Quakers had also taken their stand. Apart from these one can only find a thin stream of literature from unknown writers. *Views of American Slavery. Anthony Benezet and John Wesley* (Phila., 1858) *passim;* Anthony Benezet, *Some Historical Account of Guinea* (London, 1788); R. Coupland, *Wilberforce (Oxford,* 1923), pp. 77-79; Edwards, *op. cit.,* pp. 113-15.

32. Wesley, *Journal,* III, 461.
33. Warner, *op. cit.,* pp. 241-45.
34. *Ibid.,* p. 244.
35. For the economic slavery to which the Indian provinces had been reduced Wesley had this to say: "Not even the divine Cato or the virtuous Brutus plundered the provinces committed to their charge with such merciless cruelty as the English have plundered the desolated provinces of Indostan." Wesley, *Journal,* IV, 90.
36. Wesley, *Works,* VI, 282, 284, 286-89.
37. *Ibid.,* VI, 290-93.
38. Wesley, *Journal,* IV, 419-20.
39. Wesley, *Letters,* VIII, 23, 207.
40. *Ibid.,* VIII, 17.
41. "Fleecy locks and black complexion
Cannot forfeit nature's claim;
Skins may differ, but affection
Dwells in white and black the same."
Chas. Wesley, "On the Slave Trade." *Arminian Magazine* (1790), p. 502; Warner, *op. cit.,* p. 244.
42. Edwards, *op. cit.,* p. 124.
43. *Minutes of the Methodist Conference (1807)* (London, 1813), II, 402; Edwards, *op. cit.,* p. 124; Warner, *op. cit.,* p. 245.
In the Minutes of the Methodist Conference preachers in the West Indies were forbidden to marry anyone who had not previously emancipated her slaves.
44. Wesley, *Works,* VI, 339.
45. Wesley, *Letters,* VIII, 265.

Chapter 14

1. Wesley, *Works*, VI, 248; Lipsky, *op. cit.*, p. 15.
2. Wearmouth, *op. cit.*, I, 257.
3. Warner, *op. cit.*, p. 122.
4. Wesley, *Works*, VI, 257, 264; Mac Arthur, *op. cit.*, p. 25.
5. Wesley, *Works*, III, 251, 269.
6. Warner, *op. cit.*, pp. 88-89.
7. Wesley, *Works*, VI, 273.
8. *Ibid.*, VI, 274.
9. Whiteley, *op. cit.*, p. 209.
10. Warner, *op. cit.*, p. 97.
11. Wesley, *Works*, VI, 263, 269; Mac Arthur, p. 28.
12. Herbert, *op. cit.*, 106-11; Wesley, *Letters*, VI, 192-93.
13. Samuel Johnson, *The Letters of Samuel Johnson*, ed. by G. B. Hill (Oxford, 1892), I, 372-74.
14. Herbert, *op. cit.*, p. 111.
15. Wesley, *Works*, V, 511, VII, 10; *Letters*, VI, 150-51.
16. Hammonds, *The Town Labourer*, pp. 281-87.
17. Élie Halévy, *A History of the English People* (New York, 1924), 339, 372, 511, 514.
    "In the vast work of social organization which is one of the dominant characteristics of nineteenth century England, it would be difficult to overestimate the part played by the Wesleyan revival." p. 372.
    Alfred P. Wadsworth and Julia De Lacy Mann, *The Cotton Trade and Industrial Lancashire* (Manchester University Press, 1931), pp. 356-61; Hammonds, *The Town Labourer*, p. 288; G. D. H. Cole, *Persons and Places* (London, 1938), pp. 70-71.
18. S. E. Keeble, *Proceedings of the Wesleyan Historical Society* (1926), XV, 220-21.
19. *Ibid.*, XV, 220.
20. *Ibid.*, XV, 221; Mac Arthur, *op. cit.*, pp. 141-42.
21. Hammonds, *The Town Labourer*, pp. 282, 285.
22. *Ibid.*, pp. 288-289; see also Francis J. McConnell, "New Interest in John Wesley," *Journal of Religion* (October, 1940), XX, No. 4, 341-43.
23. Hammonds, *The Town Labourer*, p. 282.
24. *Ibid.*, 272-73, 284, 286-87.
25. "Townsend was once what I had liked to have been, a Methodist, and what I should have been still, had I not been what I am." Jeremy Bentham, *Works* (Edinburgh, 1843), X, 92.
26. Philip D. Brown, *The French Revolution in English History* (London, 1918), pp. 37-38, 148-49, 27-29, 99; Edwards, *op. cit.*, pp. 83-85.
27. Brown, *op. cit.*, pp. 13, 16.
28. *Ibid.*, p. 148; Edwards, *op. cit.*, pp. 85-86.
29. Edwards, *op. cit.*, pp. 87-91, 95-96.
30. Albert V. Dicey, *Lectures on Law and Opinion in England*

(London, 1905), pp. 399-405.
"Practically both the preachers and the philosophers appealed to much nobler feelings than the mere desire to avoid pain or to enjoy pleasure. Evangelical teachers and philosophic radicals urged their disciples, though in very different ways, to lead better and nobler lives; they appealed as regards matters of national concern, to the public spirit and to the humanity of Englishmen; they excited among all whom they could influence the hatred of palpable injustice, and felt themselves, and kindled among others, a special abhorrence for that kind of oppression which manifestly increased human suffering. . . . It is indeed a coincidence that one can link together the names of Wesley and Bentham, but it is no mere coincidence." Dicey, *op. cit.*, p. 402.

31. *Methodist Magazine* (1812), p. 720.
32. Wearmouth, *op. cit.*, II, 66, 68.
33. *Ibid.*, II, 73, 185, 189.
34. *Ibid.*, II, 273; Warner, *op. cit.*, p. 133.
35. Wearmouth, *op. cit.*, II, 227, 230; *Primitive Methodist Quarterly Review* (1882), p. 393.
36. "Appendix to First Report of Commissioners on Children's Employment (Mines)," *Parliamentary Papers* (1842), XVI, 568, 608.
37. Thompson, *op. cit.*, pp. 96-98; Wearmouth, *op. cit.*, II, 253, 248.
38. Thompson, *op. cit.*, pp. 96-98.
39. Wearmouth, *op. cit.*, II, 214, 216; *Proceedings of the Wesley Historical Society*, XV, 219-21, 139-40.
40. Wearmouth, *op. cit.*, II, 216.
41. *Ibid.*, II, 217-18.

Chapter 15

1. Even Marjorie Bowen, a critic of Wesley, grants that Methodism brought companionship, hope, and comfort to the outcast and wretched. Marjorie Bowen, *Wrestling Jacob* (London, 1937), p. 255.
2. John Richard Green, *op. cit.*, IV, 1618.
3. Warner, *op. cit.*, pp. 276-77.
4. Edwards, *op. cit.*, p. 147.

Chapter 16

1. Augustine Birrell, *Miscellanies* (London, 1902), pp. 34-35.
2. "He was a man whose eloquence and logical acuteness might have rendered him eminent in literature, whose genius for government was not inferior to that of Richelieu, and who devoted all his powers in defiance of obloquy and derision to what he sincerely considered the highest good of his species." Macaulay, "Southey's Colloquies on Society," in *Works* (London, 1913), VII, 454-55.
The Cambridge History of English Literature (New York, 1928) calls Wesley's *Journal* "one of the great books of the world," X, 417.

3. Leslie Stephen, *op. cit.*, II, 410-11.
4. Southey, *Wesley*, II, 330-32.
5. Wesley, *Journal*, IV, 520.
6. *Ibid.*, IV, 401-2.
7. *Ibid.*, IV, 408-9.
8. Wesley, *Letters*, VIII, 267.
9. John H. Overton, *John Wesley* (Boston and New York, 1891), p. 212.
10. Telford, *op. cit.*, pp. 351-52.

BIBLIOGRAPHY

Abbey, Chas. J., *The English Church and Its Bishops*, 2 vols. (London, 1887).

Abbey, Chas. J. and Overton, John H., *The English Church in the Eighteenth Century*, 2 vols. (London, 1878).

Addison, Joseph, *The Spectator*, ed. G. Aitken, 8 vols. (London, 1898).

Addison, Joseph, *Works*, 6 vols. (London, 1877).

[Allestree, Richard T.], *The Whole Duty of Man* (London, 1842).

Andrews, Alexander, *The Eighteenth Century* (London, 1856).

The Arminian Magazine

Baldwin, Stanley, *This Torch of Freedom* (London, 1936).

Balleine, George R., *A History of the Evangelical Party in the Church of England* (New York, 1911).

Barr, Josiah H., *Early Mehodists under Persecution* (New York, 1916).

Baudouin, Chas., *Suggestion and Auto-Suggestion*, trans. by E. and C. Paul (New York, 1921).

Bebb, E. D., *Nonconformity and Social and Economic Life* (London, 1935).

Belden, Albert D., *George Whitefield* (Nashville, Tenn., 1930).

Benezet, Anthony, *Some Historical Account of Guinea* (London, 1788).

Berkeley, George, *Works*, ed. by Alexander C. Fraser, 4 vols. (Oxford, 1901).

Besant, Sir Walter, *London in the Eighteenth Century* (London, 1902).

Birrell, Augustine, *Miscellanies* (London, 1902).

Boswell, James, *The Life of Samuel Johnson*, ed. by G. B. Hill, 6 vols. (Oxford, 1887).

Bowen, Marjorie, *Wrestling Jacob* (London, 1937).

Brailsford, Mabel R., *A Tale of Two Brothers* (New York, 1954).

Bready, J. Wesley, *England before and after Wesley* (London, 1938).

Broome, William, "The Poems of William Broome," in Alexander Chalmers, *The Works of the English Poets*, Vol. XII (London, 1810).

Brown, Philip D., *The French Revolution in English History* (London, 1918).

Burke, Edmund, *The Writings and Speeches of Edmund Burke*, 12 vols. (Boston, 1901).

Burnet, Bishop Gilbert, *History of His Own Times*, Vol. VI (Oxford, 1896).

The Cambridge History of English Literature, Vol. X (New York, 1928).
The Cambridge Modern History, Vol. VI (New York, 1934).
Cameron, Richard M., *The Rise of Methodism* (New York, 1954).
Campbell, John L., *Lives of the Lord Chancellors,* Vol. VII (London, 1857).
Carlyle, Dr. Alexander, *Autobiography* (Edinburgh and London, 1861).
Carlyle, Thomas, *Works,* Vol. XXVI (London, n.d.).
Chalmers, Alexander, *The Works of the English Poets,* Vols. VIII and XII (London, 1810).
Chambers, J. D., *Nottinghamshire in the Eighteenth Century* (London, 1932).
Cheyney, Edward P., *Modern English Reform* (Phila., 1931).
Churchill, Charles, *The Poetical Works of Charles Churchill,* Vol. I (London, 1844).
Cole, G. D. H., *Persons and Places* (London, 1938).
Collier, Frank W., *John Wesley among the Scientists* (New York, 1928).
Collins, John C., *Voltaire, Montesquieu, and Rousseau in England* (London, 1908).
The Connoisseur (London, 1757).
Copeland, Arthur, "Woodrow Wilson's Opinion of John Wesley," *Methodist Review* (New York, 1915), Vol. XCVII, Ser. 5.
Coulton, G. G., *A Medieval Garner* (London, 1910).
Coulton, G. G., *Ten Medieval Studies* (Cambridge, 1930).
Coupland, R., *Wilberforce* (Oxford, 1923).
Courthope, W. J., *A History of English Poetry,* Vol. V (London, 1905).
Cowper, William, *The Poetical Works of William Cowper* (London, 1926).
Crabbe, George, *Works,* 5 vols. (London, 1823).
Cross, Wilbur, Introduction to *The Complete Works of Laurence Sterne* (New York and London, 1924).
Dicey, Albert V., *Lectures on Law and Opinion in England* (London, 1905).
Dimond, Sydney G., *The Psychology of the Methodist Revival* (Oxford, 1926).
Dobrée, Bonamy, *John Wesley* (New York, 1933).
Dock, George, "The Primitive Physic of Rev. John Wesley," *The Journal of the American Medical Association* (Chicago, Ill., 1915), Vol. LXIV, no. 8.
Edwards, Maldwyn, *John Wesley and the Eighteenth Century* (London, 1933).
Eliot, George, *Adam Bede* (Boston, 1887).
Ellis, James J., *John Wesley* (New York, 1891).
Elton, Oliver, *A Survey of English Literature, 1730-80,* Vol. II (London, 1928).
Encyclopedia Britannica, 14th Edition.

Faulkner, John A., *Wesley as Sociologist, Theologian, Churchman* (New York, 1918).
Fielding Henry, *The History of Tom Jones*, 4 vols. (London, 1926).
Fielding, Henry, *Joseph Andrews*, 2 vols. (Oxford, 1926).
Fitzgerald, Percy, *The Life of Laurence Sterne*, 2 vols. (London, 1864).
Forster, John, *The Life and Times of Oliver Goldsmith*, 2 vols. (London, 1871).
The Gentleman's Magazine.
George, M. Dorothy, *England in Johnson's Day* (London, 1928).
Gibbins, H. de B., *English Social Reformers* (London, 1892).
Gibbon, Edward, *Autobiography* (New York, 1907).
Goldsmith, Oliver, *The Miscellaneous Works of Oliver Goldsmith* (London, 1919).
Green, John Richard, *A Short History of the English People*, 4 vols. (London, 1893).
Green, Richard, *The Works of John and Charles Wesley: A Bibliography* (London, 1896).
Griffiths, Arthur, *The Chronicles of Newgate, 2 vols.* (London, 1884).
Halévy, Élie, *A History of the English People*, Vol. I (New York, 1924).
Hammond, J. L. and Barbara, *The Town Labourer* (London, 1917).
Hammond, J. L. and Barbara, *The Village Labourer* (London, 1911).
Harrison, G. Elsie, *The Clue to the Brontës* (London, 1948).
Herbert, George, *The English Works of George Herbert*, Vol. II (Boston and New York, 1915).
Herbert, Thomas W., *John Wesley as Editor and Author* (Princeton, 1940).
Hervey, John, Lord, *Memoirs of the Reign of George the Second*, 2 vols. (London, 1848).
Hillis, Newell D.,*Great Men as Prophets of a New Era* (New York, 1922).
Hobson, J. A., *God and Mammon* (London, 1931).
Hughes, Hugh Price, *The Heart of Wesley's Journals* (London and Edinburgh, n.d.).
Johnson, Samuel, *A Dictionary of the English Language*, 2 vols., 8th edition (London, 1799).
Johnson, Samuel, *The Letters of Samuel Johnson*, ed. by G. B. Hill (Oxford, 1892).
Kennett, White, *A Compassionate Inquiry into the Causes of the Civil War, 1703-4* (London, 1704).
Kennett, White, *Sermon Preached before the House of Commons*, January 30, 1705-6 (London, 1706).
Knox, Vicesimus, *Essays, Moral and Literary*, 2 vols. (London, 1827).
Lackington, James, *Autobiography* (London, 1830).
Lecky, W. E. H., *A History of England in the Eighteenth Century*, 8 vols. (London, 1891).
Lipsky, Abraham, *John Wesley* (New York, 1928).

Lunn, Arnold, *John Wesley* (New York, 1929).

Mac Arthur, Kathleen W., *The Economic Ethics of John Wesley* (New York, 1936).

Macaulay, T.B., *The History of England,* 3 Vols., Everyman Edition (London, 1915).

Macaulay, T. B., *Works,* Vol. VII (London, 1913).

McConnell, Francis J., "New Interest in John Wesley," *Journal of Religion* (October, 1940) XX, no. 4, 340-58.

Massey, William, *A History of England during the Reign of George the Third,* Vol. II (London, 1865).

Mc Carthy, Justin, *A History of the Four Georges,* Vols. I and II (New York and London, 1885-1901).

The Methodist Magazine

Milton, John, *Paradise Lost,* ed. by Merritt Y. Hughes (New York, 1935).

Minutes of the Methodist Conferences (London, 1812, 1813).

Montesquieu, Chas de, *Oeuvres Complètes,* ed. par Laboulaye, Vol. VII (Paris, 1879).

The Monthly Review (1791).

Moore, Cecil A., *English Poetry of the Eighteenth Century* (New York, 1947).

Neilson, Francis, *The Roots of Our Learning* (New York, 1946).

Newton, Thomas, *The Works of the Right Reverend Thomas Newton,* 3 vols. (London, 1782).

Nichols, John, *Literary Anecdotes of the Eighteenth Century,* 6 vols., Vol. III (London, 1812).

North, Eric M., *Early Methodist Philanthropy* (New York, 1914).

Overton, John H., *The Evangelical Revival in the Eighteenth Century* (London, 1886).

Overton, John H., *John Wesley* (Boston and New York, 1891).

Parliamentary Papers (1821) X; (1842) XV, XVI.

Pattison, Mark, *Memoirs* (London, 1885).

Perry, George G., *A. History of the English Church,* 3 vols. (London, 1890).

Pike, G. Holden, *Wesley and His Preachers* (London, 1903).

Pomfret, John, "The Choice," in *The Works of the English Poets,* ed. by Alexander Chalmers, Vol. VIII (London, 1810).

Porter, Frank G., *Wesley, a Forerunner of Social Reform, The Methodist Review,* CIII, 5th Series, Vol. XXXVI (New York, 1920).

Pratt, James B., *The Religious Consciousness* (New York, 1927).

Primitive Methodist Quarterly Review (1882).

Proceedings of the Wesley Historical Society.

Rogers, James E., Thorold, *Six Centuries of Work and Wages,* 2 vols. (London, 1824).

Rowden, Alfred W., *The Primates of the Four Georges* (New York, 1916).

Ryle, J. C., *The Priest, the Puritan, and the Preacher* (New York, 1855).

St. David, Bishop of, *Sermon before the House of Lords,* January 30, 1727-8 (London, 1728).
Schilling, Bernard N., *Conservative England and the Case against Voltaire* (New York, Columbia University Press, 1950).
Schofield, Robert E., "John Wesley and Science in 18th Century England," *Isis* (December, 1953), XLIV, part 4, no. 138.
Seymour, Aaron C. H., *The Life and Times of Selina, Countess of Huntingdon,* Vol. I (London, 1844).
Shelley, Percy Bysshe, *The Complete Poetical Works of Percy Bysshe Shelley* (London, 1927).
Shepherd, T. B., *Methodism and the Literature of the Eighteenth Century* (London, 1940).
Simon, John S., *John Wesley, The Last Phase* (London, 1934).
Smollett, Tobias, *The Works of Tobias Smollett,* Vol. I (London, 1925).
Southey, Robert, *The Life of Wesley,* 2 vols. (New York, 1925).
Southey, Robert, *Life and Correspondence,* Vol. I (London, 1849).
Stackhouse, Thomas, *The Miseries and Great Hardships of the Inferior Clergy in and about London* (London, 1722).
Starnes, De Witt T., and Noyes, Gertrude E., *The English Dictionary from Cawdrey to Johnson* (Chapel Hill, 1946).
Stephen, Leslie, *History of English Thought in the Eighteenth Century,* 2 vols. (London, 1927).
Sterne, Laurence, *The Complete Works of Laurence Sterne,* Vol. I (New York and London, 1904).
Swift, Jonathan, *Works,* ed. by Sir Walter Scott, 19 vols., (London, 1883).
Sydney, William C., *England and the English in the Eighteenth Century,* 2 vols. (Edinburgh, 1913).
Tawney, R. H., *Religion and the Rise of Capitalism* (New York, 1926).
Taylor, Ernest R., *Methodism and Politics, 1791-1851* (Cambridge, 1935).
Telford, John, *The Life of John Wesley* (London, 1886).
Thackeray, W. M., *Works,* Vol. XIX (London, 1886).
Thompson, D. D., *John Wesley as a Social Reformer* (New York, 1898).
Thomson, James, *The Works of James Thomson,* Vol. I (Edinburgh, 1774).
Tickner, F. W., *A Social and Industrial History of England* (London, 1915).
Toynbee, Arnold, *Lectures on the Industrial Revolution of the Eighteenth Century in England* (London, 1913).
Trapp, Rev. Jos., *The Nature, Folly, Sin, and Danger of Being Righteous Overmuch* (London, 1758).
Trevelyan, G. M., *English Social History* (London, 1943).
Tyerman, Rev. Luke, *The Life and Times of John Wesley,* 3 vols. (New York, 1872).
Views of American Slavery Taken a Century Ago, Anthony Benezet and John Wesley (Phila., 1858).

Vulliamy, C. E., *John Wesley* (London, 1931).
Wadsworth, Alfred P., and Mann, Julia De Lacy, *The Cotton Trade and Industrial Lancashire* (Manchester University Press, 1931).
Walpole, Horace, *The Letters of Horace Walpole,* ed. by Mrs. Paget Toynbee, 16 vols. (Oxford, 1903-05).
Warburton, Bishop William, *Works,* Vol. X (London, 1811).
Warner, Wellman J., *The Wesleyan Movement in the Industrial Revolution* (London, 1930).
Watson, Richard, *Anecdotes of the Life of Richard Watson, Bishop of Landaff,* 2 vols. (London, 1818).
Wearmouth, Robert F., *Methodism and the Common People of the Eighteenth Century* (London, 1945). (Referred to as Volume I in References.)
Wearmouth, Robert F., *Methodism and the Working Class Movements of England, 1800-1850* (London, 1937). (Referred to as Volume II in References.)
Webb, Sidney, *The Story of the Durham Miners (1662-1921)* (London, 1921).
Wedel, T. O., "On the Philosophical Background of *Gulliver's Travels,*" *Studies in Philology* (Chapel Hill, N. C., 1926), XXIII, 434-50.
Wellbourne, Edward, *The Miners' Unions of Northumberland and Durham* (Cambridge, 1923).
[Wesley, John], *Desideratum: or Electricity made plain and useful.* By a Lover of Mankind and of Common Sense (London, 1760).
Wesley, John, *The Heart of Wesley's Journal* (London and Edinburgh, n. d.).
Wesley, John, *Journal,* 4 vols. Everyman Edition (London and New York, 1930).
Wesley, John, *The Letters of John Wesley,* ed. by John Telford, 8 vols. (London, 1931).
Wesley, John, *An Extract from Milton's Paradise Lost* (London, 1763).
Wesley, John, *Primitive Physic: An Easy and Natural Method of Curing Most Diseases,* 21st Edition (Phila., 1789).
Wesley, John, *Sermons on Several Occasions,* 3 vols. (New York, 1831).
Wesley, John, *The Works of John Wesley,* 7 vols. (New York, 1831).
Wesley, John and Charles, *The Poetical Works of John and Charles Wesley,* 13 vols. (London, 1870).
Wesleyan Bicentennial (Wesleyan University, Middletown, Conn., 1904).
Wesley Historical Society, *Proceedings.*
Whitely, J. H., *Wesley's England* (London, 1938).
Woodforde, Parson James, *The Diary of a Country Parson,* Vol. I (London, 1924).
Young, Arthur, *An Enquiry into the State of the Public Mind among the Lower Classes* (Dublin, 1798).
Young, Arthur, *A Six Weeks Tour* (London, 1769).
Young, Arthur, *Travels in France during the Years 1787, 1788, 1789* (London, 1924).

INDEX